Praise for *The Second Nuclear Age*

"Penetrating. . . . Bracken is an example of why fresh and fearless thinking is required when considering the near-term future of geopolitics. . . . Everyone interested in nuclear proliferation in the Middle East should read [this book]."

—Robert D. Kaplan, Stratfor Global Intelligence, author of *The Revenge of Geography*

"An alarming and compelling wake-up call. . . . Read this book. We should not wait for the first nuclear crisis of this century to start thinking about what to do differently."

—Admiral Mike Mullen, USN (ret.), former chairman of the Joint Chiefs of Staff

"Paul Bracken argues that we have already entered a second nuclear weapons age—and that the United States needs to face that reality. His book is well worth reading."

—Graham Allison, Harvard University, author of *Essence of Decision* and *Nuclear Terrorism*

"Put Paul Bracken in charge of our nuclear policy for the twenty-first century. *The Second Nuclear Age* is a superb analysis of why and how a continuation of our cold war nuclear forces and doctrines will fail, and how we can make them safer and far more strategically useful."

—R. James Woolsey, former Director of Central Intelligence

"In this book—which could hardly be more timely—Paul Bracken dissects the dangerous and often neglected realities of 'the second nuclear age' and argues for bold, innovative, and often provocative ways to think about how to avert those dangers. . . . He helps ensure that one of the most important, complex, and controversial issues of our time will get the hard-headed attention it deserves."

—Strobe Talbott, president of the Brookings Institution and former deputy secretary of state

ALSO BY PAUL BRACKEN

Managing Strategic Surprise:
Lessons from Risk Management and Risk Assessment
(Editor, with Ian Bremmer and David Gordon)

Fire in the East:
The Rise of Asian Military Power and the Second Nuclear Age

Advanced Weaponry in the Developing World
(Editor, with Eric Arnett and W. Thomas Wander)

Reforging European Security:
From Confrontation to Cooperation
(With Kurt Gottfried)

The Command and Control of Nuclear Forces

THE SECOND NUCLEAR AGE

STRATEGY, DANGER, AND THE NEW POWER POLITICS

PAUL BRACKEN

 ST. MARTIN'S GRIFFIN ⚙ NEW YORK

THE SECOND NUCLEAR AGE. Copyright © 2012, 2013 by Paul Bracken.
All rights reserved. Printed in the United States of America. For information,
address St. Martin's Press, 175 Fifth Avenue, New York, N.Y. 10010.

www.stmartins.com

Design by Kelly S. Too

The Library of Congress has cataloged the Henry Holt edition as follows:

Bracken, Paul J.
    The second nuclear age : strategy, danger, and the new power politics / Paul Bracken.—1st ed.
        p. cm.
    Includes bibliographical references and index.
    ISBN 978-0-8050-9430-5 (hardcover)
    ISBN 978-1-4299-4504-2 (e-book)
    1. Nuclear weapons—Political aspects.   2. Balance of power.   3. Deterrence (Strategy).
4. International relations—History—21st century.   I. Title.
    JZ5665.B73 2012
    327.1'12—dc23

                                                                        2012015062

ISBN 978-1-250-03735-0 (trade paperback)

St. Martin's Griffin books may be purchased for educational, business, or promotional use.
For information on bulk purchases, please contact Macmillan Corporate and Premium Sales
Department at 1-800-221-7945, extension 5442, or write specialmarkets@macmillan.com.

First published in hardcover by Times Books, an imprint of Henry Holt and Company

First St. Martin's Griffin Edition: November 2013

10 9 8 7 6 5 4 3 2 1

For Nan

CONTENTS

THE SECOND NUCLEAR AGE

THE BOMB RETURNS FOR A SECOND ACT

Atomic weapons have returned for a second act. This isn't a welcome message, and yet it's one that we ignore at our peril. The question is not whether nuclear weapons are good or bad, or whether they should be eliminated or limited in some manner. Rather, the challenge we face is to assess, with clear eyes, the new geopolitical dynamics wrought by the bomb's emergence in what I call the second nuclear age.

This time the bomb's spread has nothing to do with the cold war, which was the first nuclear age and remains the context for so much of our thinking about nuclear weapons. In the past two decades, new nuclear powers have emerged from "natural causes," the normal dynamics of fear and insecurity that have long characterized international affairs. Perhaps the United States could have done more to stop the spread of nuclear weapons, cracking down harder on India or Israel, on North Korea or Pakistan. But any such efforts would have looked like a historical grand design to freeze existing power realities into permanent history, preserving U.S. military predominance through arms control. In an era of shifting great powers, rising regional powers, and great uncertainty about the shape of world order, such efforts were bound to fail.

I don't believe it's possible to avoid the problems of a new nuclear age by arguing that nuclear weapons are dangerous or horrible. That argument didn't work in the cold war, and it is equally impractical now. Getting the bomb out of the international system remains extraordinarily difficult because the second nuclear age, unlike the first, is decentralized, with many independent nuclear decision makers, in key regions and globally, among the world's major powers. The bomb is a fundamental part of foreign and defense policies in the Middle East, South Asia, and East Asia and has become deeply embedded in these regions. An even larger system has taken shape with interactions and interconnections linking these regions and the major powers (the United States, Russia, China, India), all of whom have the bomb. We must also add subnational groups to this mix, terrorists and militias who can take advantage of a nuclear context even if they don't possess a bomb of their own. These major powers, secondary powers, and groups have fundamentally different cultures and perceptions, and they are far more diverse than the nuclear actors of the cold war. A grand design for world order that gets rid of the bomb, especially one that greatly advantages the United States, may certainly be desirable. But conflating its desirability with feasibility isn't good policy analysis. Getting rid of the bomb isn't going to happen anytime soon.

What is required is a longer-term perspective on the problem. Some have argued that the way to think about the spread of the bomb is that it's like a slow-motion Cuban missile crisis. It should be treated as a sequence of individual tactical moves and countermoves to get away from direct confrontations that could lead to war. This is how the United States has handled the spread of the bomb for the past two decades.

But I don't agree with this argument. Instead, a longer-term strategic framework is needed. Basing policy on the skill of individual moves and countermoves overlooks the relationship that these actions have with one another. If individual moves have no deeper relationship, then policy will blow in the wind between fleeting political dispositions and bureaucratic rigidities. This, too, is how the United States has handled the spread of the bomb for two decades. Tough rhetoric is followed by years of inaction. In the cold war there was a recognition that if policy fell into the grip of either one of these forces the risk of a nuclear disaster would grow considerably.

Treating the second nuclear age as a slow-motion Cuban missile crisis overlooks how the context of a crisis changes, as countries arm to the teeth or embrace dangerous strategies like launch on warning. It ignores how arms control can alter the conditions and consequences of a crisis. Most of all, it doesn't consider how a larger structure of competition shapes the environment of conflict.

Instead of isolated tactical moves and countermoves, we need to look at the second nuclear age as a long-term problem—a fifty-year problem—if we are to get the perspective and context to understand it. A multipolar nuclear order is taking shape. It will have its own interactions, and as it matures it will undergo dynamic changes. India isn't going to give up its nuclear deterrent, and neither are the other major powers. To call this a crisis is to confuse the term with much deeper forces that drive international relations. It muddies the discussion to call the multipolar nuclear order a crisis, even if it does lead to particular crises.

Understanding this system of major and secondary nuclear powers and groups is critical to averting a security disaster and big shocks that the international system may not be able to absorb. Regional nuclear arms races, crises in the regions, and nuclear competition among major powers are likely parts of the second nuclear age. But it is this bigger system, this larger set of major and secondary countries, that has to be recognized if policies to manage the second nuclear age are to be effective.

There are grounds for optimism. The world made it through the cold war with skill and luck. The United States and its allies avoided a security disaster like the loss of Europe or a large slice of the developing world going over to communism, which is what the cold war was about. Nuclear war didn't erupt either.

The problem facing the world in the second nuclear age is that few people have thought about how atomic weapons reshape the strategic rivalries in the world's most contested regions, or at the global level. Even less thought has been given to managing these conflicts in a nuclear context. *Management* is the operative word here—understanding the dangers, instabilities, and dynamics of international relations in the new nuclear context. It's a more practical goal than radically redesigning the world's future. A dose of humility is needed, because if the major powers cannot stop Pakistan, North Korea, and other nations from getting the bomb, it is hard to believe that these nations can be talked into giving it up.

The management approach has received scant attention because it has been deemed more important to prevent the emergence of a second nuclear age, not to manage it. The nuclear nonproliferation treaty (NPT), U.S. leadership, and democracy were supposed to avert the bomb's second act. That was the argument put forth after the cold war, when it was said that the bomb would fade into the background. The two largest nuclear powers, the United States and Russia, might retain their arsenals, but as sources of influence and instruments of strategy this wouldn't matter. The bomb would exist as an irrelevance.

The United States actively promoted this viewpoint. It dramatically lowered its dependence on nuclear arms, cutting back their numbers by two-thirds, and instead fielded revolutionary nonnuclear military technologies. America didn't need the bomb for deterrence anymore; conventional weapons could do the job better. The motivation was also strategic and moral, to get nuclear weapons out of international affairs, and because the United States no longer wished to threaten others with nuclear annihilation, except in remote and largely unimaginable circumstances. Sure, the United States needed to deter a massive Russian or Chinese nuclear attack, but who, honestly speaking, could imagine this possibility after the 1990s?

For all practical purposes U.S. dependence on nuclear weapons went to zero. Nuclear forces were left to rot, technologically and intellectually. There was also a strategic holiday when it came to any thinking about nuclear weapons—that is, any thinking that went beyond the narrow confines of nonproliferation or disarmament. That Pakistan, India, China, Iran, or Israel might see value in such weapons, that they would innovate technologically and strategically, wasn't imagined. The United States projected its own antinuclear ethos onto the world. But not everyone shared these values.

The United States did nearly everything it could to foster global antinuclear policies after the cold war. I cannot think of any policy in American history, not the Monroe Doctrine, not liberal internationalism, not containment, that had more widespread, bipartisan support in domestic politics, or more energetic backing. The problem is this: it just didn't work. Other countries simply didn't buy it. They were sovereign nations in charge of their own destiny, so they could choose to keep the bomb or get it. The spread of the bomb and other advanced military technologies wasn't some aberration or false start, a path that was briefly followed until people woke up to the dangers. The bomb became deeply established in international relations, at the global and regional levels.

I don't believe any U.S. policy to prevent a second nuclear age would have worked, short of a colossal effort on the scale in dollars and blood of World War II. This is because it wasn't just a handful of rogue nations like North Korea that went nuclear. Major powers did, too. India, the world's largest democracy, joined the nuclear club. China upgraded its nuclear forces along with the rest of its military. Add Russia to this group and three of the four BRICs (Brazil, Russia, India, China), the most vibrant comers in the twenty-first century, are modernizing their nuclear arsenals. Even Britain and France didn't give up their nuclear weapons, in great part to preserve their declining influence as other countries rose in power. Looking back, these are natural developments in the international system as responses to the rhythms of geopolitical change.

Major powers such as Russia, China, and India, along with the secondary nuclear powers Pakistan, Israel, North Korea, and very likely Iran, aren't sure where the world is headed. From their perspective there are many different possibilities for the future. The decline of U.S. capacity, political and economic, to enforce order in various regions, the absence of promised new structures (governance institutions, democracy, self-interest) to do so, and the spread of advanced military technologies of all kinds have made it unlikely that they would take the extraordinary step of unilateral disarmament.

But another cause stands out for the spread of the bomb, beyond mere uncertainty about the security environment. Distrust of the United States has also fueled the spread of the bomb as a counter to American military interventions. China, Russia, India, Pakistan, North Korea, and Iran hardly desire a world that is "safe" for U.S. strong-arm tactics with conventional forces. In their eyes, the bomb counters America precisely because it is so risky. Because if there's one thing the bomb does, it increases the risks in any military showdown, with the prospect of a large increase in the level of violence. This suits many countries just fine. It's exactly what they want, given that they can't possibly compete against the United States in conventional technologies.

There are nine countries with the bomb. Eight have modernized their nuclear arsenals, with weapons of longer range and with a diverse menu of delivery means and warhead types. The one exception is the United States. In the world of the second nuclear age, it is misguided for America to continue the charade that nuclear weapons are useless. Other countries sure don't think so, and they are the ones that count.

What is now developing goes beyond merely getting the bomb. Strategic innovation is increasing among those in the nuclear club, and even among those about to join it. As countries acquire these weapons, they consider new ways to use them to advance their strategic purposes. Some of these ideas are clever. Some are nuts. But good or bad, these strategy innovations will play an enormous role in setting the danger level in various regions of the world. Strategy innovations will also influence how the major powers respond. Yet we may miss these altogether because of America's conviction that the atomic bomb is useless.

No, the bomb didn't make a permanent exit after the cold war. It wasn't killed off by the NPT or by U.S. power. It surely wasn't written out of the script by democracy, as the case of India makes clear. It just went offstage for a time, as the theater was prepared for the next act. Natural opportunities for a comeback role opened up, and will continue to do so in the future. This isn't a bit part by any means; the bomb is returning with a featured role in the drama.

STRATEGIC IMPLICATIONS

Two questions stand out in the new environment. One is highly practical. How can the world manage its affairs as safely as possible in a second nuclear age? This was the question the great powers faced in the late 1940s, at the dawn of the first nuclear age. Though that era was very different from this one, there is a lot to be learned from understanding how things were handled and mishandled in that experience.

The second question is whether it's possible for countries to survive the second nuclear age. Nuclear weapons may be an enduring feature of the international system. But, then again, they may not be. If the dangers of an international security catastrophe—an uncontrolled nuclear arms race in a volatile region, the destruction of Israel or another country—are as great as they look, then it may be impossible for a multipolar nuclear order to endure very long. The question then may be how catastrophes in the second nuclear age can be exploited to create a much more restricted global nuclear order, or even one that abolishes the bomb altogether.

Countries whose strategic personalities hardly mattered in the cold war now have their own nuclear forces. Their geography and politics are quite different from one another and are far different from those of the two superpowers during the cold war. This diversity of actors raises a crucial point. It is very doubtful that a single overarching conceptual framework such as deterrence or containment can adequately handle the large variations of strategic personality. When there were only two big nuclear players, such a simplification made some sense, but even then it had glaring weaknesses. The political structure of the world that leads to the underlying instability in the first place now is going up against nuclear deterrence. It can hardly be certain that deterrence will always win this contest. At any rate, that's putting a lot of faith in deterrence.

To put it simply, the political structures in the Middle East, South Asia, and East Asia now have a nuclear context. They never did in the cold war, at least not directly. The road to nuclear war through these regions always went through Washington and Moscow because they controlled the triggers. The U.S. and Soviet governments served as safety valves to make sure that whatever happened in these regions didn't go nuclear. The locals might have wanted this to happen, or not, but the superpowers surely did not.

The shifting of nuclear risk to the regions raises another critical distinction. This isn't a book about nuclear strategy. Rather, it's about strategy in a nuclear age, a very different subject. Looking at the second nuclear age using the terminology of the deterrent frameworks of the first nuclear age, such as first-strike (and second-strike) missile survival, military versus urban targeting, and conventional versus nuclear attack, does not come close to describing the challenges the world faces. This approach leaves out the causes of conflict in the

Middle East, South Asia, and East Asia, conflicts that now have a nuclear context. To leap over these political causes to an altogether different framework that minimizes their impact, namely nuclear deterrence, means overlooking the principal sources of risk. It substitutes a familiar calculus that worked in the cold war for fundamentally different strategic realities. Convoluted discussions of nuclear strategy—for example, which U.S. targets China might fire at, or the implications of Israel's greater nuclear throw weight against Iran—miss the main risks of the second nuclear age because they do not include the political conflicts that play out in a far more dangerous context.

TWO NUCLEAR AGES

The idea for this book came from my desire to see what had carried over from the first nuclear age to the second. The two ages are fundamentally different, and indeed I've never met anyone who sees today's nuclear dynamics playing out the way they did in the cold war. It simply is not plausible that China and the United States would build massive counterforce arsenals against each other. I've yet to meet anyone who thinks it is.

But there's a deeper link connecting the two nuclear ages. As Rudyard Kipling put it: "They are whimpering to and fro—And what should they know of England who only England know?" Kipling is saying that no one can understand England if they've never looked at it in terms of its similarities and differences with France and Germany. The world faced nuclear weapons before, and there are lessons to be drawn. The bomb was poorly understood at first. Mistakes were made. Strategists focused on the wrong problems. Official strategy bore almost no relation to how nuclear weapons were actually used by leaders. The competition was dynamic, not static, with rhythms and changes over the years, and even fads, in technology and strategy.

These are all important lessons, and they are dangerous to forget. It would be astonishing if something like them didn't occur again. The point is just this: the two nuclear ages are more usefully studied in tandem than apart. In both, leaders faced challenges of unimaginable violence and a need to impose some limits, some rationality, to break the momentum for escalation, arms races, and a competition that could itself lead to the very disaster the arms were designed to prevent.

In both nuclear ages, likewise, leaders have believed the bomb to be useful. Why else did the United States and the Soviet Union build so many of them? And why else are Pakistan and North Korea, and all the rest, basing their national existence on them? They find such weapons useful, too.

The Kipling line points to another key issue. Not all nuclear-weapons states are alike. China's nuclear buildup is part of a larger military transformation. Israel's nuclear arms serve entirely different purposes. North Korea is different still, a starving rat with a nuclear bite. Lumping these countries together makes no sense. They're too different, as are their strategic situations. Yet the unexamined use of cold war jargon does this, using a vocabulary invented in the 1950s to describe a competition between two continental-sized industrial powers. Minimum deterrence, nuclear war fighting, counterforce and countervalue—these terms are used today as if their meanings are self-evident or in no need of clarification when applied to vastly different situations.

The second nuclear age lacks a global overarching struggle like the cold war. But it does have an overarching theme: the breakdown of major power monopoly over the bomb. The United States, Russia, China, France, and Britain, the victorious powers of World War II, once had exclusive rights to it. They were even granted their monopoly positions by treaty, in the NPT, and in their permanent seats in the United Nations Security Council.

But their nuclear monopoly has broken down, just as it has in economic and political power, with profound implications. The original five nuclear powers have not been able to control membership in the major power nuclear club, as India has "used" the bomb quite successfully to force its way in, and to leverage its way to greater international status with it. But the greatest breakdown, surely the most dangerous, has been in failing to prevent secondary powers from getting the bomb. Today no circuit breaker exists in the path to nuclear war; there is no requirement that escalating crises must involve a major power in order to go nuclear, as was the case in the cold war. This is what the breakdown in the major power monopoly means: the circuit breakers have been pulled out of the global wiring system for nuclear war and peace.

CAN THINKING MAKE IT WORSE?

Can merely thinking about these problems, by itself, increase tensions and make matters worse? Can it heighten suspicions and fears, by excessively focusing on dark possibilities? I believe the honest answer to these questions is yes. But it should proceed anyway.

In the first nuclear age the same question came up. Strategists like Henry Kissinger and Herman Kahn thought about the unthinkable, in the parlance of the day. In so doing they raised many unpleasant issues. But they did something else that was much more important. They broke the government's monopoly on the conversation about nuclear weapons. They broadened it to allow a much wider national debate that brought in moral and political considerations, as well as technical and strategic ones. One didn't have to agree with them to appreciate the service they performed. Before their work, the U.S. government had nuclear weapons wrapped in so much secrecy that no one could understand just how bungled the thinking was about issues of nuclear war and peace.

It's easy to forget how much the U.S. government didn't understand its own forces in the early cold war. Had it maintained its stranglehold over nuclear issues, the breakthroughs that dampened the arms race and put limits on crises wouldn't have happened. Arms control, the importance of survivable nuclear forces, the key role played by command and control, banning weapons in space—and other provocative deployments—would not have happened. Strategic communications between Moscow and Washington, as each told the other what it found to be most destabilizing, wouldn't have happened, either. It would have been judged too secret to discuss with the enemy. Accidental war would never have been raised as a concern. Early articles on the topic were shut down by the White House, as newspaper and magazine publishers were told to yank the story. Interlocking alerts and back-channel contacts were taboo subjects. The list goes on.

Progress was made only after these independent strategists broke the government's monopoly over the conversation. I am convinced that this lowered the risk of nuclear war. Had the broader debate been kept hushed up because of its sensitivity, or its horror, this wouldn't have taken place.

The issue can be put even more starkly. The strategists of the early cold war usefully exaggerated nuclear dangers—and in so doing performed a valuable service. Focusing attention on dynamics that were not especially likely led to concentrated efforts and high-level attention to make them even less so. Smart people were brought in to look at the problems. Political leaders asked questions the bureaucracy wouldn't ask.

One of the key lessons learned from this experience was the dangerous tendency to focus only on "likely" possibilities. But no one had any real idea of what these likelihoods were. Their probability was often more a matter of personal outlook and feeling than anything grounded in fact. This suited the bureaucracy just fine. They didn't want to explore hard problems.

What needed attention wasn't the "likely" as defined in a narrow way by a bureaucracy. The disastrous unexamined possibilities were what needed attention, and these received little. Crises in Berlin, Cuba, and Taiwan—none were anticipated by the government. All were judged as "unlikely." This is another useful reminder from the first nuclear age for the second. Absent a wider debate, governments will put a gloss on events that has a history of being wrong. They won't ask probing questions. Anything that is dubbed "unlikely" will be dismissed as impossible and ignored entirely.

Too much denial of nuclear reality, too much restraint, and too much hope in avoiding a second nuclear age has other risks. When coercive facts demolish the cheery view that nuclear weapons have few uses, it leads to shock. But this shock comes not from an enemy surprise attack, but rather from a failure of analysis and from an inadequate perception of the world as it is. Reckless or irresponsible escalation then becomes much more likely, based on inadequate deliberation and plans that have received little or no thought before-hand. Especially with nuclear weapons, there will be a sharp increase in paranoia, as happened at times during the cold war. There was a domestic political momentum in the United States during the first nuclear age to the extreme, at times to the paranoid. It was captured in movies and TV shows such as *The Twilight Zone*. Yet a combination of restraint, skill, and luck limited these excesses compared to what might have happened.

Now, in the second nuclear age, imagine a nuclear terrorist inci-dent, or an Israeli security disaster. If the U.S. government hasn't thought about these things beforehand there could easily be a sharp ideological shift, driven by emotion, not rationality. There could also be ill-considered escalations, including U.S. nuclear responses, that might make a bad problem worse.

In the second nuclear age American domestic political sentiment is up for grabs. A mishandled nuclear crisis that exposes giant gaps in America's military power could produce a surge in paranoia and fear. A regional nuclear shock would lead to official investigations and a search for the guilty, just as 9/11 did. But the catastrophe we are talking about here would make 9/11 pale in comparison.

This leads to a fundamental conclusion, one that was also true in the first nuclear age. If we don't manage the second nuclear age, the second nuclear age will manage us.

PART ONE

ENDURING TRUTHS

· 1 ·

GAME CHANGER

War games have been used for a long time to discover and test strategies. The U.S. Navy gamed out the war against Japan for twenty years before Pearl Harbor. Reflecting on this afterward, Chester W. Nimitz, the commander of the U.S. fleet in the Pacific, said that little surprised him during the war because he had seen it played out so many times before at the Naval War College in Newport, Rhode Island. Only the kamikaze attacks came as a surprise—they hadn't been imagined in the Newport war games.

During the cold war, analysts at the Rand Corporation used games to explore the strange new world of nuclear strategy. What contributed to deterrence? How might a nuclear war start? What, exactly, did it mean to "win" a nuclear war? This last question led them to drop the term *war* from their work. New terms were used to capture a shift in strategic emphasis: crisis games, politico-military exercises, escalation games—the idea was that nuclear wars were not something the United States might win or lose like World War II. The focus shifted to managing them, not winning them, so that they didn't go all the way to nuclear annihilation.

Games use another tool, the scenario. Scenarios set the stage for a game's interactions. Scenarios—the term and the idea were borrowed from Hollywood by Rand analysts in the 1950s—are hypothetical plot outlines of plausible future developments. They are not forecasts or predictions like "China will fire missiles at the United States on March 12, 2015." Rather, they describe the context and the dynamics as seen by the different actors, along with the interactions that may lead to conflict.

As nuclear weapons have spread in recent years, basic questions needed to be asked about the difference a nuclear context makes. To discover these questions as they apply to the Middle East, games have been played in the United States and Israel. I have been involved in some of these exercises and find them insightful—and troubling. The questions they raise are not unlike those asked at the start of the first nuclear age, updated to today's environment. Would a nuclear Iran just sit on its bomb or would Iran use the bomb in some way? How might a nuclear war start, and how might it end, in the Middle East?

In free-form games, teams are set up for the principal actors—the United States, Israel, Iran, Egypt, Syria, Hezbollah, and Hamas. The members of each team are told to role-play what they believe their countries or groups would do. The participants are diplomats, retired officials, and military officers. Academics are often included for good measure and to wander around the teams and pick up insights on what is taking place.

Games can be controversial even before they start. The U.S. government's official policy is nuclear nonproliferation. The United States, working with the international community, the International Atomic Energy Agency (IAEA), and the UN, is determined to stop Iran from acquiring nuclear weapons. With official Washington declaring that Iran won't get the bomb, a game presupposing that it will suggests that the current policy will fail. Some officials fight the scenario for this reason. What, they ask, is the point of wasting time over something that isn't going to happen? Better, they argue, to focus on stopping Iran from getting the bomb than gaming out what happens if it does.

Something else is going on here beyond a narrow objection to not sticking to official U.S. policy. It's one of the features of games that make them so thought-provoking. Some people in Washington and Tel Aviv smell a rat when they see a game featuring a nuclear Iran. They know that government departments rarely oppose official policy out in the open. They fight it behind the scenes, saying that they are only preparing for contingencies that might develop. This is the way policy often changes, not from some meeting of big shots at the White House. Smaller changes set the stage for a policy shift. It might be the subject of a game or words used in a staff paper. These small changes give early warning of what's really coming. Many experienced old hands know this, and they don't like gaming a nuclear Iran one bit because they foresee a policy change ahead. They even have a name for it: "soft acceptance" of a nuclear Iran.

Most people, though, accept their game roles. Games bring different agencies together in a protected and confidential setting. Often these agencies have never talked to one another before, except through official bureaucratic channels.

The team interactions make games an example of organizational learning, not just individual learning. In an MBA program they call it "experiential learning." It contrasts with individual learning, where you sit passively at a desk and listen to a talking head flip through his or her PowerPoint slides, usually with no interaction, or at least no dynamic interaction. By the time the audience reaches the end of a PowerPoint briefing, most people want to flee the room, not to prolong the agony of listening to scripted questions and answers.

Games force senior officials to pay attention to problems that many of them would rather not think about. No one can guarantee that a game won't veer into areas of sensitivity that go well beyond official policy. Hiding behind official policy is much safer. A leader won't get into trouble with a good official story, as long as it isn't challenged.

This is much easier to ensure in a one-way briefing, speaker to audience, than it is in a free-form game. That's why some senior officials steer clear of games.

Games have the opposite characteristics of an official study. It is harder to rig them with predetermined conclusions. People get emotionally involved in games. There are unanticipated moves. Mistakes are made. Some think that's bad, that it's a departure from objective rationality. But I think it is the advantage of games because it's more realistic.

Some of the most interesting insights about the cold war came from crisis games played by the Rand Corporation, the Hudson Institute, and other think tanks. Games were employed to discover dynamics that no one had ever thought about before. The course of play wasn't tightly scripted the way a study often was. Games do something no other methodology I know does: show you things you hadn't thought about before. Each team can pretty much do what it thinks the real-world players would do. There's an umpire who rules out impossible actions. No one is allowed to have perfect intelligence on the enemy. Nor are "laser zappers" permitted, weapons that immediately kill all the bad guys with the push of a button.

Let's consider a game of a nuclear Middle East to see some of the things that come up and make nuclear weapons a game changer for the region. This generic synthesis of several games shows that a country doesn't have to detonate a nuclear weapon to use it. It's a lesson from the first nuclear age as well, but it seems to have been forgotten in the discourse about a nuclearized Middle East.

The game starts with an incident: Hezbollah kidnaps Israeli soldiers, or there is a big terrorist strike inside Israel. Israel hits back with air strikes on villages believed to be Hezbollah ammunition dumps. Next, the West Bank and Gaza flare up.

After the Israeli air strikes on Lebanon, Hezbollah fires Scuds with cluster bomb warheads into Haifa and Tel Aviv. These weapons came from Iran. There even are Iranian "advisers" with them.

Hezbollah also has Mach 2 anti-ship cruise missiles. They had a slow cruise missile in the real war in Lebanon in 2006, but it exploded prematurely when it struck an Israeli combat ship. Had it gone off as intended it would have exploded inside the Israeli ship, probably causing a catastrophic kill. But that was an ancient, slow-flying missile. Everyone wondered what it would mean if Iran gave modern, faster missiles to Hezbollah. No Israeli ship could defend against them; it would know it had been hit only from the light flash of the explosion.

The weapons Hezbollah used in the game were deadlier, and they killed a lot more people. But that wasn't their main effect. They slowed down the game's rhythm. The expectation of most players was that the deadlier conventional weapons would accelerate Israeli attacks. But they did the opposite. Israel slowed the tempo.

This wasn't the pattern of pre-nuclear war games in the Middle East. Israel immediately went on the offensive after an Arab provocation. In the Gaza war of 2009 and the Lebanon war of 2006, Israel quickly upped the ante. The other side might get in the first punch, but Israel was going to immediately answer with quite a wallop.

But not here. I noticed that players, on whatever team, were perking up, curious about how Israel was going to handle this. The side conversations, what I have dubbed "the shadow game" in some academic writings, are where participants talk informally, out of their roles, over coffee and lunch. It's the water-cooler conversation where people give their candid views of what they see. Side conversations are often where the most interesting insights are found. The official game is written up for lessons learned. But often the most penetrating insights are watered down as participants default back to their bureaucratic rather than game roles.

There was a lot more Israeli caution here. Hesitation even. And everyone saw it. No air strikes on Syria. The Israeli navy backed off from the Lebanon-Syria coast for fear of losing a ship. If a ship was lost, Israel would have to escalate. And that was the heart of the matter, something I don't think anyone really appreciated beforehand.

Escalation in a nuclear context wasn't like escalation in earlier conflicts without the bomb.

The bomb was a game changer. Israel knew how to escalate in a
conventional war or against an intifada or an insurgency. These were
bread-and-butter problems for the Israel Defense Forces and the
Mossad. But a nuclear context was different. Conflict was no longer
about how much pain to inflict before the other side gave up. Now
the game was about risk. It was like suddenly switching tables in a
casino from a roulette wheel with betting limits to one without any
limits. Even in the roulette game with limits there was chance for a
run of bad luck. But in the limits game it couldn't get that bad for
Israel. The United States would come in after a decent interval and
make up the loss anyway.

The nuclear roulette wheel had no limits, and this changed not
only the big decisions but also the small ones, like pulling back war-
ships from the Lebanon coast. An unwanted escalation spiral might
drive the game in a very bad direction.

Israel wasn't at all confident in this game. What would Iran do?
That's what the Israel team needed to know. The Mossad couldn't say.
They debated but couldn't agree on what the red lines were. Maybe
Israel's red lines were different from Iran's. That could spell national
disaster. Maybe at the higher levels of escalation there weren't any
recognized limits. Or maybe escalation would throw the game into
the hands of dame fortune. A glitch—a mistaken warning blip on
Iran's radar, a garbled message to its rocket forces, a "mad major"
in the Iranian Revolutionary Guards—might tilt the game to catastrophe.

Israel liked the old game much better. But this didn't matter,
because now the tempo increased. Iran, Syria, Hamas, and Hezbollah
pressed harder. Israeli civilian casualties climbed from the cluster-
loaded Scuds. The Israel team debated a big escalation to shock Iran.
It was tricky, though, because there were several factors that had to
be considered. There was also Egypt to think about. A big attack on

anyone might tip Egypt to actively fight Israel. This could mean a two-front war, as in 1973.

But the biggest unknown was the results of escalation itself. If escalation led to more escalation, Israel could be worse off. Some on the Israeli team argued that perhaps they should de-escalate. Put out peace feelers, work the back channels, and ask the United States to demand an immediate cease-fire. Do something to slow down the tempo of the war. That's what drove their decision to hold the Israeli navy and other forces back.

But how to de-escalate when Iran was emboldened? The conventional rockets kept coming in from southern Lebanon. So the Israel team began to think the unthinkable. They considered firing a demonstration nuclear shot, a missile warhead that would explode 100,000 feet over Tehran. This was an option in top-secret war plans devised years earlier. It was designed to suddenly nuclearize a crisis. Israeli plans since the 1970s had called for doing this as a last-ditch alternative to firing all-out atomic attacks.

A high-altitude nuclear detonation would shatter windows in downtown Tehran, but it wouldn't kill anyone, or hardly anyone. Surely it would shock Iran into a cease-fire. Iran would pressure Hezbollah to stand down and fold its cards. That was the hope of the Israel team anyway.

But what about the United States? Should Israel just do it, or discuss it with Washington first? This was debated, but the Israel team couldn't agree one way or the other.

Events overtook debate, as they so often do. Iran upped the ante by declaring a full nuclear alert. This was done "to defend against nuclear Israel." Atomic rockets on truck launchers were flushed from their peacetime storage bases, along with hundreds of conventionally armed rockets and shorter-range missiles that could hit U.S. bases throughout the Middle East.

Iran's tactics were fascinating. Tehran barely had a nuclear force. But a great deal of thought had been devoted to it. When a country has only a few weapons it is acutely aware of how easy it might be for the enemy to knock them out. Iran also understood the psychology of the West. Iran's enemies didn't want to kill millions of innocent people, so the Iranian government placed some mobile missiles in city parks in Tehran, Esfahan, and Mashhad. Camouflage nets were placed over many parts of these cities to conceal the missiles and to mislead American satellites. But in some city parks Iran's missiles were deployed right in the open for every U.S. and Israeli satellite to see. Iran wanted its enemies to see these urban missiles.

Other nuclear rockets were mixed in with hundreds of conventionally armed missiles. Effectively, the conventional missiles served as decoys because U.S. and Israeli intelligence couldn't tell a conventional missile from a nuclear one. Iran even had dummy missiles. They looked real enough, at first. Given time, CIA experts might be able to distinguish them from subtle differences. But the mobile missiles—nuclear, conventional, and the dummies—kept scrambling about to new locations. This process was faster than the intelligence cycle times needed to make accurate estimates.

Putting missiles in cities meant that tens of thousands of innocent people would be killed if Israel or the United States attacked them with conventional arms. Iran then might hit back at Israel with atomic weapons. As for an Israeli nuclear attack, that would drive casualties into the millions because it meant firing bombs directly into Iran's cities. No one thought Iran would hold back after that.

Iran also kept a few nuclear missiles in hardened, underground silos. It looked as if these were for quick-reaction firing, ready to launch on short notice. Mobile missiles could take hours to move and set up. Someone in Iran had thought through the various possible scenarios to understand that Iran needed a prompt firing deterrent, just in case Israel or the United States got any ideas about preemption. These silo-housed missiles could fire as soon as an enemy attack was picked up on radar. They could be set to what is called "launch on warning"—a classic cold war tactic.

No one was quite sure exactly how hard the silos were. Some participants argued that they could be taken out with conventional precision weapons, such as cruise missiles. Then, someone asked about Iran's launching on warning. Could a local Revolutionary Guard commander order them to fire? Maybe he had standing orders to launch if a blip showed up on a radar screen.

Iran's nuclear alert did something else. It stretched Israel's relations with the United States to the breaking point. The U.S. team wanted to act as if nuclear war was completely unthinkable. They didn't want to go there, even hypothetically, not in any way, shape, or form. It was amazing to watch this dynamic play out. Several participants on the U.S. team had been schooled in nuclear nonproliferation through graduate programs and government service. Their careers had been built around stopping the spread of the bomb, and they brought this view into the game. Nuclear war was something you had to prevent, that was the goal.

But the Iran team didn't see things this way. Not at all. Someone had thought through the missile dispersal scheme, putting some of them in cities. There was genuine forethought in having mobile missiles and missiles in silos, too. The combined deterrent effect of both deployments made it very hard to preempt Iran. Iran had a small, crude nuclear force, true, but its political strategy for using that force was complex—shrewd, even. This came as a surprise to the United States team. They had come into the game convinced that Iran would never be crazy enough to fire at Israel. The two nuclear deterrents, of Israel and Iran, would produce a mutual standoff. But this wasn't happening. The dynamics were taking an ominous new turn, and it didn't look good.

Another surprise to the United States and Israel teams arose from the communications they had with each other. Two allies in lockstep, of course, at least that was the official line. But certain delicate matters that should have been discussed in peacetime were ignored because it would have meant actually discussing how nuclear weapons might be used. Nobody on the U.S. team wanted to touch this one. But now the topic couldn't be avoided. How far would the United States really go to support Israel? Would America authorize strikes on Iran? Should Washington demand a no-first-use pledge from Israel? How could Israel be restrained? In the time-compressed, stressed fever of a crisis it was impossible to analyze all of these questions adequately.

So the two teams spoke past each other. It was like watching parallel play among young children. Israel wanted to know concretely what the United States would do to stop Iran. The United States had said that Iran wouldn't be allowed to go nuclear. Now Tehran had done so. Moreover, Iran was threatening Israel with nuclear weapons. The U.S. team responded to the Israeli question with a message that Washington "would take all measures necessary." But the Israel team wanted to know exactly what that meant. Would the United States join in a preemptive strike on Iran?

The U.S. team was worried that the crisis would accelerate the bomb's spread. There were secret Saudi Arabian and Egyptian nuclear programs. Japan, Brazil, and Algeria were also possible candidates for going nuclear.

But the Israelis weren't in any mood to receive a U.S. lecture on the dangers of nuclear proliferation. Their survival was at stake. So they ordered two Jericho missiles alerted under a special plan certain to be photographed by American satellites. They were timed to move to their launch positions just as the U.S. satellites were passing overhead. It was a plan that had been worked out years ago to "introduce" nuclear weapons into the Middle East. The intent of this esoteric communication from Tel Aviv to Washington, obviously, was to shock the White House. "We hope it leaks to the media, too; maybe we should make sure it does," one Israel team member said.

Israel's move forced a U.S. decision. Washington wanted to restrain Israel, defend Israel, and scare the living daylights out of Iran. So the United States publicly gave Israel a nuclear guarantee. Making it public was an escalation, because it put the American reputation on the line. If one atomic missile hit Israel, the United States solemnly announced, well, that would be it for Iran. The guarantee was cleverly worded. Maybe too cleverly. It didn't specify which weapons America would use. The term *nuclear* made reference only to Iran's attack on Israel.

There was more going on than in the game play itself. At the sidebar coffee breaks, in the shadow game, several U.S. team participants expressed genuine frustration with the designers for putting them in this terrible position. There was also anger at the Israel team and, actually, with Israel. "Why the hell didn't the United States force Israel to sign the NPT long ago, to give up the nukes? Then we wouldn't be in this crazy situation," one of them said.

The U.S. team wanted to end the crisis and avoid nuclear war. But here they were getting pulled more deeply into it. What if payment on the U.S. guarantee was demanded? This wasn't some college seminar, after all, where the different sides of a problem were debated, the bell rang, and students went out to play Frisbee.

So many issues hadn't been thought through. The Joint Chiefs were screaming for guidance. What if the United States actually had to launch against Iran? What, exactly, would they fire at? And with what—conventional or nuclear weapons? The chiefs needed to know in order to make plans and get airplanes and ships in position. The United States hadn't fired an atomic bomb in anger since 1945. It hadn't conducted a realistic nuclear exercise since the end of the cold war. That was a long time ago. You can't just pick up the phone and order someone to do something that hasn't been considered for decades.

The chiefs pointed out some unsettling facts. Iran's atomic missiles, presumably the legitimate targets, couldn't be located. Perhaps Iran's cities should be hit? Would the United States use nuclear or conventional weapons? One argument was that only a nuclear attack would teach Iran (and others) the appropriate lesson. But what exactly was that lesson? The individual playing the president said that he didn't want to go down in history as the first leader to kill five million people in an afternoon.

Some on the U.S. team argued that it was immoral to use nuclear weapons against civilians. They called instead for a massive conventional strike, one that would destroy Iran's military power for decades. They added that if Iran's leaders ordered nuclear retaliation in response to a conventional strike they would be put on trial for war crimes in the Hague, and hanged. That sounded great, but the president asked if Iran would simply kick back and watch an attack unwind over ten weeks' time, withholding an atomic strike on Israel (and others) as it rolled in. The president was very angry. He asked why better options and intelligence hadn't been developed over the years as the world watched Iran go nuclear. Iran's bomb program wasn't exactly a surprise, after all. It was the most closely watched of any in history. While every damn centrifuge had been counted, no one was looking at what the whole thing meant for the United States. Everybody talked about deterrence. But now Iran had an *offensive* deterrent. Why hadn't anybody seen this coming? Why hadn't anyone thought about this before?

Attention shifted back to Israel. The Israelis didn't like the U.S. nuclear guarantee one bit. It gave Iran and Hezbollah a green light to throw more conventional missiles at Israel. Tension, fear, and stress increased. This wasn't faked, at least in my view. It spilled over to the lunch and coffee breaks. People were getting angry outside of the game. But at whom? That, they weren't sure about.

Distrust infected the Israel team. Maybe it was paranoia. They smelled betrayal, that the United States was going to hide behind its global nonproliferation responsibilities to ignore that this was a life-or-death crisis for the Jewish state. Was America selling Israel out with cheap talk about stopping the spread of the bomb, while Israel went down the drain? Maybe it was like 1975, they said, when the United States watched South Vietnam go down while debating lofty issues of presidential power and purpose. Given Jewish history, who could blame them for thinking like this?

The crisis was spinning out of control.

Iran's next move jacked the tensions to a fever pitch. It was an inspired move, actually. Without saying anything, Iran evacuated its big cities. The population packed into buses, cars, and trucks and rode out of Tehran, Mashhad, Esfahan, out to the distant suburbs and beyond. In a day, Iran's cities were at 25 percent of their normal population. The United States watched this fantastic exodus over satellites. Soon, CNN put videos taken on the ground on the Web.

Iran was now poised for nuclear attack. On the brink. The missiles were ready to fire, on a hair trigger, and most of Iran's population would survive an Israeli counterstrike.

Israel, by contrast, was in chaos. There was nowhere for the Israelis to go. Ben Gurion Airport near Tel Aviv was closed by the rockets bombing it. Hundreds of thousands of Jews were mobbing the coastal marinas, desperately trying to escape to Cyprus in small boats. TV showed the panic. Deterrence, and the myth of Israeli invincibility, the bedrock of Israeli security, were disappearing.

But suddenly Iran declared that in the interest of world peace it would step back from the brink, having exposed the true nature of "the Zionist nuclear entity." This came as a welcome relief, especially to the U.S. team. They wanted out.

So the game ended. I believe this abrupt termination was artificial, but it was no accident. I've played in games that just got too intense. The design team had to break it off to prevent the animosity from getting out of hand.

Lessons were drawn, as they always are after a game. The United States needed better intelligence. Cruise missiles are a problem. The list went on with the usual items.

But there was an overarching lesson. Iran had thrown Israel into pandemonium without firing a shot. The population was terrified.

The economy was in ruins. Israel's reputation as the Prussia of the Middle East was smashed. Yes, nuclear war had been avoided. Deterrence worked. But who in Israel, the United States, or, for that matter, Iran would claim this was the real lesson? Iran had used a small nuclear force to overturn Israeli deterrence and rupture the Middle East order. That is what people took away.

Next time the revolver might be fired with a nuclear bullet in the chamber. And there was little doubt that there would be a next time. This was the Middle East after all. Tehran was now empowered with a tremendous psychological victory. Iran had stood up to the Israelis and the Americans and had gotten away with it. The sidebar conversations dealt with this impact. Who was going to invest in Israel when their plants might be blown up? Many participants thought that Israelis would see the writing on the wall and that many would get a second passport to get out, just in case.

What fascinated me almost as much as the lessons of the game was the mood. Games have moods, just as dramas do, which after all is what these exercises really are. Fear is the overriding mood I've seen in nuclear crisis games. I've seen it in games I was involved in during the cold war. I'd run crisis games for the Pentagon and others, and there was high drama in them. I've also seen this kind of fear in the faces of leaders who had lived through the Cuban missile crisis and other near misses, people such as Robert McNamara, McGeorge Bundy, Ted Sorensen, and Andrew Goodpaster. In each instance, whether in Pentagon simulations or in actual crises, it's this fear more than anything else that stands out. It's a very different type of fear than the fear of being in combat, like in the film *Saving Private Ryan*, hitting Omaha Beach, or among people I've known who fought at Hue or in Fallujah. Because in the nuclear games the participants aren't getting shot at. It's not *their* lives that are at risk, at least not directly. It's that they have to make transcendent, life-or-death decisions for millions of people. It's a very different kind of fear. The stress is over making a wrong choice—and losing cities.

The players in this game were too young to have known this type of fear. They had never experienced the cold war, the duck-and-cover civil defense drills and air-raid sirens. The horrific potential of the cold war for them was portrayed as a sick, comic insanity, as portrayed in *Dr. Strangelove*. You laugh at it. You see how foolish it was.

Or you treat it like an academic debate. I don't think any of the game participants believed such monumental life-and-death choices could actually exist. Yet they surely did exist for leaders in the first nuclear age. Now, as we enter the second nuclear age, they are back. This is another lesson, one I've learned in other games in recent years. It doesn't have to be the Middle East. It could be South Asia or East Asia. Long-suppressed nightmares are returning. In different form, yes, but still the ultimate horror of the vast destruction inherent in these weapons is there. It's only been offstage.

These choices are no longer academic debates. People have been taught all kinds of things. An older generation wants to make the nuclear nightmare go away by inoculating the young with protective ideas. Nuclear weapons are useless and we should get rid of them. Strengthen the NPT. Get rid of ballistic missiles. Deterrence will work. This game was a rebuttal to these parlor fantasies.

· 2 ·

A MOST USEFUL WEAPON

It has become commonplace to hear how horrible nuclear weapons are, how they are the scourge of the earth and how they should be condemned at every turn. In today's sensibility they are seen as relics of the cold war, and, what is worse, thinking about them is often dismissed as "cold war thinking." When old American cold warriors turn against the bomb and urge the United States to get rid of it, as has happened recently, this is one more sign that the bomb must be headed for the strategic trash can.

Would that we could get rid of the bomb so easily. The view that the bomb is obsolete is hard to square with two facts: other countries aren't giving it up and the United States in an earlier time sure didn't think it was useless.

The major powers that have the bomb haven't given it up. Indeed, they're modernizing their nuclear arsenals. India, a rising major power, a democracy even, has gone out of its way to get the bomb. Secondary powers who have it, such as Israel and Pakistan, haven't given it up either. Other secondary powers are trying to get it. If the bomb is so terrible and so antiquated, then all of these countries must be wrong. But they certainly don't think they're wrong.

The second fact, that the United States didn't find the bomb to be useless in the cold war, is more delicate. This is because it gets to a very hard truth that people would now like to forget. The United States found the bomb a most useful weapon, no matter what retired cold warriors say about it today. And if America found it useful, should it be surprising that Pakistan and North Korea do, too?

The bomb is terrible, certainly. My only point in bringing up its usefulness is that we need to see nuclear weapons in the strategic context of the time. In one of my classes at Yale I go through a net assessment of the atomic bomb in the cold war. I present the downsides, the horror, the innocent deaths, Hiroshima, and nuclear annihilation. But then I go through the upsides of why the United States found nuclear weapons useful. The students have never seen anything like this before. They've been given a one-sided picture of nuclear weapons. Overlooking the fact that the United States found nuclear arms to be useful in a larger geopolitical context is a dangerous oversight. Doing so will lead us to miss why other countries find the bomb useful today.

Few people in the United States want to face the fact that nuclear weapons were very useful weapons in the cold war. But it's important to understand why they were useful if there is to be any chance of seeing why others do as well. It's hard to discuss this topic in a calm, rational way because American thinking about nuclear weapons has changed so fundamentally. The bomb has been delegitimized because U.S. government policy has changed to what can be called "nuclear disarmament for others." This transformation grew out of a new way of thinking about the cold war. It is now argued that the cold war was won by Western values. Liberty, free markets, and democracy triumphed over tyranny, state control, and military overspending. Nothing, it is now said, could stand in the way of Western values winning out.

It's a triumphal story. And in this telling the bomb has no role, at least no positive role. Let's be clear. Western values were superior, by a long shot. And those values were important. But leaving the bomb out of the story isn't an honest account of the cold war.

In many accounts the bomb doesn't so much have a subordinate role in the cold war but rather a damned one. It is condemned, associated with phony missile gaps and anticommunist hysteria.

The philosopher Paul Ricoeur speaks of how certain memories are "overly remembered" while others are forgotten. The bomb is remembered not for any role it actually played in the cold war—that is, whether it was a big factor or a small one. Instead it is "overly remembered" as an evil object, one that nearly led to catastrophe. Cartoon versions of the cold war go even further. They ridicule the bomb. Black-and-white video clips of schoolkids scrambling under desks in civil defense drills as the sky lights up with an atomic flash. *Dr. Strangelove*. The bomb as comic nightmare.

Perhaps making fun of nuclear weapons will make them go away. Maybe that's the goal. Laughing at old movies will show a younger American generation the evils of the cold war. Perhaps it will. But I wouldn't bet on it. So far the argument hasn't persuaded North Korea, Israel, India, China, Russia, Pakistan, and Iran to see the bomb this way.

To understand how these nations see the bomb today, it helps to understand how American policy makers viewed nuclear weapons in the cold war. The strategic problem facing the United States wasn't how to offer the world superior political and economic values. The Western democracies always had greater appeal on economic grounds, and on their general political character. The problem was bringing these advantages to bear in local situations. No one was voting on which side offered superior values. For example, in the 1948 Berlin crisis, the first big crisis of the cold war, the people of Berlin did not want communist rule. They wanted to stay with the West, prosper, and raise their families without the secret police knocking on the door at 2 a.m. Winning the values contest was easy for the United States and the West.

The hard part was to stop Soviet expansion, coercion, and tyranny. The bomb played its biggest role in just these situations. Because if these local contests had been lost, the cold war's history would look quite different. In the late 1940s, Western Europe could have come under Soviet domination. Add its GDP (Gross Domestic Product) to the Soviet Union's and it would have been an economic power almost as great as the United States. A similar dynamic would have been at play in Asia, if communism had taken over in Japan, Indonesia, and Thailand.

Some of these developments, had they occurred, could have been reversed. Some not. Getting the Soviets out of Eastern Europe took fifty years. Had they gained control of all of Western Europe it could have taken much longer. Had larger swathes of Asia gone over to communism, Asia would not have seen the triumph of capitalism in anything like the form it did.

The point is this. Had communist advances occurred beyond what they did there would have been a far more intense, dangerous competition than the actual competition that took place. The ferocity, spending, and risk of the cold war would have been much greater than anything actually seen.

Few people think about the cold war this way—that it could have been waged with a far greater intensity than the cold war we actually got. At higher levels the danger of an "eruption" to a nuclear war would have been significantly greater. The extremes the cold war took, in Korea, Vietnam, Indonesia, and Cuba, and in U.S. domestic politics with McCarthyism and red scares, would have been many times greater than they were. The risks were not only of nuclear war. There would have been far higher military spending, which would have undermined the mass consumption society that came to define

American moral and political superiority. A greater degree of competition might have led to garrison-state politics, of a kind that troubled many American experts at the time.

POLITICAL AND MORAL FACTORS

Nuclear weapons are not like most security issues. It's important to get this on the table at the beginning. Debating their use or deployment is not like debating U.S. policy in Afghanistan, or whether to cut the defense budget by 10 percent. These are issues that can be discussed in a neutral, clinical way. The alternatives are laid out and honest people give their best arguments.

The bomb isn't like that. Debating it comes with greater moral and emotional considerations since the outcome of the debate has political and ethical consequences. That the United States invented the bomb and used it on two Japanese cities, and that the bomb's spread could produce biblical levels of destruction, makes it a very different matter than debating counterinsurgency theory or the use of drones in Afghanistan.

Debate about the bomb is more like arguments over genocide, the Holocaust, the internment of Japanese-Americans, or the rape of Nanking. Trying to think through any of these topics without recognizing their political and moral significance doesn't work. The bomb isn't just another weapon.

The relevance of this today is that a wider conversation is needed, one that puts living through a second nuclear age not only in a strategic framework but also in a political and moral framework. This isn't something that can be done by a government agency. It can't be done with pious calls to eliminate the bomb, either. Today, the problem isn't U.S. bombs, it is those of the other countries.

How do we develop such a political and moral framework? One approach is to look to the past to see how that debate worked out and why it mattered. Even though past conditions no longer apply, past debates can point to how political and moral factors were brought into the debate. In the first nuclear age there was a high-level national debate over these political and moral factors. That debate uncovered new issues that the government itself had never thought of. Nothing like this is taking place as the world enters a second nuclear age.

What is forgotten today, or what critics choose to overlook, is how the cold war debate changed the problem of nuclear weapons. What came out of it was that the challenge wasn't to beat the Soviets in an arms race, or to contain them. Rather it was to manage a long-term competition (something else to remember) to avoid a security disaster—in such a way that the competition itself didn't get out of control. The problem was to ensure that the arms race itself didn't cause the very disaster that defense policy was trying to prevent. This was what strategists, moralists, and others were thinking about.

The conceptualization had an enormous impact on cold war dynamics. Take the arms race. It is generally believed that there was an all-out, largely wasteful arms race between the United States and the Soviet Union. Actually, in the United States most weapons that were proposed were never built. The cobalt bomb, a radioactive killer weapon designed to prevent recovery from nuclear attack. Bacteriological weapons. The B-70 bomber. Thousands of additional ICBMs (Intercontinental Ballistic Missiles). Supersized hydrogen-bombs. Mobile missiles. Near-doomsday machines. The neutron bomb. Space-based lasers. Tsunami makers using atom bombs stationed on the sea floor. All of these were proposed, and all of them were rejected.

Why? The reason is that they were adjudged to be over the top, in a political or moral sense (or both). Had they been built, they would have driven the arms race to a much higher, more dangerous pitch.

Moreover, something that wasn't proposed, at least by the U.S. government, was "bought" instead: arms control. This idea didn't come out of the government, but rather from think tanks, universities, and religious and moral thinkers who stepped back and asked a simple question—What was the United States doing in the way it waged the cold war?

The very idea that outside experts of all stripes would have a view on strategic matters was itself a new concept. Because traditionally it was the military that had the only views that counted on strategic questions. But in the cold war the outsiders' views counted. They reframed the debate in a basic way.

This had far-reaching effects. It is not generally remembered today how the moral concerns over nuclear weapons drove one of the most remarkable technological transformations in military history. The concern originated with World War II population bombing, quickly followed by the atom bomb, and then the H-bomb. The United States in the 1960s began research to make conventional strikes more precise and controlled, to avoid killing innocent civilians. This program eventually led to a dramatic de-emphasis of the atom bomb itself, in favor of precision conventional weapons. By the mid-1960s the role of the bomb had declined enormously in U.S. strategic plans and thinking.

A comparable debate never occurred in the Soviet Union. That regime built institutions that can only be described as transcendentally mad. This is worth remembering, too. Autocratic regimes don't have the moral compass that democracies do. That they are capable of building unimaginable horrors is understood, given the history of the twentieth century. This predisposition is unlikely to magically disappear in the twenty-first century.

The U.S. cold war debate lowered the risk of nuclear war. There's no scientific way to prove this, but I believe it to be the case. The debate embodied America's commitment to not giving up, but also to not going too far. Balancing strategic purpose with restraint is possible. It need not lead to the extremes of militarism or weakness. To think otherwise underestimates American democracy.

NUCLEAR WEAPONS AND THE COLD WAR

The cold war wasn't about nuclear weapons. I run in to students who think that it was, so it's important to correct the misconception that the cold war was first and foremost a nuclear arms race. The cold war had an arms race and a nuclear component, but that wasn't its essence. Rather, the cold war was a long-term contest between two industrial powers for control of Europe and the developing world. The cold war's deadly toll wasn't in Europe, nor was it from a nuclear exchange. These outcomes could have happened but did not. The high casualties were from regional and internal wars, in Southeast Asia, Korea, Africa, and other places. This is important to understand because there was a global dynamic, with regional patterns and variations.

Global-regional connections are extremely important to any understanding of the cold war, most especially to its nuclear dynamics. They are extremely important in the second nuclear age, too. The cold war was driven by the regional dynamics of local actors that stood far apart from the global struggle. Regional conflicts had a dynamic of their own that was far different from the superpowers' interests or even understanding. But these regional actors didn't have nuclear weapons, at least outside of Western Europe, and even that was a specialized case because of the bloc discipline installed by the North Atlantic Treaty Organization (NATO) and the Warsaw Pact.

Global-regional connections, as we will see, apply to the second nuclear age as well. This time, however, the regional actors have nuclear weapons, as well as fundamentally different purposes from those of the major powers.

The presence of nuclear weapons in the cold war enlarged the conceivable destruction far beyond anything that went before it. Military technology had been moving on this path for some time. The world wars saw unlimited submarine attacks on civilian ships, poison gas, population bombing, and death camps.

Yet adding the atomic bomb to this portfolio of horrors dramatically increased the scale of catastrophe. Think of it this way. The population bombings in World War II killed half a million Germans and Japanese each. Draw this four-year campaign, 1942 to 1945, as a horizontal time line. Now stand it up vertically and visualize that it could be done in an afternoon. A million people killed in one day. That was with kiloton weapons. Megaton weapons, like the hydrogen bomb, made the violence that much more horrific.

There were several ways that this development affected strategy, primarily by placing a nuclear context on the use of force. Countries that had been rivals forever now had to consider the possibility that if a crisis flared up, it could escalate to nuclear levels. The question, then as now, was how to manage this change in context.

A nuclear context radically changed the character of rivalry. Many of my students enter my classes believing that the military is built to fight and win wars. I know many military people who believe this, too. Seen this way, the main divide is between war and peace. If there's peace, why would anyone need to use force? If there's war, then force should be decisive, even all-out if necessary.

The cold war starkly diverged from this pattern. In a nuclear context, the military couldn't be used in an all-out way without inviting comparable destruction on oneself that was unacceptable. So avoiding nuclear war, "managing" an arms race, and dampening incentives to inflame a situation took on much greater importance.

The nuclear context of the cold war lessened the clear divide between peace and war. In its place there was a spectrum in the use of force. It ranged from peace to war. But in between there were many, many possibilities and options. The cold war was waged in this spectrum, between the two extremes of peace and nuclear war.

Rather than using force to fight and win wars, a far greater diversity of purpose came into effect. Force could be used to punish. It could demonstrate resolve. Or it could be used as a demonstration—of recklessness or caution. Force could be used for deterrence or for revenge.

All of these purposes existed before nuclear weapons were invented. But a nuclear context profoundly changed them. Now they had to be looked at not only in terms of their costs and benefits, but for their impact on estimates of the result should they intensify. Even small uses of force became important. If the United States did X, and the Soviet Union responded with Y, where would this lead if the chain of actions continued? That was the question.

Nuclear weapons thus made the calculation of "next moves" central to strategy. A mistake, a careless decision, or a misestimate could lead to a lot more than political embarrassment.

Big decisions over war or peace were broken down into lots of smaller ones about the use of force and where it might lead. And even the smallest decisions got high-level attention. In the Berlin crisis of 1948, the decision as to the kind of rifles U.S. guards carried on trains running to Berlin, M-1s or carbines, was kicked all the way up to the White House.

The skill needed to identify these smaller decisions was learned on the job. It was not anticipated. Everything said here about the calculated use of force to achieve various purposes, basing decisions about using force on estimates of an opponent's reaction, breaking down sweeping decisions on war or peace into much smaller "chunks," and high-level attention given to micro moves—none of this was foreseen. It was "discovered" by national leaders and, even then, usually after they got into a crisis.

This is worth keeping in mind for the second nuclear age. The early years of the cold war were very dangerous because much of what would become "obvious" strategic lessons weren't known or even thought about beforehand. Just like learning how to drive or swim, it didn't come automatically. There was a steep learning curve. That's why the 1950s and early 1960s were more dangerous than the 1970s and 1980s, when at least the obvious lessons of nuclear rivalry had been learned by both sides.

The early cold war revealed something else that may well be part of the second nuclear age. The superpowers didn't understand their own forces. Consider just one example. Defending Western Europe using conventional weapons was one thing. But a nuclear defense was altogether different. Secretary of State John Foster Dulles traveled to Western Europe in 1957 to assure the West Germans that the United States would use the bomb to defend them, even though it might lead to a nuclear war between the United States and the Soviet Union. Dulles, and virtually all of Washington, had framed the deterrence problem as one of German incredulity about this promise. In the lingo of the day the question was asked: "Would America really trade New York and Chicago to defend Hamburg and Munich?"

Dulles was stunned to discover that this issue wasn't what concerned West German chancellor Konrad Adenauer. Quite the contrary. Adenauer pleaded with Dulles *not* to be defended with the bomb. A nuclear defense meant firing hundreds of atomic bombs, which would destroy German cities, leading to the destruction not only of the German state but also of the German people. That's how Adenauer saw it, with good reason. In my first job after college I worked on this problem, in the 1970s, using computer simulations of a "tactical" nuclear war in Europe, with battlefield atomic bombs aimed at Soviet tank columns.

I couldn't believe the U.S. plans. They assumed that all the nuclear weapons would be fired at Soviet armored and mechanized divisions in the countryside, far from German cities. It was as if Germany had no cities, and this was the assumption in the 1970s! That was fine except that World War II showed how quickly the fighting got into urban areas. Somehow this bit of history had escaped the planners in Washington.

Moreover, once the first Soviet tank divisions were destroyed by tactical nuclear weapons, it seemed to me pretty clear that word would get out fairly quickly to stay away from open fields in the countryside. You would be amazed how fast word gets out over the radio if traveling in the open country means you will be hit with fifteen kilotons. Somehow, none of this penetrated U.S. plans.

Even years into the cold war the U.S. government did not understand nuclear weapons, even though they were building them by the thousands. Washington didn't understand how our allies viewed their security concerns in a nuclear context. The same issue came up in the game changer exercise of chapter 1. Even in a simulation, a game, the U.S. team made up of senior officials completely missed how a key ally, Israel, saw nuclear developments. Maybe this is all a coincidence. That is, the history of the 1950s reflected in Dulles with Adenauer, the plans devised for European defense in the 1970s, and the war game scenario of a nuclear Middle East all show that the U.S. government hadn't thought through some pretty obvious issues. But I don't think it is a coincidence.

Another point. While all the many uses of force discussed earlier came up in the cold war, one of them got more prominence and emphasis than any other: deterrence. An outsized attention to deterrence was a distinctive feature of the first nuclear age. The bomb was viewed mainly through the prism of psychology. And deterrence, more than anything else, is psychological.

This one-sided emphasis meant that the "performance" of nuclear weapons was judged more in psychological terms than in any other way. Tactics, command and control, alerting dynamics, deception, et cetera, received far less attention than they should have because policy makers believed that such details didn't matter. They could be "managed" by deterrence, meaning that these other issues wouldn't ever arise.

I am not criticizing the reliance on deterrence during the cold war. It *was* the most important use of nuclear weapons, but the bomb had other functions as well. It's the imbalance of attention, thought, and effort that's noteworthy. The reason that this is important to highlight is that America got through the first nuclear age with an overdependence on the deterrent aspects of nuclear weapons. It may not be so lucky in a second nuclear age. I've played a lot of crisis games in recent years and have often been struck by the importance of factors that have little to do with deterrence, such as command and control, tactics, geography, inexperience, bad weather, or outright mistakes. There is a strong bias in favor of deterrent strategies, and an aversion to thinking through anything else that has to do with nuclear weapons. This bias could lead to underappreciating the likelihood that other countries may not hold the same view as the United States.

A nuclear context also had consequences that went beyond the "moment of choice" dramas in crisis management. It fit the economy and politics of the time. This is the second way nuclear weapons affected the U.S.-Soviet rivalry. It doesn't usually get the attention it deserves, but it was the main reason so many nuclear weapons were built. It is not clear how the bomb will or won't align with the economy and politics of the twenty-first century, but the question needs to be asked. It wasn't clear how this alignment would work out in the cold war either.

Nuclear weapons allowed the United States to wage the cold war with one hand tied behind its back. Consider the defense burden. The peak U.S.-defense budget (1953, during the Korean War) was 11.7 percent of GDP. The average defense budget in the years between Korea and Vietnam was 10 percent. After Vietnam it went down sharply. The Reagan defense buildup peaked at 6 percent of GDP. At the end of the cold war, in 1991 under President George H. W. Bush, it was only 4.6 percent.

Had the United States needed to spend more it surely could have. After all, America spent 40 percent of GDP to defeat Japan and Germany in World War II. But to do so would have had dire consequences. The rise of the mass consumption society in the 1950s and 1960s would have been one of the first casualties. Had the United States spent more of its national wealth on defense, the funds would have had to be diverted from something else, and that surely would be consumption.

This was precisely the Soviet Union's problem. It consistently spent 25 percent of its GDP on the military—most of that money diverted from consumption. The country was stuck in the 1930s, with an industrial economy long on investment, a grotesquely oversized military and state bureaucracy, and undersized consumption. Everyone thinks that the Soviet economy was a disaster, which it was at the end. But this was not from some mistake. It was a strategic choice. In certain narrow ways the Soviet economy was a success because it accurately reflected Stalin's vision of what an industrial economy should be. The problem, obviously, was that it was optimized for the 1930s, not the 1980s.

What is rarely acknowledged today, or is intentionally overlooked, is how defense economics fit the U.S. nuclear emphasis of the era. Nuclear weapons allowed the United States to get away with defense on the cheap, so to speak. Over a fifty-year period a smaller U.S. defense program contained a larger Soviet one.

Let's shift attention from dollars to people. The peak size of the cold war U.S. Army was twenty divisions, in 1953. The Soviets had more than two hundred divisions. The Soviet divisions were smaller, true. But the Soviet military was vastly larger than anything America had at its disposal.

Consider some math. There's an old rule of thumb that there should be a division for each one million population. In World War II the United States raised 89 army divisions and 18 marine divisions. Given the U.S. population in the 1950s of 165 million, this would have meant about 165 divisions. With better technology than the Soviets had, this would have been a force that could have defended Western Europe.

But the problem was that the United States wasn't in Europe. It had a small force there, and plans to put a big one in if war broke out. If Europe fell, either from a Soviet military attack or a political seizure of some kind, it would have taken years to draft, train, and land a U.S. force to retake it. A D-Day-style landing on the beaches of France was unimaginable once the Soviets had the bomb. The threat of four or five nuclear bombs dropped on the landing beaches made such a strategy impossible.

So what about keeping a huge force in Europe full time? Let's consider the economic and political consequences of this. This would mean a vastly enlarged U.S. defense effort far beyond anything seen in the actual cold war. America had the draft, which meant that soldiers were cheap, at least economically. But a 165-division force would have disrupted American society. Imagine a draft twenty times greater than what it actually was, with extended age eligibility to, say, thirty-five years of age. Men in their early thirties pulled out of their careers, families broken up, new industries never built. It is hard to conceive of this. And one reason it didn't happen is because the atomic bomb allowed for a much smaller army, measured in dollars and manpower.

Push this a little further to see the alignment of nuclear weapons with politics and economics. Domestic tensions in the 1950s and early 1960s were growing under the surface of American prosperity. McCarthyism, civil rights, the baby boomers. To overlay on this social situation conscription requirements twenty times larger would have strained domestic politics to the breaking point. Think of the impact on race relations in the 1960s and 1970s, or the consequences of drafting far greater numbers of college students for such a vastly enlarged defense program. Several scholars, such as Yale's Harold Lasswell, argued that the United States might turn into a garrison state at this level of defense. It was not a groundless fear. But it's important to note that Laswell's concern was over a form of defense, super-high defense budgets and a giant standing force, and this never materialized.

The effect of a large standing, peacetime military was still a matter of great concern. President Dwight D. Eisenhower worried about it, and said so in his famous 1961 farewell address. For the first time in its history, Ike said, the United States had a peacetime standing military, and also for the first time a peacetime arms industry. All citizens, he warned, should be concerned about their unwarranted influence in the corridors of power.

The cold war, as Eisenhower noted, wasn't fought by Ford and General Motors, as World War II was. It was fought by highly specialized defense companies who quickly saw that they needed to anchor their programs with congressional support.

Eisenhower, the president who coined the term and articulated fears of a military-industrial complex, was also the president who presided over the vast increase of U.S. nuclear weapons. This wasn't a coincidence. Nuclear arms fit in with prosperity at home, by not allowing the defense budget to distort the economy. When Ike came into office there were few nuclear weapons. He ushered in an era of what was called at the time "Nuclear Good & Plenty," after a popular candy of the day. Each box of Good & Plenty contained dozens of small pieces of candy-coated licorice, and kids would scatter them around to play with them. The American nuclear buildup under Ike was a lot like that. Every service went nuclear—the army, the navy, and the air force. If something could float or fly or drive, the Pentagon put a nuclear warhead on it.

A nuclear context aligned with other aspects of U.S. strategy. Cold war histories usually describe American policy in terms of containment and deterrence. This is true, but it doesn't go far enough. It is important to recognize that the challenge America faced wasn't to win the cold war, to contain the Soviets, or even to deter them. It was to do these things without pushing the arms race, or international politics, to levels so dangerous that it would produce the disaster that deterrence was trying to prevent. That is a tremendously important point to keep in mind. Strategy isn't just about what the goals are. It's also about how they're achieved.

For example, the United States could have easily doubled or tripled its defense program had it chosen to do so. This would really have pressed the Soviets, with their smaller GDP. But the United

States didn't do this. And the reason was that it was too dangerous. World War I had erupted out of an arms race, between Germany and Britain. The political impact of an all-out arms race waged by the United States in the early cold war would have raised the risks of war, probably by a great deal. This is because the Soviets were so weak economically, as is now known.

There were related political decisions America could have made in the cold war but didn't because they would have overexcited international politics. Russia's traditional enemy in the Far East was Japan, its adversary in the Russo-Japanese war of 1904–5. Japan's victory in that war had far-reaching political consequences in Russia and Asia, and it remained a sore point for the Soviet Union. Recognizing this dynamic, the United States waged the entire cold war without trying to get Japan to rearm. Tokyo spent less than 1 percent of its GDP on defense throughout. Nor did the United States back the ultra-right in Japan as a kind of threat to keep the Soviets off balance. That, too, was considered too dangerous.

Likewise, America could have, but didn't, build up a militaristic, nationalistic regime in West Germany. Germany is not exactly a nation lacking in military traditions, as Europeans in the 1950s and 1960s remembered all too well. But the United States always kept West Germany on a short leash, tightly hemmed in by NATO.

Unleashing Russia's historic enemies Japan and Germany, this time with the economic heft of America's GDP behind them, would have put Moscow in a vast geographic pincers. But Washington never did this.

America also could have gone after Soviet vulnerabilities in Eastern Europe. Washington always proceeded gingerly on this front. It was a key fault line and was studied several times. I worked on some of these studies at the Hudson Institute. Large CIA and covert operations, assassinations, arming the Polish unions, parachuting a million anti-tank rifles into Poland and Czechoslovakia—all studied and, thankfully, utterly rejected by the American government.

Only late in the cold war, under President Jimmy Carter and picking up under President Ronald Reagan, did limited U.S. political actions focus on Poland and the others. At this point in the cold war the Soviet empire was in decline.

On the weapons front, the United States canceled many weapons that would have given it a military edge in the narrow sense, and which the military services wanted. The neutron bomb, mobile medium-range missiles, ABM (Antiballistic Missile), SDI (Strategic Defense Initiative)—all never built. In 1961 the Russians exploded the biggest bomb ever made, a fifty-megaton behemoth they parachuted out of an airplane in the Arctic north. The spectacular photos of the explosion were published in every newspaper and magazine in the world. The Pentagon rushed to President John F. Kennedy saying that America needed to match it. He turned them down flat.

Why didn't the United States take these actions? Because, once again, the challenge was to win the cold war without overdoing the arms race, without destabilizing Europe and the international system that could lead to disaster.

THE FIRST NUCLEAR AGE WAS DYNAMIC

Another very important lesson to remember is that the first nuclear age wasn't static. The tendency today is to look at the cold war as a slow-moving, steady competition. Most historical accounts of the cold war focus on containment and deterrence as if they were timeless grand strategies planned at the beginning of the cold war and stuck with until its end.

But the cold war was much more dynamic than this. By "dynamic" I mean that there were big changes in major parts of the cold war over time. The reason this point is so important is that those who think that the second nuclear age will be static, and easily stabilized by overarching strategic doctrines like containment or deterrence, incorrectly presuppose that the first nuclear age was static. They fail to understand the important dynamics that were anything but easy to manage. Indeed, there are many reasons why the second nuclear age may be even more dynamic than the first nuclear age.

What drove the dynamics of the first nuclear age? Technology, politics, and strategy all changed over time. There were even fads and fashions that came and went. There were ebbs and flows in the cold war's intensity. Sometimes it looked as if war might break out. A year later the main concern was arms control.

Consider the role of nuclear weapons. In the 1950s the United States was in the nuclear buildup phase as the costs of mounting a conventional defense of Europe were judged to be too high. Each service fought for its share of the nuclear pie. More nuclear weapons were considered better in this era of "Nuclear Good & Plenty," and atomic factories cranked out bombs as if they were pieces of candy. Ten years later, in the mid-1960s, wars of national liberation and counterinsurgency were the central focus, and the U.S. government started to de-emphasize nuclear deterrence. In the 1970s détente became the focus. It had a nuclear component, certainly, but it was to cap the arms race from what had started in the 1950s. In the 1980s, nuclear weapons returned for a time to American strategic thinking. This time it wasn't to reduce them but rather to use them in political ways to intimidate the Soviet Union.

To see this dynamism in action, consider the first crisis of the first nuclear age. Better than any abstract discussion it shows how events shaped policy just as much as policy shaped events. This also is an important lesson from the first nuclear age to keep in mind for the second.

GAME CHANGER 1.0: THE 1948 BERLIN CRISIS

The crisis game in chapter 1 was played to understand the dynamics of a nuclear Middle East. The first nuclear age began with a real crisis, and it was a game changer, too. It set the rules and style of the political and military dynamics that were to follow. In this respect, the 1948 Berlin crisis had far-reaching consequences. It established precedents for the first nuclear age, crystallized rules of engagement, and established red lines that endured throughout the cold war.

It's worth emphasizing that a crisis did this. In the absence of a good understanding of the political and military dynamics beforehand, a crisis focuses attention on problems that would otherwise be ignored. National leaders, and the bureaucracy, can't ignore a crisis. It forces participants to respond to events rather than to the problems of bureaucratic infighting.

Berlin is important for another reason. The first nuclear crisis of a second nuclear age is likely to have a disproportionate impact precisely because it will establish rules and red lines for many years afterward. Once these are established, it is possible to overturn them—but it is much harder to do so because precedents and expectations have been set. Indeed, cold war dynamics can usefully be examined as a rivalry to establish advantageous precedents for acceptable behavior.

The Berlin crisis arose out of worsening U.S.-Soviet relations after World War II. Berlin was under four-power rule, with the United States, the Soviet Union, France, and Britain sharing joint control of the city. Berlin, however, was deep inside the Soviet zone of Germany, surrounded on all sides by Soviet armies.

In the spring of 1948, the Soviets began impeding Allied access to the city with temporary roadblocks, exhaustive vehicle searches, and similar actions. The United States protested, and there was a lessening of the Soviet chokehold on the city.

But America did something more than just protest. Three atom bombs were tested in the South Pacific in April and May 1948. These were widely reported, with photos of the mushroom clouds in every major newspaper in the world.

On June 24, 1948, the Soviets laid down a full ground blockade of Berlin, preventing all car, truck, and rail access. Amazingly, few in America anticipated this, despite the earlier harassment. They just hadn't thought of it in the Pentagon or in the White House. This is something to remember, too, the move that should have been foreseen but wasn't.

President Harry S. Truman faced a tough choice. The military situation on the ground was untenable. Unlike the United States, the Soviet Union had kept its army together after the war, and it had more than 350,000 troops in fifteen divisions in Germany. Moscow didn't yet have the bomb—the first successful Soviet test would not happen until August 1949—but the Soviets did have another 180 divisions in western Russia that they could throw into Germany. Further, Stalin had an armed communist underground in Western Europe left over from fighting the Nazis, which stood waiting for a signal to rise up against the Western Allies. Sabotage, labor disruption, strikes, and terrorism could have disrupted not only Berlin but France, Belgium, and the Netherlands as well.

The United States had only 60,000 occupation troops in Germany. These were skeleton forces, mainly military police and civil affairs units. Combat forces had been withdrawn after the war. There was only a single infantry division and a few armored cavalry units. British and French forces were even weaker.

The global situation also has to be understood in order to see the choices Truman faced. NATO did not exist yet. Indeed, to Truman and most others in Washington, this was what the crisis was all about. It wasn't about Berlin directly, but rather it was a Soviet attempt to forestall the creation of an American-led bloc in Western Europe. If Stalin could split the Europeans and prevent them from coming together, he could then continue his "salami tactics," taking one country at a time as he had so successfully done in Eastern Europe.

Truman had other problems. Mao Zedong was winning in China in 1948. The prospect of losing both Western Europe and China to communism at the same time wasn't something Truman could stand. The effect on the global power balance was obvious.

Moreover, the 1948 presidential election was coming up in November. The American people were fed up with war and were in no mood to support a big military program so soon after World War II.

Truman had a weak hand to play. You might ask yourself, What would you do in his shoes? It's an interesting question. But for Harry Truman it wasn't an academic exercise.

He turned to the Pentagon for ideas. The generals' plan was to send an armored column toward Berlin. If it was blocked, which was virtually certain, there were no plans for what to do next, other than attack the Soviet Union with the atomic bomb. In other words, "send up an armored column, and if that doesn't work, launch World War III." Truman declined the advice.

The Berlin crisis is usually presented in terms of Harry Truman's brilliant decision to resupply Berlin by air, once ground access had been cut off. This was a stroke of genius, and a gutsy move. But it raises certain larger questions. Why didn't the Soviets just shoot down the supply planes, or even just a few of them, to put the ball back in the American court about what to do next? Why didn't they just take the city with their larger army? And why didn't they unleash political warfare to wrack Western Europe with strikes, demonstrations, and sabotage? These are the critical questions.

Let's look at the U.S. options from Harry Truman's viewpoint. The United States had the bomb and an air force. It was bigger, with much better technology, than its Soviet counterpart. America had the B-29, used against Hiroshima and Nagasaki, and the new B-36, one version of which was designed for atomic warfare. The United States also had a global air base system that ringed the Soviet Union with airfields in Japan, Spain, Germany, Libya, and—with Britain—in Egypt.

What Truman did was to ratchet up pressure on the Soviets through forward stationing of bombers and stepped-up "routine" training exercises. The plan was to gradually increase these bomber exercises to pressure the Soviets to back down.

If Stalin signaled communist labor unions to strike in France and Belgium, that would disrupt the Western alliance. But it would also raise the stakes. The United States would have to respond. Increased exercises and other actions would follow. If Stalin escalated, it would only harden the U.S. position—at a higher level of danger to Moscow. If Stalin were to take Berlin in this situation, he'd face a serious prospect of war. The tactic was later dubbed "brinkmanship." Think of two individuals fighting on a cliff. One of them tries to steer the fight closer to the edge, but not too close. There are really two contests going on at the same time. One is the fight itself. The other is maneuvering it to the edge, where it becomes so treacherous that one or the other party decides that it's just too dangerous to continue. Or they both fall into the abyss.

It's important to emphasize that this wasn't nuclear blackmail. That's a different concept altogether. Nuclear blackmail means saying, "If you don't open up Berlin, I'm going to hit you with the bomb." Academics often argue about nuclear blackmail in the cold war. They say that it's dangerous, or that it doesn't work. But my assessment is different. Nuclear blackmail was never used in the cold war, not one time. There was never a single instance of a nuclear ultimatum. Truman never did it. He never came close to it. Nor did any other president.

Truman wasn't threatening to bomb the Soviet Union. He was threatening to go to higher levels of risk. That's very different. It was the key innovation of the Berlin crisis. And it set the pattern for the United States for decades to come.

Some examples show how the threat of going to higher levels of intensity worked in practice. In July, a month into the blockade, three B-29s were sent on a highly publicized around-the-world flight, testing landings on foreign airfields and demonstrating what the United States had and the Soviets didn't: a ring of bases on its adversary's perimeter and an air force that could use them.

In the same month Truman ordered sixty B-29s to be deployed

from the United States to Britain, and thirty more to Germany. These airplanes did not have atomic bombs with them, but the Soviets didn't know that—and in fact the bombs could have been delivered to their bases in Britain and Germany in days, with the planes fitted with nuclear bomb racks in hours. The B-29 bases in England even had special storage facilities for atomic bombs built in the summer and fall of 1948 in preparation for just this contingency. Runways in Germany were lengthened to handle the B-29s, and one hundred fighters were sent there to protect the airfields. Thousands of maintenance personnel were sent to Britain and Germany, including an entire air force maintenance depot. All of this was done with highly public announcements. It wasn't any bluff.

There was a larger pattern to the moves. The United States was moving its airpower forward, from America to the Soviet perimeter. Bombers leapfrogged around these bases on stepped-up "routine training flights." Moscow was kept guessing about what might come next, and where. And the Soviets didn't like it one bit. For at this time they didn't have a single base outside of their territory. (This asymmetry was one of the motivations behind the later Cuban missile crisis.) The Americans could reach them but they couldn't reach the Americans. Airpower, the bomb, and geography created the advantage.

Even more provocative exercises were coming. In July 1948 seven hundred U.S. Air Force planes converged on Idlewild (now John F. Kennedy International) Airport in New York to demonstrate the ability to rapidly concentrate on a single target from widely scattered bases. The exercise was dramatically covered in the media. Bombers typically are spread over several bases to protect them from a surprise attack. If they were all on one airfield the whole force could be taken out by one blow. This tactic meant they had to take off and converge to hit their target. From the Soviet side, this July exercise had little ambiguity. It was a test run for an attack on them.

In September 1948 there were more exercises with the new B-36 bomber. Six B-36s overflew several U.S. cities, and forty-nine B-29s were flown in to the United States from Misawa, Japan; the Azores; Furstenfeldbruck, Germany; and other distant bases to "bomb" New York, Chicago, Dallas, and San Francisco. Fifty thousand people watched the exercise at Mitchel Field on Long Island, just outside New York City (today the site of the Nassau Coliseum), including President Truman and his Republican challenger in the November election, Governor Thomas Dewey of New York, who watched the exercise sitting together in the observation stands.

This display of political unity could hardly go unnoticed in Moscow. The message was clear. If U.S. bombers could stage from overseas to "attack" American cities, they could surely fly the other way. The United States could strike the Soviet Union from almost 360 degrees. It was impossible to build air defenses against such a nimble threat. And the threat would continue, no matter who won the presidential election.

The Soviets did try some pathetic countermeasures. In October they held a live-fire air exercise in their German occupation zone. But the fact that they were inside their own territory only showed how geographically boxed in they were. Their air force was archaic— it even included an old biplane from World War I.

Truman calculated that Stalin didn't want war over Berlin. If he had, he could have just taken the city. Throughout 1948 the air exercises kept getting bigger, and closer to Soviet territory. Truman challenged the Soviets to give in, call off the blockade, or face ever-mounting risks.

Let's suppose, for a moment, that the Soviets did harass the air resupply of Berlin. The United States, in response, could have moved atomic bombs to Britain and Germany, and leaked this tidbit of intelligence to the *New York Times*. Or, more provocatively, it could have landed three nuclear-armed B-36s in Berlin and put them on runway alert, ready to take off in minutes. The U.S. Navy could have closed the Suez and Panama canals to Soviet shipping. Or it could have sunk one Soviet ship for every day the blockade lasted. None of these actions was taken. But they could have been.

The Berlin crisis begins with Harry Truman having few good cards to play. He could have given in and let Berlin fall. This would avoid a conflict, but likely with disastrous consequences down the road. America's alliances with Western Europe might have collapsed before NATO ever got started. The key alliance of the cold war would have gone down the drain. With Mao's looming victory in China (which would come in October 1949) the momentum of the cold war might have shifted. I think the United States still would have won the cold war. But it would have taken far greater efforts—and greater risks.

What made Harry Truman a great president was his judgment. He didn't blindly accept the options handed to him by the Pentagon. He never used a nuclear ultimatum. And he gave Stalin a face-saving exit out of the crisis. Which is what happened when the Soviet blockade finally ended in May 1949.

Truman stood up where he could, in Europe, in Berlin. But he didn't try this everywhere. In China, for example, he didn't use a slow-motion increase in tensions, nor did he send in the U.S. Army to reverse Mao's victory. He saw that it wouldn't have worked to tell Mao to back off, even backed by U.S. airpower. Truman's genius was in accepting certain conflicts, declining others, and knowing the difference between the two.

The bomb, along with nimble airpower, turned a weak U.S. hand into a winning one. It was a powerful lesson not just in strategy but also in innovation. No one had ever thought of using airpower this way; it was devised essentially in real time by a creative group of air force officers to give political leaders options they didn't know they had. Absent this, the United States might have been forced into using nuclear blackmail, ultimatums to Moscow that the U.S. leadership thought were very dangerous.

So one big lesson was that the bomb was useful, but not in a way that critics thought. Most strategists at the time believed that war with the bomb meant large-scale nuclear firings, hitting targets and destroying cities. The Berlin crisis showed an entirely different path for strategic innovation.

There were many other such lessons learned during the first nuclear age. They may not definitively translate to the realities of the second nuclear age, but they're a good place to start in trying to understand its dynamics.

· 3 ·

LESSONS OF THE FIRST NUCLEAR AGE

Most lessons about the first nuclear age are banalities. "Choose peace instead of thermonuclear war." "Don't get into a nuclear crisis." This is fine advice, I suppose, if you accept the alternatives they offer. But they're not very useful if you don't. Harry Truman's choice wasn't between peace and war. John F. Kennedy wasn't the one who put missiles into Cuba. The challenge facing these presidents was to avoid a U.S. security disaster while not getting into a nuclear war in the process. That's a big difference in the formulation of the choices.

Nonetheless there are lessons of the cold war that are more likely to apply to the second nuclear age. My purpose in reviewing these is to use history as a way to focus attention and good thinking on the right set of problems.

Some of the lessons offered here, no doubt, will be controversial. They dredge up bad memories. Despite this, it's essential to think about them. Marshall McLuhan said something I've always liked: "To the blind all things are sudden." If the United States is blind to the dynamics of the first nuclear age, it won't foresee the dynamics in the second.

EIGHT LESSONS OF THE FIRST NUCLEAR AGE

There are many lessons of the first nuclear age that have little relevance for the world we are in now. The lessons selected here seem to me most likely to occur again. They're a statement of problems to look out for in a second nuclear age.

FIGURE 3.1

EIGHT LESSONS OF THE FIRST NUCLEAR AGE

1. You Don't Have to Fire a Nuclear Weapon to Use It
2. Words Matter
3. Nuclear Head Games
4. Individuals Matter
5. . . . And So Do Institutions
6. Getting the Risks Wrong
7. Technology and the Strategy Lag
8. Thinking About the Unthinkable

You Don't Have to Fire a Nuclear Weapon to Use It

This is the single most important lesson of the first nuclear age. Nuclear war didn't occur. But nuclear weapons were used every single day. There were many innovative ways to use the bomb without actually firing it.

Some people get upset when told that nuclear weapons helped prevent a national security disaster and served to dampen cold war dynamics. Many have grown up in a world where nuclear weapons have been thoroughly demonized, absent any discussion of their usefulness. While it's laudable to point out the horrors of nuclear war, focusing entirely on the bomb's evils leaves out things the United States couldn't ignore at the time. This is good to remember in thinking about ways North Korea, Pakistan, Israel, and others may use the bomb in the second nuclear age.

The bomb was used right from the beginning, as Harry Truman did in the Berlin crisis. The diverse ways it was used show real creativity. Its use was limited only by the imagination of leaders, their staffs, and strategists.

Despite this, many observers at the time missed what was happening. Some early nuclear strategists argued that in the nuclear age there could be no such thing as strategy. The bomb was just too devastating to develop any meaningful concept of strategy for it.

The problem with this viewpoint was that it failed to see that creativity and innovation were developing around the definition of what using the bomb meant. Using the bomb need not mean firing nuclear weapons.

Consider a few of these uses. The bomb was used to deter a nuclear attack on the United States. That's clear. More than seven thousand bombs were put in Europe to deter an attack there as well.

But not just for deterrence. Nuclear weapons were also used for communication and bargaining. Harry Truman used worldwide bomber exercises to ratchet up risk and to communicate to Moscow what he was doing. He used the bomber runs to bargain with the Soviets. "Okay, go ahead, shoot down our airplanes supplying Berlin. Then you'll face bomber probes all around your country, and if you fire on them see what I do next!" If that's not using the bomb I don't know what is.

President Eisenhower ordered the "Long Tom" atomic cannon to Korea in 1953 when the armistice talks there stalled. Film clips were sent to the newspapers of the Long Tom firing an atomic artillery round (I'm not kidding) with a mushroom cloud in the distance. President Kennedy used nuclear B-52 alerts in the Cuban missile crisis to communicate to the Soviets about the seriousness of that showdown.

The Soviets used the bomb, too. In 1956 they threatened to wipe out Paris and London if the French and British governments didn't evacuate their armies from the Suez Canal, which they had just seized. The Soviets had no army or navy in the Middle East. They had a weak hand, like Truman had in Berlin. Indeed, it isn't even clear they had missiles that could reach Paris in 1956. But the French didn't know this. There's a common view nowadays that this particular Soviet threat was just cold war bluster and wasn't something that should have been taken too seriously. But this crisis, and the Soviet threat, was a big reason the French started their own bomb program shortly thereafter. And, as is now documented, the Israelis went along for the ride with the French, too, eventually getting their own bomb with cooperation from France. The Suez crisis was not only a Soviet use of the bomb, it had a larger unanticipated consequence, nuclear prolif-eration to two countries, France and Israel. I would hardly dismiss this as cold war bluster.

The bomb was used in other ways. It held alliances together. Amer-ica's atomic shield was NATO's political cement. Had there been no bomb, the much larger Soviet army would have required a far more massive U.S. defense program. Washington used the bomb to cement an alliance with Japan as well. It forestalled any Japanese desire to get its own nuclear arsenal.

It is impolitic to say so now, when nuclear nonproliferation is the fundamental principle of U.S. policy, but Washington "gave" the bomb away to many other countries. Atomic bombs were given in the 1960s to Turkey, Greece, West Germany, Italy, and the Nether-lands. There were special keys, and later codes, that were needed to fire them. So, technically speaking, the United States controlled these bombs. But the controls were quite lax in many instances. In the fog of war their control could hardly be guaranteed. That was the whole point. Any of these countries might have fired on its own—and that was the core of the U.S. threat. The fiction of U.S. control was even put into a strategy of "threats that leave something to chance." By winking at the Soviets that the United States might not be able to keep control of these atomic bombs in all situations, Moscow had to calculate that the NATO deterrent just might fire. If the Soviet Union attacked, or if it rocked the boat too hard, well, all bets were off about what might happen next.

Other "uses" of the bomb had little to do with military affairs. This is an important lesson, too. Charles de Gaulle used the bomb to stake out an independent foreign policy for France. He quit NATO's integrated military command in 1965, and acted as if France were a third major power in the world, outside of the two cold war blocs.

The French program never really had much to do with fighting a war, or even with deterrence. When asked why France needed an independent nuclear deterrent, de Gaulle famously shot back, "So we get invited to arms control conferences." As it turned out, France didn't get invited to arms control meetings, but de Gaulle's strategy paid off nonetheless. France became a third force in Europe, with a military not under NATO (and therefore American) control. France used the bomb to get much more than it deserved. Its foreign policy was much more independent than that of other European powers. The bomb was critical to this. Had France not been a nuclear-weapons state, no one would have taken it seriously. The view would have been that France was just one more fading colonial power beholden to the Americans.

Another use of the bomb was for political mischief. The bomb provoked antinuclear movements and domestic political protests. In the 1980s new U.S. missiles were installed in Europe, to counter Soviet missiles deployed earlier. European public sentiment was opposed to this move. The antinuclear movement in West Germany and Britain threatened to bring down their governments. The movement was well intentioned, I have little doubt. It was against nuclear war and the arms race. But NATO had been foundering in the late 1970s with lots of internal bickering. Moscow saw a chance to split the alliance even further, using the nuclear issue. Antinuclear emotions were stoked everywhere, as the Soviets tried to drum up bigger street demonstrations and more domestic opposition.

None of this is to say that using the bomb always worked, that it was wise or moral, or that it didn't lead to negative consequences. President Eisenhower, as described, tried to save money by cutting the size of the army and navy, buying nuclear weapons instead. This turned out to be a dangerous illusion and was reversed after he left office. The Soviet attempt to split NATO in the 1980s also backfired. It actually produced a counterreaction.

But, and here is the point, the bomb was used. Any survey of its past or future uses needs to consider cases that are foolish, ill-considered, or reckless, and not only those that make sense using our standard of rationality.

Some uses of the bomb never stood a prayer of working. Threatening to atomize Moscow or Beijing in the 1960s if they continued to support the North Vietnamese just wasn't plausible. Virtually all strategists saw this immediately. The Soviet Union and China didn't control Hanoi. And they exploited this fact to their advantage, sending supplies with confidence that nothing would come of it.

Some uses of the bomb were poorly thought out. The Soviet leader Nikita Khrushchev got into a humiliating showdown in Cuba with nuclear weapons. It was one reason he was later kicked out of power.

My point is that leaders in the second nuclear age will use the bomb, too. And there are many different ways to use it, not just one or two. Some countries in the second nuclear age will no doubt show great imagination in this regard. A lot of innovation should be anticipated. It is likely that some of the innovative uses will be poorly thought out and dangerous, and others may be calamitous. But these uses can't be ignored. Ill-conceived, reckless uses of the bomb may be the most dangerous of all, but this doesn't mean they won't be tried.

Words Matter

It's often said that sticks and stones can break our bones but words can never hurt us. But it isn't true, in international politics or in the school yard.

With a nuclear context there is a need to be extraordinarily careful about what is said. The reactions of adversaries and allies have to be anticipated. Cheap talk—ill-considered rhetorical statements— can be truly dangerous.

An example occurred in 1956, when Hungary challenged Moscow's control there. President Eisenhower had promised to "rollback" communism in Eastern Europe. When Radio Free Europe's broadcasts hinted that the United States might intervene to help the Hungarians oust the Soviet army, it inflamed the crisis. There is ambiguity about exactly what was broadcast. But in Budapest it was linked with the talk of rollback. Yet Eisenhower had no intention of challenging the Soviets in Hungary. The Soviet army came in big, killing 2,700 people and installing a more pliant regime.

While defenders of the Eisenhower administration point to the ambiguities of what was said at the time, and that no one had any good reason to expect American intervention in Hungary, a different conclusion was reached by most observers. When there is any prospect of a clash between nuclear powers, tight controls are needed on what is said. Allowing agencies like Radio Free Europe to craft their own message is dangerous. Such actors may not see the larger picture and may let rhetoric get ahead of policy.

Words can preempt. They can dramatically raise the risks. Preemption is usually thought of too narrowly, in military terms, like firing on a missile base, but there are verbal forms of preemption, too. In the Cuban missile crisis, President Kennedy delivered a TV address to the nation in which he revealed the presence of Soviet missiles in Cuba. He put Moscow into a corner before the Soviet government was ready. No shots were fired, but his speech intensified the crisis. This was exactly what Kennedy wanted. He could have waited. Or he could have worked through secret back channels. But Kennedy wanted, and got, a sharp escalation. His speech said to the world that the United States knew the missiles were there, and the Soviets had better take them out. There was no way he could back down after this. He burned his bridges. He knew it. Moscow knew it, too.

Words can change the balance of power overnight. President Nixon did this with his trip to China in 1972. As Henry Kissinger points out in his memoirs, international politics changed immediately. The fiction of a bipolar world was gone for good. The Soviets now had to plan for a two-front war, against two nuclear-armed opponents. Imagine if China didn't have the bomb. The impact of the Nixon visit would have been far less dramatic. Yet, and Kissinger emphasizes this very point, not a single division, not a single weapon, had moved.

Finally, leaders can be trapped by their words. This has happened many times. But in a nuclear context the stakes are bigger. Jimmy Carter said that Americans had "an inordinate fear of communism." Maybe so. But when the Soviets invaded Afghanistan in 1979, these words made him look weak. It was widely argued that the Soviet military buildup, conventional and nuclear, emboldened Moscow to take this step. No one will ever know for sure, but against the backdrop of Carter's curt dismissal of communism, and the embassy seizure in Tehran, it changed the course of his presidency.

Nuclear Head Games

The bomb's psychological effects dominated all others in the first nuclear age. This led to the emphasis on strategies that used psychology for their principal effect, most especially deterrence. And it led to something else—convoluted efforts at crafting illusory estimates in the opponent's mind about where things might go if the opponent took certain actions. I call these "nuclear head games."

Nuclear head games were played by every cold war president. Liberal, conservative, hawk, dove, it didn't matter. Leaders will play them in the second nuclear age, too. Indeed, they already are, as later chapters will show.

Some examples will illustrate nuclear head games at work. When Lyndon Johnson announced the first air strikes against North Vietnam in August 1964, nuclear B-47 bombers were launched from Torrejon air base in Spain, and other bases, so the Soviets wouldn't get any ideas about rushing to North Vietnam's aid. Johnson knew the Soviets would see this on their radars, but he kept it secret from the American public.

Talk about head games. Johnson orchestrated three parallel actions: the TV address to the nation announcing the attack on North Vietnam; the air strike itself; and a nuclear alert. Johnson's TV broadcast was originally planned for 7 p.m., Washington time, on August 4, 1964. When the aircraft carriers were delayed, this slipped to 8 p.m., and then 9 p.m. Problems continued and the broadcast aired at 11:37 p.m. Never before had a military attack been timed to coincide with a TV announcement. But it was hardly the last.

In 1969, Richard Nixon, eager to find a way out of the Vietnam War, ordered the military to go on higher nuclear alert, knowing that the Soviets would see it. This, too, was kept secret from the public. The top-secret order from General Earle Wheeler, the chairman of the Joint Chiefs of Staff, to commanders at Strategic Air Command (SAC), the Pacific, European, and Atlantic commands, and NORAD (North American Air Defense Command) is worth reading:

TOP SECRET EYES ONLY SENSITIVE JCS

1. We have been directed by higher authority to institute a series of actions during the period 130000Z–250000Z Oct, to test our military readiness in selected areas world-wide to respond to possible confrontation by the Soviet Union. These actions

should be discernible to the Soviets, but not threatening in themselves. They may include, but are not necessarily limited to, the following type actions:

A. Stand-down of flying of combat aircraft in selected areas or commands, to improve operational readiness.

B. Implementation of radio and/or other communications silence in selected areas or commands.

C. Increased surveillance of Soviet ships en route to North Vietnam.

D. Increased ground alert rate of SAC bombers and tankers.

2. To initiate actions within the time frame specified, certain commanders have been directed to stand-down training flights and introduce varying degrees of EMCON [emissions control of radios and radars]. These initial actions will cover the first four days of the 14-day period.

I have spoken to the senior SAC commanders who received this order from the White House. They were in the dark as to its purpose. So they went back to "higher authorities" to ask what was going on. They thought, naively, that if they knew this, they could improve the plan. They were told by higher authorities (Henry Kissinger, the national security adviser), in no uncertain terms, to mind their own business. If their counsel was needed, they would be asked for it. They never were. In other words, "Shut up and follow orders." This is often characteristic of nuclear head games. The political leadership is playing its own sophisticated game that it doesn't want even the military to know about.

President Nixon has been ridiculed and portrayed as some kind of lunatic for doing this. But this view is hard to reconcile with our knowledge of the man. When it comes to foreign policy Nixon was nobody's fool. He was one of the shrewdest presidents. Henry Kissinger, likewise, was not exactly a neophyte in international politics. Both men knew perfectly well that the Soviets wouldn't see this as an imminent nuclear strike.

By carefully making sure the nuclear alerts wouldn't be seen in Moscow as an impending nuclear attack, Nixon showed considerable subtlety. It was actually a head game to make the Soviets think that a big escalation against North Vietnam was coming, so they in turn might cajole Hanoi to be more conciliatory in the peace talks. The move also told the Soviets that they had better not rush new aid to Hanoi or it might lead to a confrontation with the United States. Nixon was really quite clear about all of this. He described it to Herman Kahn after he left office when the two men met periodically for discussions in Nixon's home in New Jersey.

Some people may denounce this kind of behavior. Or they'll point out that it didn't work. They may be right. After all, Hanoi and Moscow never gave in to Nixon's ploy.

But that isn't the point. Leaders played these head games anyway. Take Jimmy Carter. He was the first president ever to ride in the U.S. "doomsday airplane." This was a special plane kept at Andrews Air Force Base, equipped to launch U.S. nuclear forces. In a well-publicized move, he flew it back to Georgia on his first trip home after taking office in 1977, knowing full well that the Soviets would read about it in the *New York Times*. Moreover, during the trip he exercised the firing of the SIOP (Single Integrated Operational Plan), the giant nuclear war plan, which Moscow also learned of.

President Carter is an interesting example of using nuclear head games. Most people think he was the sort of president who wouldn't do this sort of thing. Certainly one will not read about it in the many books he's written since leaving office. But Carter authorized provocative moves against Soviet nuclear-weapons submarines, as part of a systematic campaign to make top Soviet leaders believe their subs were vulnerable to destruction. The idea was to convince them that their nuclear deterrent wasn't as safe as they thought, and that they had better not start something they couldn't finish.

The U.S. Navy hounded the Soviet subs, riding their backs to a point that there were collisions. If ordered, the U.S. ships could have fired on the Soviet subs, destroying or disabling them. There were all kinds of spooky aspects to this program, including phony "eyes only" messages leaked to known Soviet spies for relay back to Moscow. These were synchronized with naval exercises against their sea bastions, the oceans near the Soviet homeland where they deployed their nuclear subs. Some aspects of this operation have been described in popular books such as *Blind Man's Bluff* and the fictional *The Hunt for Red October*. But these accounts are way down in the weeds. They miss the larger purpose, scope, and central direction of the program. This wasn't a case of a bureaucracy going too far. It had presidential backing. Special organizations in the Pentagon managed it, whose names and existence were classified far beyond top secret. The program continued, and intensified, under President Ronald Reagan.

One can argue forever that such head games are dangerous and shouldn't be used. But every president used them. Nuclear head games in the second nuclear age will likely look different. The cultures and personalities involved are dissimilar from the cold war. But they will be played. They already are.

Individuals Matter

The sheer accident of who happens to be in power can have an enormous impact when it comes to nuclear weapons. This is important because it challenges the view that nuclear dangers are so great they swamp individual personality differences. It would be great if nuclear deterrence was "automatic," and if it worked all the time. But deterrence is like all other psychological variables: it will vary by person and condition. This has troubling implications.

The Kennedy years are fascinating here. I do not believe it is any coincidence that in the history of the cold war it was the Kennedy administration that took the world to the highest level of nuclear danger. In 1961 John F. Kennedy and his self-styled New Frontiersmen came to power vowing to get America moving again. They were action oriented, energetic, always on TV playing touch football (never golf).

But youth also brought inexperience. The Bay of Pigs fiasco in April 1961 embarrassed the Kennedy administration. So did the subsequent summit meeting in Vienna with Khrushchev that June, where Kennedy appeared weak. When the Cuban missile crisis erupted, they had to prove themselves, and this led to Kennedy being especially tough on the Soviets by announcing on TV the discovery of the missiles and calling the unprecedented nuclear alert.

If deterrence were automatic regardless of who was in power, the world would be much safer. Because the need to qualify statements about deterrence with "well, it depends on who's in charge" is troubling. It makes the whole deterrence equation less reliable.

. . . And So Do Institutions

The view that nuclear risks are, at bottom, entirely psychological can go too far. It leaves out institutions. The way institutions count isn't because they foul things up, though they do. Nor is it because they have their own bureaucratic interests, though they have those, too.

Institutions matter because they introduce new dynamics into a problem, dynamics that cannot be appreciated in psychological terms. In his book *Diplomacy*, Henry Kissinger describes Europe in the early twentieth century. The technical military system of mobilizing armies was misaligned with the slower-moving diplomacy of the era. Leaders had little appreciation of this misalignment until the summer of 1914, when the dynamic of alerts, mobilizations, and countermobilizations swamped political decision making. The distance was immense between what leaders sought and what happened in the field—and they didn't understand how great the gap was.

Those at the top may have formal authority. But this doesn't give them control. And, as Kissinger argues, they may not understand this. There are many reasons for this development to be especially large in a nuclear context. One is technology, which takes on unprecedented importance. The technology of the first nuclear age led to "new" dynamics in decision making that few appreciated until they appeared in actual crises. Leaders came to rely on big technical systems, without appreciating it, like warning systems, satellite reconnaissance, computers, and command and control. These systems introduced dynamics that were not even thought of by many political leaders. Accidental launches, interlocking alerts, and enormous increases in the vulnerability of the leaders themselves to attack.

One pernicious aspect of the nuclear age was the time compression of decision making. Kissinger describes this, too, in his depiction of the outbreak of World War I. By the early cold war, in the 1950s and 1960s, it had become a far more acute problem. A missile fired at the United States from the Soviet Union could reach its target in thirty minutes. The U.S. government established processes to handle the response, and these involved many thousands of people. Missile launch centers, intelligence warning centers, alerted bombers, "alternate" command posts (in case the president and vice president were killed)—all this created an enormously complex intervening layer between the political leadership and the military. No one fully understood this system, how it would work, or how it could provoke dangerous responses in the enemy's systems. There are obvious reasons for this. It could never be tested under realistic conditions because that would mean detonating real atomic bombs.

I recall conversations about this with the former national security adviser McGeorge Bundy and the former secretary of defense Robert McNamara. They were in the apex in 1962 during the Cuban missile crisis, the highest alert ever taken by the United States in the cold war. Both of them were surprised at the scale of the U.S. alert, even though both had reviewed the plans beforehand.

Most scholars of deterrence have assumed away such dynamics, boiling the problem down to a contest between two leaders. It is then emphasized that this two-player game is non-zero sum, using the language of game theory. Just because one side loses doesn't mean that the other side wins. But this doesn't adequately describe the problem.

There's a contrast in how scholars of international security and management have framed their respective fields. I've noticed this because I have a joint appointment in the business school and the political science department. Every MBA program in the world devotes part of its curriculum to what's called "organizational behavior," or OB for short. It deals with ways to design and manage complex organizations.

While OB is not an exact science, like physics, it still offers a lot of valuable insights—for example, whether a business should organize its departments around its technology or its customers. Another example: OB says that it is important to distinguish between authority and control because they are by no means the same thing. OB gives no hard and fast answers about how to organize, because that will depend on the particulars of the situation. But it does offer many penetrating questions. It tells you what to look for, including issues that you may not have thought about beforehand. No bank or technology company would undertake a new venture today without taking an OB look at what it was doing.

When it comes to international relations, there is no counterpart to OB. Rather, there's a belief that organizations don't matter all that much. I've spoken with a former secretary of state who told me that "it's all about people." "Moving boxes and lines around on a chart doesn't really do anything," I was told. I countered that OB dynamics were central to the way GE, Goldman Sachs, IBM, and Apple operate and how they analyze their competition, so it would be surprising to me if OB didn't matter in strategic competition between nations. I got nowhere with my case.

I think part of the reason that scholars of international relations and hands-on leaders underestimate the importance of OB is that most of what they do is under conditions of low-stress normalcy. There are ebbs and flows of tension, yes. People talk about a tough day at the office. But nothing like the turbodynamics of the outbreak of World War I, or of a nuclear crisis. As a result there is a tendency to judge complex systems in terms of their performance under normal conditions. A deterrent system will perform well almost all of the time. The enemy doesn't attack. There isn't a crisis. And, so, everything works fine. That a deterrent should be judged on its performance under extreme conditions, rather than on normal day-to-day conditions, does not appear to occur to many staffers or leaders.

Organizational dynamics are as close to universal as anything I know of in social science. There's no way for any country to avoid them.

Let's look at a specific case from the cold war. The example is not nuclear, at least it isn't exactly nuclear. It's the Soviet biological warfare program. But I bet it applied to Soviet nuclear forces, too.

The Soviets signed a treaty with the United States in 1972 outlawing offensive biological weapons. They immediately cheated on it. Quite literally, just months after the treaty was signed, they established a huge organization to expand their offensive biological warfare effort. But the lesson that the Soviet Union cheated on a treaty isn't the point I want to make. It doesn't come close to describing the craziness of the dynamics taking place.

One might think that a biological weapons program, especially a Soviet program, would be centrally run. The risk of getting caught violating the treaty or of something going wrong point to the need for central control. The Soviet propensity to overcentralize everything is well known, so it should have applied here, especially.

But it didn't. There was formal centralization of authority, but

not of control. The program had three divisions. One
was established in 1973 called Biopreparat. The othe.
were run by the Ministry of Defense and the Ministry of ...
ture. There was a bureaucratic competition among the three parts t.
outdo one another in budget. Each tried to steal "market share" from
the others. They tried to supply the customer, the Soviet military,
with more biological agents than they could possibly use.

At the program's peak in the 1970s and 1980s, the Soviets had
70,000 people making these weapons. More than forty large facilities across Russia made "absolute" anthrax (a superdeadly strain),
bubonic plague, tularemia, Ebola, smallpox, and other bacteria and
virus weapons. These were the "fill" for empty bombs, shells, warheads, and spray canisters.

But this was only the peacetime program, producing test and
development batches to make sure the system worked. The astound-
ing feature was the plan for going to war. On mobilization, an all-
out production of additional thousands of tons was planned. Tens of
thousands of new temporary workers were to be called up for surge
production. Second and third shifts were to be added, using largely
untrained personnel.

Vats and pasteurizing machines were constantly monitored as
managers were aware of the deadly effects of spills and leaks. But there
was an enormous disconnect between the various departments in this
system. The political leadership in Moscow was clueless about these,
failings that could plague them (literally) in a crisis.

For example, while great attention was given to plant safety, at
least in theory, no attention whatever was given to the distribution
system that would fill the bombs and shells on mobilization. This is
like Pepsi focusing on making soda, but ignoring the distribution
system of getting it to the supermarkets and restaurants. The Soviet
plan called for hundreds of thousands of empty bomb canisters to
be sent by truck and rail to the plants, to be filled with botulinum,
anthrax, et cetera, and then shipped to the front.

The distribution system was never tested. How could it be? Soviet quality control—underpaid technicians filling thousands of canisters with anthrax and tularemia—accident-prone railroads and airplanes, shoddy work everywhere, cynical indifference would have led to an unimaginable horror if it had been undertaken. Spillage and leakage from the loaded shells would make the outbound rail movements cut a swath of death hundreds of miles across the Soviet Union as the trains chugged their way to the front in Europe.

In 1979 one hundred grams of anthrax, about two shot glasses' worth, leaked at a plant in Sverdlovsk when a worker "forgot" to replace a filter on a roof ventilator. The leaked anthrax was super-strength. It contaminated a region more than thirty-five miles downwind, killing one hundred people. It missed the city of Sverdlovsk because of the wind patterns that day. Had the wind shifted, perhaps tens of thousands of people would have suffered an agonizing death. This was from two shot glasses' worth of the stuff, in peacetime, when there was no production surge, and no "temps" working the plants.

Soviet mobilization of this apparatus would have led to a horror show beyond Dante's imagination. To think that anyone in the Kremlin truly understood this system defies credulity. If told to prepare for war, this system would have done so. Orders are orders. But what would be the consequences?

Mikhail Gorbachev was briefed on this fantastic system when he took power in 1985. He signed certain documents and received a briefing from the program's experts. I imagine that the brief presented the facts of the matter in a straightforward way. The number of tons produced per month. The cooking schedules. The number of awards given to plant managers for smooth administration.

But the madness of the program could hardly have been presented to him by anyone inside this system. A fish doesn't know it lives in water. The experts, no doubt, saw everything as "normal." After all, the schedules were followed and the quotas were met.

Gorbachev was at the apex, and officially in charge. But he could be only dimly aware of the larger insanity in which he was embedded had this institution ever been put in motion. To take one example, SS-18 ICBM warheads were to be filled with a biological agent, to be fired at the United States along with thousands of nuclear warheads. As to the rationale for this, adding biological missile attacks to a giant nuclear strike, little thought seems to have been given. It was simply an institution doing its job—oblivious to matters outside of its narrow focus.

The institutions of the second nuclear age are different from those of the first. But bureaucratic dynamics are as universal as anything is. Experience shows that empire building, mindless expansion, squirrel-like specialization, oblivious concern for larger issues, and covering up mistakes cross national borders and cultures.

Getting the Risks Wrong

Throughout the first nuclear age there was an enormous misdirection of attention and resources to unlikely risks, while at the same time ignoring more dangerous ones. Sometimes this was conscious, sometimes not. Risk could build up in one area, with little or no recognition of it.

The most vivid example of misallocation of resources and attention was the preparation for a bolt-from-the-blue surprise attack on the United States by the Soviet Union. I'd estimate that something like 70 percent of U.S. strategic attention and budget was given to this problem. Yet its likelihood was extremely low. This isn't just a retrospective judgment, it was actually made at the time. Surveys in the late 1950s and 1960s of strategic analysts at the Rand Corporation, the Hudson Institute, and other think tanks showed that their experts believed the bolt from the blue was an extremely remote possibility. Yet it was the driver of tremendous attention and billions of dollars.

Part of the reason for this was intellectual laziness. Nuclear missile attacks were very easy to model on a computer. There were accepted formulas for calculating blast damage and fallout. So that's what the American government did. Using the formulas substituted for thinking.

But this gave an exceedingly narrow picture of risk. It provided a view of the situation at the ultimate levels of nuclear war. Crises and nuclear head games were much harder to model. They involved psychology, judgment, and estimation of the other side's countermoves. This was hard to put on a computer. Yet it was the right problem, so to speak. It was hard to conceive of a nuclear war that didn't arise out of a crisis or a lower-level military conflict.

There were politico-military crisis games that explored less intense crises. These were incredibly important because they were at least looking at the right problem, the way a nuclear war could escalate from them. But even here, there was little follow-up to see if the lessons that emerged from these games made it into plans and systems. It was exceedingly hard to get senior leaders to pay attention to such problems.

Robert McNamara emphasized this point to me in discussions several times. He said that in his experience the most critical problems of nuclear war and peace, Vietnam, and other big problems that he faced were precisely the ones that received little or no analytic attention. People would argue to the death about whether the air force or navy should hit a particular target in Vietnam. But there was no one analyzing whether hitting that target would bring Hanoi to the negotiating table.

This is one reason McNamara developed a verbal agreement with Presidents Kennedy and Johnson not to fire a retaliatory strike at the Soviet Union without a long, deliberate wait to assess the situation and to estimate what the United States should do next. I've often been asked what the United States would do if it was attacked by the Soviet Union. I think that McNamara's answer was that he knew what he wouldn't do, and that was to immediately order a counterstrike. He told me he wasn't going to be stampeded into a disastrous decision at 3 a.m., or let the president be put in this position. It's fair to say that McNamara didn't have much confidence in the system to sort out the confusion or present coherent options in the stress of a nuclear attack.

Getting the risks wrong came up in other ways, too. In 1968 the United States had 530,000 troops in Vietnam, a large air force—and nothing left over to defend other places. Europe was stripped of troops and weapons. So was South Korea, even though war in Korea was more than a hypothetical possibility. The North Koreans seized a U.S. Navy ship, the *Pueblo*, on January 23, 1968. The Tet Offensive in Vietnam began a week later, on January 31. Had North Korea attacked South Korea in 1968 the United States would have had to seriously consider using nuclear weapons to stop it or else accept defeat. The U.S. Army there was understrength and underequipped, effectively serving as a cash cow to be milked for resources for Vietnam. In the context of the Tet Offensive, with U.S. attention devoted to Vietnam, it would have been an ideal opportunity for North Korea to attack South Korea. The loss of South Korea to the North would have been a security catastrophe for the United States. Indeed, this was the party line of many communist countries: one, two, three, many Vietnams.

No one can say what would have happened if North Korea had attacked South Korea in January 1968. My argument is not about predictions. But it is reasonable to say that the U.S. government would have seriously considered using nuclear weapons in Korea if the North Koreans had attacked. There were hundreds of nuclear weapons in South Korea at the time, and plans for using them were highly developed. Absent using nuclear weapons, the United States had few alternatives to protecting an important ally, South Korea, and fewer still to ensure the survival of its own army stationed there.

In this example, the risk of nuclear war was determined by a conventional war in Vietnam. The risk didn't involve a Soviet missile attack on the United States. Nuclear risks were rigidly and narrowly defined in terms of the two sides' nuclear forces, the so-called nuclear balance. Most experts at the time debated nuclear deterrence as the risk of a Soviet missile attack, and they measured it in terms of throw-weight and silo kill probabilities. But the risk of nuclear war was growing, because of events in Vietnam, and no one in Washington even recognized it. Whatever the risk of a Soviet nuclear attack was, the chance of a nuclear war erupting in Korea was surely higher, and it was completely missed.

In the first nuclear age the United States did a poor job of assessing the risks of nuclear war. The second nuclear age may be no different, for the United States, and for many other countries, too.

Technology and the Strategy Lag

Technology was a large factor in the cold war. While it had been important for some time, in the nuclear age it contributed a new dynamic to the rivalry. Falling behind, potentially, meant losing the arms race, or much worse.

Technology had many unintended effects. Technological dynamism often outpaced strategy. The common wisdom is that strategy should come first. It should take primacy. That way, strategy can be used to direct which technologies would have to be acquired to execute it.

But it didn't work like that. Technology often led strategy. Technology had its own dynamic, and it might not be in sync with politics. There's a commonsense reason for this. Only after something was bought did people figure out how to use it.

There were many examples of technology leading strategy. Only after bombers and missiles were bought in the 1950s did it occur to anyone that there was a problem in basing them. If they were too close to the Soviet Union, they could be easily taken out. Further, having bases too close to the enemy might actually invite an attack. So a distinction was drawn between "hard" (survivable) forces and "soft" (nonsurvivable) forces. Soft forces could lead to a use-it-or-lose-it situation. One side might not want to fire, but if it thought the other side was going to fire, it might feel compelled to do so.

This all makes perfectly good sense—but the distinction became clear only *after* the soft weapons were fielded.

Cruise missiles are another good example. Originally they were bought in the 1970s to carry nuclear bombs. Only after large numbers were acquired did it occur to anyone that their real utility was in precision conventional attack. They were cheaper than airplanes, and you didn't risk a pilot. This is all rather obvious. But it took more than a decade to affect actual deployments.

Thinking About the Unthinkable

One final lesson of the first nuclear age is especially controversial: the importance of thinking about the unthinkable.

It is important to point out a distinction in the wording here. The lesson for the United States is to think *about* the unthinkable, not to think the unthinkable. They are different. I am not calling for nuclear strikes on anyone, but rather for thinking about the options in a world where many others may consider doing so. Nuclear weapons exist. They are spreading. Given this, the United States may face a situation where other countries may use them. The others may be enemies or they may be allies. What the United States does can have an enormous impact on them. If American thinking is of good enough quality, it can lower the chance that others will use them in the first place.

I recognize that thinking about the unthinkable will be criticized for focusing on hypothetical possibilities. And I acknowledge that some strategists in the cold war overestimated the likelihood of nuclear war. But thinking about a problem is the only way to understand its contours. Few problems are made better by ignoring them.

Hurricanes, AIDS, sex scandals in the Catholic Church—take your pick. None was eliminated by ignoring it. Each was made worse.

I could give many examples of how thinking about the unthinkable contributed to avoiding war in the first nuclear age, but one makes the case in an especially compelling way. It's a 1983 war game in which I was involved that contributed to fundamentally changing the way American leaders thought about nuclear war, at a very critical point in the cold war. It has never been publicly discussed before.

In the early 1980s the Soviet Union was on a twenty-year military buildup. A great deal of this buildup was in its nuclear forces. The Soviets had large programs for every kind of missile, submarine, and bomber. President Ronald Reagan came into office in 1981 seeking a way for America to respond to this challenge. During the 1980 presidential campaign all kinds of ideas for U.S. defense revitalization were advanced. And that was the problem. The price tag for pursuing all of them was toted up and found to be too high even for the United States.

The problem was what, exactly, should the United States do in the face of the Soviet buildup? At the time there were advocates for many different strategies. Launch on warning. Demonstration nuclear attacks. Limited nuclear war. Decapitation attacks on Soviet command and control. Horizontal escalation—shifting a war in Europe to the Far East by attacking the Soviet bases there. Weapons in space. An offensive strategy for NATO, with NATO armies charging into Eastern Europe to incite the Polish and Czech armies to join them. Getting China to attack the Soviet Union to create a two-front war.

The debate was characterized by intellectual and organizational chaos. The United States could not follow all of these strategies. The question was, which ones made sense? Each one on the list was advocated by experts, and staffs and think tanks took sides, oblivious to how much each would cost, or to the risks.

There was a great deal of career opportunism at work as well. Looking like you were tougher on the Soviet Union than the next guy seemed a surefire way to get promoted in the new Reagan administration. Everyone wanted to get in on the act: armchair strategists, Ivy League professors, retired generals, and the services. Anyone outside of government who could write a seven-hundred-word op-ed piece on ways to smash the Soviet Union, no matter how crazy the idea, was giving advice. And those in government were deadlocked with inertia.

There was an obvious difficulty. The Pentagon couldn't follow eight different strategies. The Joint Chiefs of Staff couldn't even agree on one. The undersecretary of defense for policy had neither the time nor the inclination to critique war plans. And the Pentagon bureaucracy could not envision anything more creative than a 5 percent budgetary increase. Moreover, the new secretary of defense, Caspar W. Weinberger, was being blamed for the chaos by the press and Congress. Outsiders said that he couldn't make hard choices.

The long-serving director of net assessment, Andrew W. Marshall, recommended that a special strategy group be set up, reporting directly to the secretary of defense—and its primary role would be to help the secretary critique various proposals and explore new options in complete confidence. The chairman of the Joint Chiefs of Staff proposed that this select group of senior civilians and consultants be complemented with military officers from each of the services and have access to the resources and facilities of the National War College, promising that the military would not interfere with the secretary getting direct advice and personally interacting with them. The proposal was less than popular with many generals.

This led to the creation of the Strategic Concepts Development Center (SCDC) to develop these outside views. Secretary Weinberger recruited Phillip A. Karber as its founding director. Karber had been running an interagency National Security Study assessing the balance of U.S. versus Soviet military forces and NATO versus Warsaw Pact forces. Weinberger told Karber to recruit the brightest strategists he could get, adding that they should not be ideological but should represent a range of bipartisan views. The only constraint was that they had to operate in complete confidentiality.

A suggestion soon developed to use a war game to carry out this assignment. Karber asked Thomas Schelling, a Harvard professor and later Nobel Prize winner, to design a game that would test out the various proposals. Schelling had run the crisis games at the Rand Corporation in the 1950s and at the National Security Council in the early 1960s. Upon taking the position, he informed Weinberger that senior government leaders were woefully unprepared to cope with the major decision points in which a crisis could escalate.

Weinberger was willing to be the first senior national security leader to personally participate in a simulation of U.S. war plans. But Weinberger was concerned about the "fishbowl effect"—where fear of public exposure and embarrassment might inhibit or distort decision making of the players on the various teams. He agreed to participate in the game—but only if Karber could devise a secret way for him and the chairman of the Joint Chiefs to do so and if Schelling would design the game as both a test of U.S. war plans and as a crisis learning experience for the secretary. Karber also wanted a "Thucydidean chronicler" to independently observe decision making on both sides, and he asked me to join the project, to wander around the game and to record my impressions of what was going on.

The game was called Proud Prophet, and it began on June 20, 1983. This wasn't any ordinary war game. Schelling's earlier games in the 1950s and early 1960s had used staffers from think tanks, the Pentagon, and the CIA to play the roles. The president might be played by a think tank analyst, the chairman of the Joint Chiefs might be played by an air force colonel. Schelling wanted to change this, and so Proud Prophet was to use actual decision makers, the secretary of defense and the chairman of the Joint Chiefs of Staff. To make it as realistic as possible, actual top-secret U.S. war plans were incorporated into the game. This wasn't easy. These plans are very tightly held and the military doesn't like showing them to anyone.

Proud Prophet was the most realistic exercise involving nuclear weapons ever played by the U.S. government during the cold war. Let me elaborate on this. Every cold war president was briefed on U.S. nuclear war plans. Some, like President Carter, practiced this aboard the doomsday aircraft. At other times the national security adviser stood in. But these nuclear release exercises are not what I am talking about here. In no sense were they a game. They involved running through a procedural checklist, and the president, or his stand-in, chose from a list of prescribed options. There was no communication or bargaining with the Soviet Union, or with allies. Most important, there was no room for innovation or improvisation. They were highly scripted drills, virtually the opposite of the free-play game played here.

Other games used senior officials to play out weighty national decisions. Communication and bargaining were played. In 1964, McGeorge Bundy played a series of escalation games about Vietnam. But these "Sigma games," as they were called, didn't involve nuclear weapons, nor did they include the Soviet Union other than in its political reaction to American actions in Southeast Asia.

Other nuclear war games in the cold war might bring in a retired ambassador to play the president. A professor might play the role of the leader of the Soviet Union. Or a retired general might play the chairman of the Joint Chiefs. Only loose versions of the actual war plans were used. The combined effect of these factors was to lessen the seriousness, the gravitas if you will, of the game.

No other game in cold war history, to my knowledge, worked like Proud Prophet. Played in real time at the secret facility of the National War College, the simulation went around the clock lasting for two weeks and had hundreds of military officers participating in Washington as well as communicating over top-secret links with all the major U.S. military commands around the world. The game simulated conflict in a myriad of regions, from East Asia to Europe and in the Mediterranean and the Middle East. Also, security had to be protected, so the fact that the secretary and the chairman were play-ing in the game was concealed from all the players except a tiny hand-ful with the need to know. The process worked like this. Each morning Karber went across the Potomac to the Pentagon or called over a red phone to the secretary and the chairman. Or, if an unexpected deci-sion was needed he called and talked it over with them on a top-secret phone line. In these calls Karber described the situation in the game and asked them what course of action should be taken. They would discuss U.S. policy, alliance reactions, and next moves. Almost no one was aware of their shadow role. In the game at the National War Col-lege, there were officials playing the role of president, secretary, and chairman, but they were essentially cutouts, to conceal from the other players the actions of the senior leadership over in the Pentagon.

One added consideration was the need to prevent a media leak that could freak out leaders in the Soviet Union and in allied coun-tries. In the summer of 1983 U.S.-Soviet relations were at a low point. A headline screaming "Reagan Administration Plays Out Nuclear Strikes on Moscow" could have been dangerous, not merely embar-rassing, because paranoia in the Soviet Union was very high.

Indeed, looking back, 1983 was a more dangerous year than any of us realized. Events after the game would show this. They are useful to mention, not because anyone knew about them when the game was played—but precisely because they did not. The players in Proud Prophet didn't realize just how obsessed, and potentially dangerous, Soviet leaders were becoming.

A civilian airliner, Korean Air flight 007, was shot down by Soviet air defenses on September 1, 1983, in part because the Soviet high command was in a supervigilant posture, virtually expecting an American attack. On September 26 the "Petrov incident" occurred. Stanislav Petrov was the duty officer in a Soviet nuclear warning center when it reported a small launch of American nuclear missiles. On his own authority, thinking that it was a false alarm, he decided not to report this to the Soviet high command. If he had, they might have gone to launching their own strike on the United States. It was later determined that the Soviet warning system had malfunctioned; there had been no American missile launch.

On November 2, 1983, the Able Archer incident took place. Able Archer was a NATO nuclear release exercise. Staffs went through the procedural drill of getting permission from NATO political authorities to fire nuclear weapons. But the codes had been changed for Able Archer; there were new message formats and periods of radio silence. The Soviets thought it was real, not an exercise. Some sources indicate that the Soviet response was extreme, arming their nuclear weapons for firing.

None of this was known in June 1983. Yet nuclear tensions between the United States and the Soviet Union were building just as the game began.

What happened in the game? For one thing, many of the strategic concepts proposed to deal with the Soviet Union were revealed to be either irresponsible or totally incompatible with current U.S. capabilities and immediately thrown out. Launch on warning was quickly disposed of; no one in his right mind was going to turn over the nuclear launch decision to computers hooked up to a radar. Attacking Moscow, to knock it out as a command center, also didn't last long. The Soviets had more than 30,000 nuclear weapons. Surely they would find a way to retaliate against the United States.

Sending NATO armies into Eastern Europe was another idea that sounded good, but only until you gamed it out against a much larger Soviet army in Eastern Europe. Then it didn't look so good. Indeed, it looked like suicide.

As far as horizontal escalation and counterattacking the Soviet Far East was concerned, well, Moscow didn't seem to care very much. The Soviets wanted to win in Europe. Losing the Kamchatka Peninsula in exchange for picking up Germany, France, and the Netherlands and destroying NATO was a deal they would take any day of the week.

American limited nuclear strikes were used in the game. The idea behind these was that once the Soviet leaders saw that the West would go nuclear they would come to their senses and accept a cease-fire. The U.S. logic here was that further escalation to attacks on cities would make Soviet leaders understand that they couldn't win. An elaborate theory had been constructed in academic and think tank communities about these limited nuclear attacks. They were supposed to limit a nuclear war. That was the idea, anyway.

But that's not what happened. The Soviet Union team interpreted the nuclear strikes as an attack on their nation, their way of life, and their honor. So they responded with an enormous nuclear salvo at the United States. The United States retaliated in kind. The result was a catastrophe that made all the wars of the past five hundred years pale in comparison. A half billion human beings were killed in the initial exchanges and at least that many more would have died from radiation and starvation. NATO was gone. So was a good part of Europe, the United States, and the Soviet Union. Major parts of the northern hemisphere would be uninhabitable for decades.

There's something here that's worth mentioning. It has become part of the lore of the cold war that the experience from war games shows that it's nearly impossible to get a conflict to go nuclear. This argument is used to show that most leaders, American and Soviet, were hardly eager to fight a nuclear war. That is surely true. Both sides had very conservative leadership throughout the cold war. But my take on this point is different. This game went nuclear big time, not because Secretary Weinberger and the chairman of the Joint Chiefs were crazy but because they faithfully implemented the prevailing U.S. strategy, a strategy that few had seriously thought about outside of the confines of a tight little circle of specialists. I have played other games that erupted, and they shared this common feature, too. A small, insulated group of people, convinced that they are right, plows ahead into a crisis they haven't anticipated or thought about, one that they are completely unprepared to handle. The result is disaster.

If there was ever a reason to do some hard thinking about what we are doing, this is it. To assume that everything will work out, that we shouldn't be overly pessimistic, and that people will come to their senses has proven incorrect in one field after another. This one is no exception.

I cannot say for certain what effect Proud Prophet had on the Reagan administration. There were a lot of things going on at the time, including President Reagan's own personal horror of nuclear weapons. Upon taking office, when he was first briefed on the nuclear strike plans he might be called upon to execute, he became physically sick. The briefing had to be canceled and rescheduled.

But after Proud Prophet, there was no more over-the-top nuclear rhetoric coming out of the United States. Launch on warning, horizontal escalation, early use of nuclear weapons, tit-for-tat nuclear exchanges—these were banished, conceptually and rhetorically. The Reagan administration switched gears. The chairman of the Joint Chiefs spent the next several years cleaning up U.S. war plans. Nuclear threats were gone, the emphasis was on meeting Soviet conventional strength with U.S. conventional forces and following a long-term competitive strategy.

It is also appropriate to note that the Pentagon never went on nuclear alert with Weinberger as secretary of defense, unlike what took place in the Kennedy and Nixon years. The Reagan administration did other things, for sure. Military spending was increased. The Strategic Defense Initiative ("Star Wars") was begun. But even Star Wars was much more of a long-term techno-economic challenge than an immediate provocation. Political challenges also took on a much larger role. ("Mr. Gorbachev, tear down this wall.")

My respect for Weinberger went up enormously because of Proud Prophet. He really understood the need to think through some pretty horrible issues. Most of the time it's easier to ignore such problems. Moreover, his use of the war game to deftly manage competing internal demands was impressive. Proud Prophet was a learning exercise that countered the drift into strategies that weren't being thought through, some of which were very dangerous. It took enormous courage for a sitting secretary of defense not only to participate personally but to be willing to test U.S. war plans to the breaking point, and then to intervene to change them. It's an example of thinking about the unthinkable, which, in my estimation, lowered the chances of conflict while advancing American interests.

Yale's Garry Brewer has made a very insightful remark about war gaming: "You can often tell more about an organization from what it doesn't game, than from what it does." In the second nuclear age this is worth remembering.

PART TWO

THE NEW POWER POLITICS

· 4 ·

THE NEW LOGIC OF ARMAGEDDON

Not many people worry about a Russian surprise attack on U.S. missiles anymore. Today schools practice lockdowns against shooters, but they no longer conduct civil defense drills. The cold war is over. But its end didn't mean the end of nuclear weapons. Far from it. North Korea, Pakistan, and India have joined the nuclear club. Israel, long in the club, is coming out of the closet. Others, such as Iran, are trying to join it. China and Russia, for their part, are improving their arsenals for twenty-first-century conditions. Other countries are thinking about going nuclear, too.

This is the second nuclear age. It's very different from the first nuclear age, but there's little understanding about precisely how it's different, or about what it will look like in the future. Just as there are lessons from the first nuclear age that likely will carry over to a second nuclear age, so too are there dynamics with no parallel in the first nuclear age. Let us examine these distinctive features of the second nuclear age at the big picture level.

THE BIG PICTURE

The spread of the atomic bomb for reasons that have nothing to do with the cold war defines the second nuclear age. Like the first nuclear age, the second has an overarching structure. Countries, technologies, strategies, conventions, and behaviors combine to make the whole more than the sum of the individual parts.

Geography plays a role as well. Until recently, North Korea could never reach Japan, yet alone the United States. India and China could get at each other, but not very easily due to the Himalayas. Israel at one time could ignore Iran because it was too distant. But no longer.

There is a larger set of dynamics emerging from these developments as they cannot be viewed in isolation from one another. A new "system dynamics" is taking form.

This is quite different from describing the spread of the atomic bomb in terms of nuclear nonproliferation. That perspective diminishes the importance of such things as innovation, learning, and changes over time as this complex system develops. The challenge of the second nuclear age is to think about dynamics and instability and not just nonproliferation and containment.

The second nuclear age has a three-tiered structure. I call it the MSG framework (for major powers, secondary powers, and groups).* The dynamics between major and secondary powers are likely to be quite different from how major powers interact with one another. The United States and Russia have missiles aimed at each other. But

---

* A definition is in order. The term *major power* is used for countries that have a GDP of more than $1.5 trillion in 2012. Some major powers have the bomb, others do not. The United States and China are major powers with the bomb. So are Britain and France. Japan and Germany are major powers that do not have it. India is a major nuclear power. Countries with a GDP of less than $1.5 trillion are termed *secondary powers*. Israel, North Korea, and Pakistan are all secondary powers with the bomb. Finally, the term *group* is used for subnational organizations such as terrorists (al Qaeda) and militias (Hamas and Hezbollah). No groups have the bomb, at least not yet.

the dynamic between them shares little of what may go on between Israel and a nuclear Iran.

Nearly all the major powers with the bomb have undertaken significant modernization efforts in recent years. Only the United States holds back from this, in the increasingly vain hope of demonstrating to the world that these weapons have no utility.

[handwritten margin note: no longer accurate]

The second nuclear age is much more decentralized than the first nuclear age, with many independent nuclear decision centers. Moreover, there is nothing comparable to the discipline of the cold war blocs to keep countries in line. There are larger structures—the NPT regime, the UN, world opinion, the United States as the number-one power ensuring world order—but these have less influence over secondary powers than the cold war alliances had.

The greatest risk of nuclear war is in the regions, not between major powers against one another. It is not difficult to imagine intense nuclear rivalries among these countries. Rivalries in the Middle East, South Asia, and East Asia aren't new, of course, but rivalries in a nuclear context are new. How these rivalries play out will be one of the most important questions of the second nuclear age.

WHEN DID IT START?

The first nuclear age had a clear beginning. On August 6, 1945, the United States detonated an atomic bomb on Hiroshima. The start of the second nuclear age is much harder to pin down. Jean-Paul Sartre, quoting Hegel, remarked that "history is what takes place behind our backs." The second nuclear age is a lot like this. It began, so to speak, behind our backs. Almost no one noticed it.

The second nuclear age was obscured by the first, in part because of the belief that the first nuclear age and the cold war were identical. Another factor masking the second nuclear age was the gripping drama of the cold war itself, with its crises and politics. Ideology had a part, too. The cold war was seen as something global and universal.

It subsumed all other rivalries to it. Rivalries that didn't fit it were either dropped from the narrative or straitjacketed into its story line.

The reason all of this matters is that it obscures the overlap between the two nuclear ages. My definition of the second nuclear age—the spread of the bomb for reasons that have nothing to do with the cold war—allows for countries to have gotten the bomb during the cold war for reasons that had little to do with that conflict.

Think of two circles, representing the two nuclear ages. How much do they overlap in time? In one view they are totally separate.

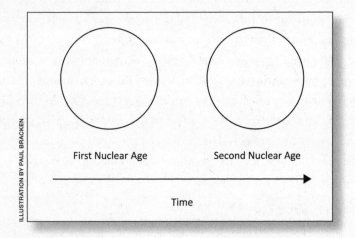

This is the common view. It says that the cold war led to the first nuclear age. It ended in 1991, with the demise of the Soviet Union. An era of nuclear proliferation then followed, in the 1990s and afterward.

This way of viewing the second nuclear age has several problems, clearly. Even at the beginning, the United States didn't get the bomb to stop the Soviet Union, but rather to defeat Germany and Japan. A larger defect in the story is that it doesn't recognize non–cold war rationales for getting the bomb by several countries during the cold war.

An alternative view of the two nuclear ages looks as follows:

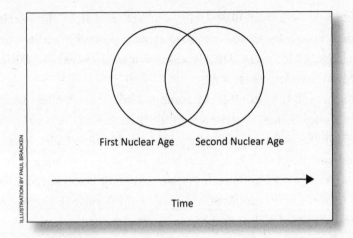

This view is controversial because it suggests that the second nuclear age began a long time ago, and that its beginning was missed because all the attention went to the cold war. The cold war, while important, was not the total story of international politics in the second half of the twentieth century. There were many other important strategic developments that happened "behind our backs."

Looking back, China's drive to get the bomb in the 1950s stands out as one possible starting point for the second nuclear age. The Chinese bomb was a declaration of independence from the Soviet Union, although few people in the West saw it this way. When the Sino-Soviet split worsened in the late 1950s, Moscow hit the brakes on nuclear cooperation with China. But China moved forward and tested its first nuclear weapon in October 1964.

China didn't come into the nuclear club as the Soviet Union's junior partner in the cold war. In the West it was seen this way, at least at first. The assumption was that the Soviet Union was the leader of the international communist bloc, and that the Soviets controlled China. It is now known this wasn't even close to being the case. Moscow understood what a Chinese bomb meant, even if Washington didn't.

It's useful to recall how China used nuclear weapons. After Mao

Zedong's victory in 1949, China was excluded from the international system by an American-led economic boycott and political isolation. China's seat in the United Nations was assigned to Taiwan. This suited Moscow just fine.

China didn't brandish the bomb to make crazy threats against the United States. American strategic literature of the era worried about this, that Mao Zedong would become a nuclear Hitler. Instead, the main use of the Chinese bomb was political. Even though China was hardly a nuclear power, its possession of the bomb forced others to treat it more seriously. China had nothing close to the nuclear capability even of Britain or France, yet alone of the superpowers. Yet China still achieved a great deal from going nuclear. It's useful to keep this in mind when people dismiss small nuclear forces as irrelevant.

It was only after China's nuclear test that the U.S. view of China changed. In particular, Senators Edward Kennedy and Robert Kennedy argued that with 600 million people—and the bomb—China had to be taken seriously. It was imperative for the United States to engage Beijing, they argued. Excluding China from the international system, the Kennedy brothers said, was dangerous and it wasn't going to work.

China's bomb also made the Vietnam War, potentially, a nuclear war. Were the United States to escalate big—say, by hitting Chinese supply lines to Vietnam or by invading North Vietnam—no one could say where it might lead. In the 1960s China couldn't launch a single nuclear weapon at the United States—it had no missiles or airplanes that could reach that far—but China could create a huge mess in Asia. Sending in volunteers, countering a U.S. invasion of North Vietnam, or firing on U.S. ships and planes would have greatly escalated the conflict. This is exactly what the Johnson administration feared. The memory of China's intervention in the Korean War was still fresh, so this was a threat that could not be dismissed. The scenario of a Chinese invasion of Vietnam to destroy U.S. forces was war gamed many times over.

China's nuclear ability thus helped to deter large U.S. escalations in Vietnam. It changed the strategic discussion in Washington, too. U.S. military commanders never understood this perspective, and it led to enormous civil-military conflicts throughout the war.

This illustrates a point worth emphasizing. Merely having the atomic bomb creates options and possibilities that wouldn't otherwise exist. It doesn't matter if there are plans or doctrines for any of these. Just the fact that China had the bomb forced the United States to make certain calculations that powerfully altered the strategy in Vietnam. Nor did it matter if the Chinese ever considered invading Vietnam. If I were told that China never considered doing this, that no plans for it existed, and that Chinese leaders were against it, the point would still stand. The existence of a Chinese bomb changed the calculus in Washington.

As it also did so for the Soviet Union. In 1969 border skirmishes with China on the Ussuri River in the Soviet Far East raised the same kinds of questions in Moscow of "where things might go." China at the time was going through the Cultural Revolution and its army was in shambles. The Soviets could have walked into Manchuria. There was nothing to stop them, save peasant infantry with rifles. But that's not what happened. Instead Moscow approached the United States about taking joint action against China to take out its nuclear production capacity, a proposal that was quickly dismissed in Washington.

China actually went on nuclear alert with its primitive nuclear force in 1969. I discovered this in 1987 on a trip I made to China. An old general I interviewed described how he was in charge of uploading atomic bombs onto aircraft in northern China that were to be flown to attack Soviet cities. He related how there was a picket line of soldiers armed with rifles around the airplanes to guard the bombs.

Going on nuclear alert against the Soviet Union can hardly be considered to be part of a "bipolar" cold war. So, even by 1969, the bomb was used for reasons having nothing to do with the cold war. Instead, there was a nuclear split in the communist bloc. It is common wisdom today that America's mistake was to see communism as a unified bloc during the cold war. This is nonsense. By the mid-1960s no serious observer or analyst in the United States did so. By the mid-1960s the cold war wasn't seen as bipolar. China wasn't in the Soviet nuclear camp.

But maybe the second nuclear age didn't begin with China after all. Perhaps it started in May 1974, when India tested its first atomic bomb. India couldn't be placed in either cold war bloc. It followed a third way, taking a path between communism and capitalism. India leaned to Moscow, yes, but held to a nonaligned foreign policy. It was hard to argue that India's bomb was part of the global cold war.

India's test sparked alarm about greater nuclear proliferation. Yet following the test India took no further steps; it didn't shrink its atomic weapons to a size and shape that could be dropped from an airplane or put on the tip of a missile. And it would be another twenty-four years before India conducted its next nuclear test.

India's test was a cause for concern, but not so much as to require a reinterpretation of the cold war framework that policy makers used to look at the world. No one was particularly upset, except Pakistan, India's neighbor and military rival. A nuclear India wasn't seen as a big change to the international order, either. It was a poor developing country, with a bad attitude toward its former colonial masters. India's bomb was seen as small potatoes in the larger cold war.

There was hardly an inkling that, with China and India both in the nuclear club, something fundamental was taking shape. For the better part of two centuries the strongest military power in Asia wasn't Asian. It was British, then American. The French even had their little slice of southeast Asia. All of this was about to come to an end.

With China and India as nuclear powers, Western military power in Asia wasn't going to last. The world entered a "post–Vasco da Gama" epoch, with Western power over Asia in irreversible decline. No longer an arena for the colonial powers to play in, nor a sideshow of the cold war, Asia was returning to the stage of world power dynamics.

The bomb in Asia was a turning point for another reason, too. It broke the Western monopoly on this most destructive weapon in history. "The club" now had two Asian members, joining the United States, the Soviet Union, Britain, and France. The West was still way ahead in the 1970s, true, but there were the beginnings of modern military power in Asia. It would soon be clear that the West's monopoly on economic growth, business, and high technology would be contested as well.

Yet again, perhaps the second nuclear age really began with the atomic bombs of Israel and South Africa. These countries used the cold war to conceal what they were doing and tried to manipulate cold war rivalries for their own purposes.

Israel's first prime minister, David Ben-Gurion, made the decision to get the bomb in the early 1950s. But it was hard for a poor desert country like Israel to do so. Israel had made the deserts bloom, but that didn't get it any plutonium.

It took the 1956 Suez crisis to do that. Suez is another excellent example of history happening behind our backs. It's one of the less-noted crises of the cold war. The crisis is usually looked at in terms of Dwight Eisenhower's skill at crisis management. In 1956 the British, French, and Israelis colluded to seize the Suez Canal from Egypt without letting the United States know about their plans. They landed parachute and ground forces to take the canal. Eisenhower was furious when he got word and forced the three to reverse course and withdraw their troops. Premier Nikolay Bulganin of the Soviet Union sent messages to Britain, France, and Israel warning them that their seizure of the canal could turn "into a World War III." Moscow might send troops to Syria or Egypt or bomb Israel.

Nearly all the scholarship on the crisis makes the same points. It was a bluff. The Soviets had no serious intention of going to war over Suez. Moscow was busy putting down the Hungarian uprising just as the crisis unfolded and was in no position to open a new front in the Middle East. The Soviets had some nuclear missiles in 1956, but not many. The personal accounts of British leaders indicated that they didn't take the threat of Soviet attack seriously.

All true. But it misses the bigger point. Few in Washington or London may have worried about a Soviet missile attack, but the French government was humiliated, having been cut loose by the United States. Coming two years after the disaster at Dien Bien Phu—which marked the end of its colonial rule in Vietnam—Suez drove home the fact that France's old glories were gone forever. Unless, that is, Paris did something to change the situation. So France decided to get the bomb. Its first nuclear test was in 1960 in the Sahara.

Few countries understood these dynamics at the time. But there was one that did: Israel. The French saw Israel as an ally who could help them hold on to Algeria. So France gave Israel nuclear "research reactors" and detonator technology. This led to Israel's plutonium facility at Dimona, and eventually a nuclear weapon.

Israel went nuclear in 1966, not with a test but with a reliable design judged certain to explode. The country had two atom bombs primed for hitting Cairo and Damascus in the June 1967 war.

Israel going nuclear can't be forced into the cold war story line at all. The United States learned of the Israeli program but decided to remain quiet about it. Not having good labels for what was taking place, yet alone policies for preventing it, the U.S. government pushed the Israeli nuclear program to the side. There is still controversy about this. A top-secret memo in 1969 discussing the Israeli bomb, from Henry Kissinger to Richard Nixon, has now been declassified. It shows the United States wanted to keep the Israeli bomb secret as much as the Israelis did.

TOP SECRET/NODIS/SENSITIVE

MEMORANDUM FOR THE PRESIDENT

FROM: Henry A. Kissinger

SUBJECT: Israeli Nuclear Program

. . . Israel has 12 surface-to-surface missiles delivered from France. It has set up a production line and plans by the end of 1970 to have a total force of 24-30, ten of which are programmed for nuclear warheads.

When the Israelis signed the contract buying the Phantom aircraft last November, they committed themselves "not to be the first to *introduce* nuclear weapons into the Near East." But it was plain from the discussion that they interpreted that to mean they could possess nuclear weapons as long as they did not test, deploy, or make them public. In signing the contract, we wrote Rabin saying that we believe mere "possession" constitutes "introduction" and that Israel's introduction of nuclear weapons by our definition would be cause for us to cancel the contract.

. . . public knowledge is almost as dangerous as possession itself. This is what might spark a Soviet nuclear guarantee for the Arabs, tighten the Soviet hold on the Arabs and increase the danger of our involvement.

. . . What this means is that, while we might ideally like to halt actual Israeli possession, what we really want at a minimum may be just to keep Israeli possession from becoming an established international fact.

Israel refused to sign the NPT, but the treaty did slow down those who had signed it, such as Egypt. The full weight of international inspection shifted to them. The United States was off the hook on this, too, because Israel couldn't violate a treaty it hadn't signed.

Without a mushroom cloud or a film clip of a shaking cratered earth, the crystallization of a second nuclear age didn't come about in the public mind. My interviews and conversations with senior Israeli officials on the history of their nuclear program convince me that this was no accident. Building a nuclear force hidden behind a treaty they never signed, and therefore couldn't break, and publicly denying that there was a program, bought the Israelis twenty-five years of freedom from harassment.

Then there's the South African bomb effort, which was deeply entwined with Israel's. The white South African government started a bomb program in the 1970s, although it had earlier roots in research. The first weapon was produced in 1982, and over the next five years a total of six were built.

The South Africans faced external and internal dangers in the 1980s. There were conventional threats from Soviet-supported Cuban forces in Angola. And of course there was the apartheid problem at home.

International events having nothing to do with South Africa's security helped the program. Israel needed uranium and also wanted to test a new design for a neutron bomb. The Israeli nuclear force had not been tested, save for zero-yield experiments to confirm the reliability of the warhead design. In the 1973 war Israel faced large Egyptian and Syrian armies that almost broke through, and so Israel wanted a weapon that could blunt this threat. A neutron bomb kills people, with less damage to buildings, making it ideal for destroying an army while sparing built-up areas. In the 1970s the thinking in Israel was that should an Arab army get close to populated settlements in a future war, a neutron bomb might come in handy. Indeed, in the late 1970s Israeli use of a neutron bomb was studied at the Hudson Institute and I participated in this research.

But a neutron bomb is a complex weapon, and a physical test is needed to ensure that it actually fires. So in 1979, in collaboration with South Africa, Israel tested a neutron bomb in the Indian Ocean

1,600 miles southeast of Cape Town, near the Prince Edward Islands. Israel promised South Africa a primitive weapon design, and in return received uranium and testing rights.

Israel thought the Prince Edward Islands were far enough from the prying eyes of American satellites. But there was an old satellite still operating, parked in orbit as a spare, and it caught the test on its sensors. There was a brief fracas in Washington, but other problems were more pressing and the matter was soon dropped.

Nonetheless, the Prince Edward Islands incident got South Africa the bomb.

If the bombs of China, India, France, Israel, and South Africa didn't register on people that a nuclear age outside of the cold war had developed, the events of 1998 surely did. So much happened that year that it looked like deep tectonic pressures were blasting through the illusions of the post–cold war world. India fired off five atomic bombs in May 1998. Pakistan responded with six shots a month later, in a kind of sick one-upmanship over India. Both nations tested ballistic missiles that could deliver these bombs to distant targets.

Nineteen ninety-eight was a critical year elsewhere as well. Iran tested a long-range missile capable of hitting Israel. Then there was North Korea, whose nuclear program had been discovered in the early 1990s but was thought to be on hold, following a 1994 agreement brokered by the United States and China. Then Pyongyang tested a missile, flying it over Japan, heedless of the chance that it might crash on a Japanese city. That North Korea would build a missile with a conventional warhead seemed odd, because it would do little damage. It was a very expensive way to land a car bomb–size explosion on Seoul or Tokyo. The only reasonable conclusion was that the missile was built to carry a nuclear warhead.

These developments took place at a blistering pace. While I believe the second nuclear age began well before then, 1998 was the turning point. The events in India, Pakistan, Iran, and North Korea were impossible to ignore and crystallized a new way of seeing the world. There may be debate about when it began, but the second nuclear age was under way.

HOW IT DIFFERS FROM THE FIRST

To understand the second nuclear age requires focusing on what's distinctive about it, as well as lessons from the first nuclear age that may carry over to it. This is what I mean by looking at the two ages in tandem.

Seven features of the second nuclear age distinguish it from the first. While there may be additional differences, these seven are a good place to start to see why it will have its own dynamics and structure.

It's a Multiplayer Game

The second nuclear age is a multiplayer game. It has many independent nuclear decision-making centers, whereas the first nuclear age essentially had two. This is the biggest single difference between the two eras, and its implications are far reaching.

Despite this obvious point, cold war concepts continue to be used to describe today's nuclear issues. For example, virtually all cold war strategic concepts (deterrence, stability, escalation, mutual assured destruction) were developed for a game with only two players, the United States and the Soviet Union. Nearly all academic theories of deterrence have two players as their premise. For all these reasons it is imperative to think more deeply about how rivalry changes when additional players are involved.

One important insight comes from the assumption that the cold war itself was a two-player game. This was a fiction, but it was a useful fiction that helped to stabilize the cold war's dynamics. The United States could hold the Soviet Union accountable for China, and the Soviet Union could hold the United States responsible for Britain and France.

The fiction of nuclear bipolarity was an agreement to pretend that there were only two nuclear powers. It was a convention that helped to rein in the nuclear desires in each side's camp. For example, it was up to Washington, not Moscow, to stop West Germany from getting the bomb. Had this convention not existed, it would have invited the Soviet side to press West Germany to stay nuclear free. Clearly, this would have raised tensions considerably.

By 1965 there were only five nuclear countries (not counting the shared weapons in NATO). The fiction of a bipolar nuclear order was pretty easy to maintain because it was unimaginable that Britain or France would take independent nuclear actions on their own, without the United States. China was different, however, and there were great concerns in Washington and Moscow about this—although not enough concerns to abandon the fiction.

Yet even in the 1960s there were multiplayer nuclear dynamics. They gave away the fiction but were small enough to sweep under the carpet.

The 1967 Middle East war was in reality a three-way nuclear crisis. Few people looked at it this way because almost no one knew about Israel's bombs. Had the 1967 war gone badly, it could have gone nuclear, as Israel had two atomic bombs ready to go. But even this tiny nuclear force, two bombs, influenced the war's dynamics. When the USS *Liberty*, a U.S. intelligence ship, was attacked in the Mediterranean by the Israelis during the war, there was alarm in Washington among the handful of top leaders in the know about Israel.

This was because the *Liberty* was part of the U.S. warning system collecting information about Israeli preparations for nuclear and chemical attack. The fear, unfounded as it turned out, was that the Israeli attack was intended to purposefully blind U.S. intelligence. With both superpowers' navies in the Mediterranean, loaded to the gills with atomic weapons, and with U.S. uncertainty initially as to who, exactly, had attacked the *Liberty* (the Soviets? the Israelis?), it was a dangerous situation.

It's easy to forget the fear that existed in Washington and Moscow at the time, but it was so great that it led to the first ever use of the hotline, a communications link between Washington and Moscow established after the Cuban missile crisis to avoid misunderstandings that could get out of control. The war began on June 5, and that morning the Soviet government sent a hotline message to Washington about its concern that the two navies were sailing straight at each other in the eastern Mediterranean, and presumably that a clash of some kind could occur between them. The *Liberty* was attacked on June 8, just three days later.

Two years later, in 1969, when Henry Kissinger wrote his memo to President Nixon, he argued that if the United States didn't acknowledge Israel's bomb, it would stabilize relations among all three nuclear parties. In other words, keep up the fiction of nuclear bipolarity. The Soviet Union wouldn't be forced to give a nuclear guarantee to Egypt and Syria, and it wouldn't have to fend off these countries' demand for their own bomb. The United States, for its part, wouldn't have to fend off a contentious domestic political argument about letting Israel get the bomb, nor would it face charges by Arab countries that while Israel had been allowed to get the bomb they couldn't do so.

Game theory sheds additional light on multiplayer game dynamics. Game theory is a highly idealized mathematical abstraction of competition. The benefit isn't in making predictions about what will happen but in understanding the dynamics of rivalry as the number of contestants increases. In their 1944 classic *Theory of Games and Economic Behavior*, John von Neumann and Oskar Morgenstern emphasized just this point, the appearance of new strategic phenomena as the number of players in a game increases.

Others built upon this idea. Martin Shubik did so with a three-player game he calls a "truel." A truel takes the idea of a duel, two opposing players shooting at each other, and enlarges it to three players. In a two-player duel the dynamics are pretty simple. Nuclear forces that are "soft," that is, vulnerable to preemptive attack by the other side, tempt the enemy to shoot first to take them out. This is, obviously, a highly destabilizing situation, but the fact that it is destabilizing is clear. This is what happened in the cold war. The Soviet Union and the United States both understood that having vulnerable forces was destabilizing and could lead to a mutually reinforcing dynamic of first strike. Measures were taken to deal with this, however, and hundreds of billions of dollars were spent to make nuclear forces survivable by putting them in hardened underground silos, aboard submarines, and on airplanes.

Now think of three countries with nuclear missiles. In this truel, far more convoluted and treacherous strategies emerge. One player, seeing that the other two are at war, can wait until they finish each other off. Then he can use his missiles to blackmail the greatly weakened survivor. Or a weaker player may try to manipulate a stronger one into attacking the third party. It may lie about some intelligence information or exaggerate the threat, all to manipulate the stronger player to act for its benefit.

In a truel a weak player can gain tremendously from manipulative behavior. And one of the most provocative findings becomes apparent: in a two-player game the stronger player almost always wins. But in a multiplayer game, this isn't necessarily the case. In fact, as Shubik emphasizes, the weakest player may win.

This isn't just some academic finding. Consider South Africa's nuclear strategy in the 1980s. The country had six atomic bombs. There were 50,000 Cuban troops backed by the Soviets in Angola. And South Africa was experiencing severe racial tensions at home.

If Cuban troops invaded, South Africa could fire one or two atom bombs at Luanda, the capital of Angola, where the Cubans were staging. But South Africa had a more convoluted strategy. It planned to suddenly "introduce" nuclear weapons into the crisis and thereby force the United States to intervene. The South Africans would announce that they possessed several bombs, go on alert in a way guaranteed to be spotted by American (and Soviet) satellites, and then threaten to fire if the Cuban army didn't pull back.

As to what the target was—Luanda, the Cuban troops, or other targets too horrific to contemplate—it didn't really matter. It just wasn't the right question. The goal was to manipulate the United States to come in to the conflict. The logic for this was a calculation that the United States wouldn't stand back and allow the first use of the atomic bomb since World War II, certainly by South Africa.

South Africa would "use" the bomb to turn a conventional crisis into a nuclear one. That was the concept. With a weak hand, morally and militarily, it could try to manipulate a bigger ally, the United States, to move against the Cubans and the Soviets. I doubt that this strategy would have worked for any number of reasons. But that's hardly the point. South Africa believed the strategy was a good one. It shows the convoluted, treacherous calculations that may be the shape of things to come in the multiplayer second nuclear age.

Let's consider some other multiplayer interactions. Two examples stand out. One deals with the interaction of strategic postures. The other deals with the pathological complexities of multiplayer strategies.

The United States is currently considering deployment of super-accurate conventional missiles aboard its nuclear weapon–firing submarines. This is to target the small nuclear forces of North Korea or the underground bunkers in Iran's nuclear infrastructure.

But China has objected to this. Beijing says that these missiles also threaten their nuclear deterrent with destruction by a purely conventional attack. Imagine that the United States could destroy fifty ICBMs in China in a clean attack using only conventional arms that hardly killed anyone. Even though this is an unlikely eventuality, China doesn't like the fact that America has the capability. There are political and symbolic considerations. It undermines China's entire military modernization. The United States would possess a low-cost way to knock China down to lower-power status.

So what do the Chinese do? One response is to remodel their strategic deterrent. They are deploying road mobile missiles that are harder to find and kill. They have also put ICBMs aboard submarines, making them hard to locate, too.

Push this scenario a little further. China's mobile missiles and nuclear weapon–firing submarines upset the balance with India. So New Delhi has to respond in some manner. Currently, India is building long-range missiles, probably with a MIRV (Multiple Independently Targeted Reentry Vehicle) capability, that can reach China with a nuclear warhead. Nuclear missile submarines are also part of India's expanding strategic arsenal. As are nuclear bombers. Thus, China's moves drive India into rebalancing its nuclear triad of missiles, submarines, and bombers.

Step back to assess what has happened here in a multipolar nuclear world. The understandable U.S. requirement to be able to hit targets in a rogue nuclear country like North Korea or Iran spills over to affect China's strategic posture. China responds in a way to counter the changes. In turn, this has an impact on India. But what India does will surely have a considerable effect on Pakistan.

You can see the cascading dynamics that occur in a multiplayer game. A U.S. policy of building weapons that can destroy hard targets in North Korea and Iran has a ripple effect on countries from China to Pakistan.

The United States wants conventional missiles so it doesn't have to use nuclear ones. The goal, actually, is to raise the nuclear threshold, to make nuclear use less likely. But the result in a multiplayer game could be just the opposite, with China, India, and Pakistan responding with more nuclear weapons.

A dynamic close to this recently took place in Europe, as a NATO missile defense plan designed to deter Iran affected a major nuclear power, Russia. In response to plans to place a missile defense system in the Czech Republic and Poland, Russia reacted by threatening to build more missiles. Moscow also threatened to put nuclear cruise missiles in Kaliningrad. The missile defense system in question was canceled by President Barack Obama, at least in part because of this dynamic. But, at the same time, U.S. missile defense fell years behind schedule, just when the Iranian nuclear threat was growing.

A closely related point is that when only two powers had nuclear deterrents it was easier to reach arms control agreements. That's what the SALT (Strategic Arms Limitation Talks) and the START (Strategic Arms Reduction Talks) treaties did. The fiction that there were only two nuclear powers was incorporated into them and it helped considerably in getting a deal. Had China—or, for that matter, Britain or France—been brought into the negotiations, it is unlikely that an agreement would have been so easily reached. In the second nuclear age it is impossible to maintain such a fiction of only two nuclear powers.

Let's consider a different type of example, one unrelated to arms buildups and interaction of strategic postures. It doesn't involve nuclear weapons but other weapons of mass destruction (WMD). Actually, what makes it so provocative is that it didn't involve even WMD.

After Saddam Hussein was captured by American troops in Iraq in December 2003, he gave long interviews to the FBI. What comes out of these is that he was playing a double game with respect to WMD. He was trying to signal Iran that he had them, while also signaling the United States that he didn't. According to the FBI interview:

Even though Hussein claimed Iraq did not have WMD, the threat from Iran was the major factor as to why he did not allow the return of the UN inspectors. Hussein stated he was more concerned about Iran discovering Iraq's weaknesses and vulnerabilities than the repercussions of the United States for his refusal to allow UN inspectors back into Iraq.

It is now known, of course, that Iraq didn't have WMD. This is the other side of the coin of Israel and nuclear weapons, when for many years the world believed that Israel didn't possess them. Iraq was a false positive; Israel a false negative. Both types of error occur. There's a lot of experience dealing with problems where both types of errors are present. Broadly speaking, it requires careful specification of the degree of caution, of how conservative one is willing to be, in balancing the two types of errors.

Saddam's bluff involved two countries, the United States and Iran. It led to a disastrous war, certainly for him. He lost his country, his regime, and his life. For the United States the war was arguably a disaster.

Again, it's useful to step back and assess Saddam Hussein's double game. The strongest player—by far—the United States, didn't win. A very weak player, Iran, seems to have come out on top, at least for the time being. Iraq was a big loser. Israel, much stronger than Iran at the start, has ended up worse off, too, facing a nuclear threat from Iran.

Stability in a multiplayer game can be very delicate, much more so than in a two-player game. This is because bluffs can have geometric effects in multiplayer games. Saddam didn't have nuclear weapons or WMD. Bluffing Iran, he precipitated a U.S. attack. Saddam's convoluted strategy, simultaneously saying "I have them" and "I don't," broke down, taking others down with him and changing the balance of power in the Middle East.

Details of personality, guile, pronouncements, technology, and intelligence may profoundly affect estimates of deterrence. This sheds more light on how the second nuclear age is different from the first. Because as far as deterrence and stability were concerned, such "details" may not have mattered all that much when it came to the risk of nuclear war. Eisenhower, Kennedy, Nixon, Reagan—I don't think it mattered who was in charge on this question. The United States never seriously considered a calculated nuclear attack on the Soviet Union at any time in the cold war. I don't believe the Soviets did on the United States. If anything the Soviets were even more cautious and conservative than the Americans when it came to nuclear matters. In the first nuclear age the details could be ignored. It is far more dangerous to do so in the second.

Nationalism

In the cold war neither superpower saw nuclear weapons as a way to wipe out a hated people. In the showdowns over Cuba and Berlin, crowds didn't pack Times Square or Red Square demanding the blood of the *untermenschen*. There were crowds in Times Square, but they were there to watch the news ticker for signs of an end to a crisis, not to scream for Russian blood. I interviewed foreign diplomats who were in Moscow in 1962, during the Cuban missile crisis. They described a terrified, silent capital city that was scared to death of nuclear war. One told me that if America had parachuted a company of marines into Moscow, and demanded that the Soviets surrender, they would have done it. I don't believe this is true, but I think it captures the mood in Moscow during the crisis.

It was too dangerous for the superpowers to stage mass rallies during a nuclear crisis. Doing so could have backed them into a corner, to be trapped by their own rhetoric. Indulging a hysterical mob could easily hinder getting out of a jam.

When it came to nuclear questions, specialists, not the mob, ran policy. The image of Robert McNamara drawing graphs of decreasing marginal utility curves of nuclear attack on the Soviet Union captures the American attitude very well. Nuclear weapons were treated in a bloodless way, an irony given the destruction inherent in them. Strategy was dissected with detached rationality. Professors such as Thomas Schelling used game theory to study nuclear war as if it were a Harvard seminar. This style of strategy didn't taunt the enemy or make hysterical calls for its annihilation. On this the United States and the Soviet Union were alike. Analysis over action, and dispassionate logic, characterized nuclear decision making.

To be sure, this approach produced its own pathologies and was parodied in movies such as *Dr. Strangelove*. In the film, the character Dr. Strangelove, a composite of Henry Kissinger and Herman Kahn, invokes studies coming from the "Bland Corporation" about the number of years society needed to recover from "mega deaths" and strontium 90 poisoning. Here, the analytical logic of Armageddon is carried to its grotesque, comic conclusion.

The second nuclear age won't be like this. It will be driven by intense, emotional regional rivalries, now set in a nuclear context. The mood will be much closer to the street.

The second nuclear age has a powerful ideology, yes, but it isn't democracy or communism. Rather, it's nationalism. Nationalism is one of the most powerful forces of the past two hundred years, and it may be the most powerful force in the world today. Yet the United States consistently underestimates it and misses the dangerous association that nuclear weapons could develop with nationalism. To Americans, other people's nationalism looks silly.

American academics despise nationalism as a throwback to some primordial human emotion. I'm hardly exaggerating when I say that course titles like "Nationalism and the Politics of Genocide" typify how it is studied today in universities.

Look at the trouble caused by Slobodan Milošević with his absurd claims of Serbian superiority in the 1990s. Americans were puzzled that anyone took him seriously. Yet he was able to mobilize wide support and engineer mass murder. Likewise, the North Korean state seals itself off from the outside world with an extreme philosophy of self-reliance, telling the population that they are the most respected people in Asia. To Americans, this would be comic if it weren't so dangerous. It's straight out of the textbook of nationalism—the fantasy that one people is inherently superior to another.

Vladimir Putin used nationalism to put Russia back together after the chaos of the 1990s. China uses it today to manage its rising inequality. Israel uses it to patch over deep internal religious and political differences. India uses it to hold together a fragmented politic. Pakistan uses it to offset the absence of governance.

All of the countries mentioned here use nationalism. They have something else in common. They are all nuclear-weapons states. The connection between nationalism and atomic weapons needs much closer attention.

Nationalism was supposed to die out, said the experts, as the world converged toward a liberal business democracy called globalization. One may not like nationalism. It may be distasteful. But discounting it as a factor is done at one's peril.

Most of the "new" nuclear states (North Korea, Pakistan, Israel, India) are themselves new, having gained independence only after World War II. They need demonstrable accomplishments to legitimize their identity. This means projects that symbolize achievement, as an expression of what a people can do when properly led by the state.

The centrifugal forces of globalization require an offsetting power to hold a country together. Nationalism is a powerful motivator because the human capacity for egotistical superiority flourishes in the face of the flattening tendencies of globalization. It protects the nation from outside threats, both real and imagined.

Nationalism and nuclear weapons are potentially a toxic mixture. The bomb may be viewed as a horrific weapon, but it's also a national accomplishment. It takes considerable technical and political skill to get one. I've been quite impressed how Indians involved in their country's nuclear program are proud not just of the bomb as a physics triumph. They're also proud of how India adroitly outmaneuvered the United States and China to acquire it.

Nationalism can drive regional tensions and rivalry. This has always been so. Leaders may need a diversion from intractable domestic problems, or they may believe their own rhetoric about their country's place in the world. But a nuclear context changes the game considerably. Alerts, nuclear head games, and apocalyptic rhetoric are new additions to old rivalries.

One of the greatest risks of nationalism and nuclear weapons is that mass opinion, the street, will become an important factor in crises. This can lead to a number of different problems. Popular outrage can back a leader into a corner when he uses over-the-top rhetoric that may come back to haunt him. The role of the street in the Arab world stands out here. From Gamal Abdel Nasser in the 1950s to the Arab Spring of 2011, crowds have a close association with power. Demonstrations are easy to start but often difficult to stop. Leaders think they can control them, and they believe that the mob attitude can be safely kept away from real decisions. But this isn't always so easy. There are many examples of leaders deluding themselves, stirring up the mob to demonstrate national conviction, only to be backed into a political corner because of it. If there is a military setback, crowd psychology can harden positions beyond any reasonable calculation of gains and losses.

Finally, the psychological effects of nuclear weapons must be considered. Passion, hatred, hysteria—these were excluded from the crises of the first nuclear age. They are far less likely to be excluded—indeed, they may well be much more important—in the second nuclear age.

Terrorism

Terrorism is most often defined in terms of indiscriminate civilian destruction. But in thinking about nuclear weapons, it's better to think of terrorists as a catalyst to escalation. They create a new opportunity for instability that was not present in the first nuclear age. While terrorist attacks took place during the cold war, with attacks on civilians in Vietnam, kidnappings in South America, and bombings in Western Europe, these were not intended to trigger a nuclear war. They had more prosaic goals.

Terrorism is a distinctive feature in the second nuclear age because of its tipping power, its potential to accelerate escalation. Just think what would have happened if the 9/11 attacks had taken place at the height of the Cuban missile crisis. U.S. restraint might have held. But then again, maybe not.

Terrorist strikes intended to escalate a crisis between two countries are an example of catalytic war. A third party, the terrorist group, launches an attack with the intention of triggering a larger conflict. A few studies were done on this topic at the Hudson Institute during the cold war, but they never got anywhere because the terrorists of that era didn't seem interested in starting a bigger war. It was more a scenario for thriller novels and James Bond movies.

Catalytic war is no longer hypothetical. Think of the 9/11 attacks by al Qaeda. The purpose wasn't to start a war between the United States and al Qaeda, but between the United States and Islam. The attack led to the United States sending large ground forces to the Middle East, with consequences that are only too apparent.

I am not talking about nuclear terrorism. Terrorists setting off an atom bomb in Manhattan is a problem, obviously. But if the goal is to launch a catalytic war, a terrorist attack need not be nuclear. If a shooting rampage in Mumbai were to come at the height of an India-Pakistan nuclear crisis, it might be enough to tip the balance to war. Plain old conventional bombings, shootings, and airplane crashes are more than sufficient.

But having said this, the destructive potential of nuclear terrorism obviously makes this another feature of a multipolar nuclear world. Nuclear terrorism has received a great deal of attention, deservedly so. But it isn't the only problem, not by a long shot.

Terrorism comes in many shapes and sizes in the second nuclear age. There is a tendency to lump too many different possibilities under a single heading. If there is to be a productive conversation about managing our way through the second nuclear age, certain distinctions are essential for clear communication. Terrorism in a nuclear age is a different subject than nuclear terrorism. Catalytic war, anonymous war, and surrogate war (Iran using Hezbollah and Hamas) are all distinct kinds of conflict. Each has different implications for deterrence, stability, and many other variables.

Second Mover Advantage

The second nuclear age piggybacks on the first, and benefits from second mover advantage, the gain that comes from learning how others have faced similar problems. Second movers have cheaper, easier challenges than first movers, because they profit from copying experience and knowledge. The basic design of the bomb itself is the clearest example. Anyone with a computer and library can learn a great deal about it. This wasn't the situation when America built its bomb in World War II.

North Korea is a second mover, learning from Russian engineers about Scud missiles. Iran learned about uranium enrichment from trade journals and from A. Q. Kahn, who developed Pakistan's atomic bomb from designs he picked up in Europe. Pakistan also received nuclear know-how from China. The list goes on. These countries didn't need to stand up a giant R&D enterprise to discover original technical solutions. They only needed clever people and a reasonably competent set of scientific and engineering institutions.

Saudi Arabia may one day be the extreme second mover, if it were to buy a bomb from North Korea or Pakistan. It would be a nuclear virgin birth, a country going nuclear without all the hassle of enriching uranium. This has not taken place, at least not yet, but it shows how different the second nuclear age is.

Second mover advantages have a number of consequences. Obviously it should lead to cheaper development of weapons of mass destruction of all kinds. But what should not be overlooked is that second mover advantages can also apply to strategy innovation. The new nuclear powers are combing through the history of the cold war to glean insights and get ideas. They undoubtedly will adapt their strategy to their local conditions, but nonetheless there are significant ideas for them to learn in using nuclear weapons.

Historical Timing

That the second nuclear age comes after the first is an obvious but nonetheless important difference between the two. There were no superpowers or IAEA to stop or slow down the United States and the Soviet Union from building their arsenals. Actually, the major powers created these institutions to lock in their nuclear monopoly.

Today countries going nuclear have to weigh the reaction of the United States and of an international nonproliferation system built to stop them. They have to factor this into the way they go nuclear. Extreme secrecy, deception, and target hardening and dispersal are critical to these countries. This applies both to getting the bomb and to using it. Because with a small nuclear arsenal, attention is needed to ensure it isn't easily destroyed.

A good example of this occurred in 1998, when India conducted its first nuclear test in twenty-four years. The Indians were afraid that the test would be discovered a few days before it went off. There would be frantic calls from the American president to the Indian prime minister. Sanctions and threats would follow, and the rest of the Indian government and body politic (who were in the dark about it) would find out.

The Indians moved their scientists to the nuclear test site one at a time so they wouldn't draw attention. Another trick was to make sure that the number of parking spaces at their labs were filled with the same number of cars from one day to the next. They shuffled cars in the parking lot to make things look normal in satellite photographs, and to distract attention from the fact that many of the key scientists and engineers had actually moved to the test site. Another trick was to disguise their scientists with fake beards and makeup.

These were very simple tricks. But on top of this, New Delhi carried out a sophisticated deception plan to fool the White House. The Indians hinted to senior American officials that a nuclear test wasn't being considered that year. It all worked like a charm. Since everything looked normal in the satellite photos, and since senior U.S. officials were led to believe that they had the inside dope on Indian politics—that a test wasn't coming—they were lulled into complacency. When the test happened, the United States was caught completely off-guard.

Some countries have perfected deception to a fine art. Iran's bomb program was hidden for over a decade. Academic groups from the United States and Europe were invited in and given "secret" briefings the Iranians knew would be reported back to their governments. Secrecy and deception also lie at the heart of Israel's nuclear program. There has never been a photograph, by satellite or spy camera, of an Israeli nuclear weapon, for example on a missile being moved from one position to another. Given the scale of the U.S. intelligence collection, this is an extraordinary achievement.

The Soviets had a reputation for clever deception, but I think this was exaggerated. On big technical programs they were as ham-fisted as they were in running their economy. One of the big reasons the Soviets got caught in the Cuban missile crisis was that they built their nuclear sites there exactly the same way they did in Eastern Europe. It was amazing. The fence lines, perimeter length, and guard post layout were an exact copy of their sites in Eastern Europe. Once the CIA saw the pictures, it immediately understood what was going on.

The Soviets weren't particularly agile or sophisticated. And that, I believe, is the lesson to emphasize. They didn't have to be because they had so many nuclear weapons. But deception skills will be paramount in the future, as will secrecy in hiding small nuclear forces in a world where major countries are out to find them. With the very different cultures involved, the United States may be hard pressed to see through many deceptive stratagems. Putting more money into U.S. intelligence for this purpose would be a good thing. It may be a high-payoff investment. But expecting intelligence to catch all the things it did during the cold war may be unrealistic.

A Post–Vasco da Gama Era

Europe and America once had a monopoly on the bomb. It is easy to forget just how European the first nuclear age was. The bomb was invented by European physicists to solve a European problem, namely Hitler. That it was first used against Japan was an unlucky consequence of the early collapse of Nazi Germany.

Another way to look at the second nuclear age, then, is as the breakdown of the Western atomic monopoly. China broke the ice here, and now others have, too. But a deeper change is under way, ending a five-hundred-year epoch that began in 1498 when the Portuguese explorer Vasco da Gama opened a sea route to India from Europe. This began a historical era of Western overseas empires and ultimately control of the world's political and economic systems.

The tendency is to think of victory in the cold war as the turning point of the modern era. But that's not how it looks to much of the world's people. For them, it's a closing of a five-hundred-year period of Western domination, not fifty years of cold war. Looking at the second nuclear age in terms of the cold war may well be a Western conceit.

Monopolies are great—for the monopolist. Think how nuclear nonproliferation looks in this framework. Today Britain and France preach the benefits of nuclear nonproliferation, yet both have retained their nuclear arsenals. The United States has kept its nuclear weapons, too, while building a global conventional force that no other country can stand up to. It looks as if the West is trying to hold on to its place in history, and to preserve its nuclear monopoly. China was allowed in, true, because there was no alternative. But think of how this looks to India, Pakistan, and Iran. To them it must seem like a corporate monopoly, fighting new high-tech entrants with legal maneuvers at the UN to prevent new entrants from starting their own businesses.

That the West also dominates the UN Security Council's permanent membership (the United States, Russia, France, Britain, China), and that just these five countries make up the "legal" nuclear states, as enshrined in the NPT, only adds insult to injury.

This global perspective will surely affect how the bomb is conceived. If a global nonproliferation regime built on shared values for all practical purposes means that these countries have to accept Western values, it isn't going to fly. Given the changes in economics and the military, it may be asking them to swallow too much.

The Economics of Defense in the Second Nuclear Age

It was once argued that the costs and technical complexity of nuclear weapons would prevent other countries from getting them. This was at a time when it was also unthinkable that developing countries would take jobs from the United States, produce cars, or design computers.

The economic pressures on countries with the bomb are different from what was expected. There is a competition for resources in defense ministries between the "new" weapons projects like atomic bombs and missiles, and "old" ones like infantry, airplanes, and tanks. As more money is spent on the new technologies less is spent on the old ones.

One consequence is that in many places conventional forces are being run down, relative to the new forces. The old mass infantry armies of Asia are everywhere being used as "cash cows" to fund the newer programs. There are cuts in funding, investment, and training to free up money for missiles, nuclear arms, information warfare, satellites, et cetera. That's where the excitement is. It's where a good defense bureaucrat or scientist in India or Iran can advance his career.

At present, few countries are seriously thinking through their *overall* strategic postures. Rather, they are entering a new technology area, expanding bureaucratic empires, and trying to curry favor with political elites to keep the money spigot open.

One danger from this is that they will build a nuclear one-trick pony. They are becoming so dependent on nuclear deterrence that if it fails, or if it is understood that it can't be used in many situations, there is little else for them to fall back on.

Strong conventional forces work like a shock absorber. In India and Pakistan it's the conventional armies that slow down crises and prevent them from going nuclear. On the Korean peninsula, the running down of North Korean conventional forces from economic weakness means that if a crisis were to come, it may quickly accelerate to a nuclear confrontation. That's about all Pyongyang has, along with chemical and biological weapons.

A country that has atomic bombs and missiles, and not much of an army, may be a very destabilizing actor in the international system. It will have few options in a crisis, other than to threaten a nuclear attack. When its rivals see this, they may feel that preemption is the only way to deal with the situation. So even a garden-variety crisis, which ordinarily would de-escalate on its own, can grow to a question of national survival for reasons that have little to do with the specific dispute that created the crisis in the first place.

Nuclear force comparisons—counting how many bombs India

and Pakistan have—take attention away from the more critical linkage of conventional to nuclear forces. Crisis stability is more likely to
be affected by this conventional-nuclear linkage than by nuclear-on-
nuclear comparisons.

With skill and luck the world made it through the first nuclear age.
But we may not be so skillful or so lucky this time. There are just too
many important differences. The second nuclear age is a multiplayer
game, but even more than that, the arrangement of major and secondary powers is altogether different. The superpowers didn't have
to worry about nuclear escalation in a region because none of the
secondary regional powers were acknowledged to have the bomb.
There was bloc discipline that came more or less automatically, and
there were years of developed conventions about what was and was
not acceptable behavior in this system.

The global-regional arrangements of the second nuclear age are
entirely different. Some secondary powers face a real prospect of
attack, and while they can turn to a major power for protection this
offers nothing like the security of turning to one of the superpowers
leading a global competition. Moreover, nationalism has supplanted
liberal internationalism and communism as a driving political force,
and this brings in emotional and perhaps even hysterical forces
of paranoia and fear. It means that the street, the mob, and the narrow
distrustful leader are in the firing chain. Add to this terrorists, who
whether they have the bomb or not will see new opportunities to be
accelerants to escalation, and it adds up to a combustible mixture.

The world did not blow up in the first nuclear age; it made it
through without a nuclear shot being fired. But there were close calls.
We know this now. The near misses came from an inadequate recognition of risks and from complicated strategic interactions not understood at the time. Still, at no time in the cold war did either side
seriously consider a calculated nuclear strike on the other. This doesn't

mean that nuclear war could not have happened. But it does mean something that's quite important, that both superpowers were extremely conservative when it came to nuclear weapons.

In the second nuclear age inadequate recognition of the risks by new nuclear powers, or by countries who have had the bomb for years but haven't thought things through because they haven't been thrust into a nuclear crisis, is likely to be greater because their forces are smaller and hence are more tempting targets. The complexities of strategic interactions are likely to be greater as well. Most of all, serious consideration of a calculated strike on the other side certainly can't be dismissed. Depending on the specifics, and the region, it seems positively likely that calculated attacks will be considered. The world made it through the first nuclear age, yes, but we may not be as lucky this time.

· 5 ·

THE MIDDLE EAST

Although nuclear weapons are not new in the Middle East, in the past they could largely be ignored because they rarely had an impact on the strategic dynamics of the region. Now they are a central problem, both in themselves because nuclear stability is hardly a given and also because they establish a new context for all the other problems that have not gone away in the region.

The United States and Israel have declared that a nuclear Middle East is unacceptable. This statement is offered as if it were the final say on the problem. It surely is not, because it says little about how Iran will be stopped from getting the atomic bomb. But declaring a nuclear Middle East unacceptable has another consequence. It has discouraged thinking about the many sizes and shapes that a nuclear Middle East might take. Many different possibilities are simply lumped together and declared to be unacceptable. Iran might get a few bombs and just sit on them. Alternatively, Iran might devise a sophisticated political strategy for using the bomb, with nuclear and other ways to keep the nuclear pot boiling. Israel could respond by relying on its current nuclear deterrent. Or Israel could redesign its deterrent, moving it to sea, in which case it would have a much larger, high-profile nuclear force. Other countries, such as Saudi Arabia, could go nuclear if Iran does.

Lumping all of these alternatives together in a one-size-fits-all model makes little sense. Israel itself is only beginning to think through the implications of a nuclear Middle East. It hasn't officially announced itself as a nuclear power, but leaks, media stories, and academic research have brought Israel's nuclear force out of the closet. When nuclear weapons were kept offstage, during the cold war and through the 1990s, there was little need for Israeli leaders or their staffs to think about how a nuclear Middle East might change the whole context of Israeli security. It was enough to declare the possibility unacceptable. Many controversies were avoided. But so too was a lot of thinking.

The small number of Israelis who were in the know about nuclear weapons were a tiny, cloistered group. As a result, the most important strategic questions have not been deeply analyzed within Israel. The extraordinary secrecy and sensitivity about Israeli nuclear forces had the effect of leaving fundamental questions unexamined. This is just beginning to change as Israel faces a nuclear Iran, but there is still an intellectual catch-up aspect to Israeli thinking about nuclear weapons.

The United States and Israel are about to go into an upper-level course on nuclear weapons in the Middle East. It is time to look at the issues that should be in the syllabus.

SHOULD ISRAEL ATTACK IRAN?

One tool that should be in this class is the concept of a branch point. A branch point is a strategic turning-point decision that leads to several different alternative futures. Once a choice is made, it is impossible to go back and unmake it. There is great uncertainty about where many of the branches lead.

The branch point is whether or not Israel attacks Iran's nuclear complex. Perhaps the United States would join in the attack, but I would argue that this doesn't affect the branch point argument made here.

Some observers and commentators say that there is no branch point. They argue that Israel bombing another country to prevent its nuclear armament is just another business-as-usual move in a violent, dangerous region. Israel has bombed nuclear facilities in the past—in 1981, when Iraq's Osirak nuclear reactor was destroyed and, in 2007, when Israel destroyed Syria's nascent plutonium reactor. Such attacks are unfortunate but not transformational, they say.

I disagree. An Israeli attack on Iran will produce a different Middle East; it will set in motion a chain of developments that will have greater consequence than the wars in 1967 and 1973. If Israel does not attack, and Iran gets the bomb, a nuclear Middle East will be the result. Either way, it will be a different Middle East.

I am not saying that Israel should, or should not, attack Iran. It is a branch point, and leaders and their staffs have an obligation to identify the consequences that will follow. Leaping to the outcome of one branch, and ignoring the others, is irresponsible. Branch points put immediate pressures and fears into a larger framework. Allowing immediate pressures to drive decisions abdicates the responsibility leaders have to take a broader, big picture look, even when the pressures are extraordinary.

Israel has two choices, to attack Iran's nuclear complex or not. If Israel waits and doesn't attack, there is a good prospect that Iran will get the bomb.

Iran, if attacked, has two choices as well. It can respond to an Israeli attack or not. By not respond I include the possibility that Iran might declare outrage and stage a few small-scale terrorist attacks, and maybe harass a few ships in the Persian Gulf. But the strategic decision is to stand down and not to counterescalate against Israel or the United States.

If Iran doesn't respond to an Israeli attack, Israel wins. Iran is disarmed, at least for a time, and although Israel will be widely condemned for the attack, it will seem like a small price to pay for getting rid of a nuclear threat.

If Iran does respond, Israel's victory could evaporate. Iranian-backed terrorism, war in the Persian Gulf, skyrocketing oil prices, attacks on Israel itself with long-range rockets would dramatically increase the costs to Israel.

This framing of the problem shows something that is usually missed in public discussions of attacking Iran. The costs to Israel depends on *Iran*'s response, not on what Israel does. The benefit of an attack depends on its costs, and these are determined in Iran, not Israel. If Iran counterescalates, and a game of escalation develops, this could be a bad outcome for Israel.

Israel can try to influence Iran's calculations about retaliation. It has been suggested that Israel strike only nuclear-related targets in Iran, avoiding civilian and other military targets. This way, leaders in Iran would see that it was a limited attack, rather than an attack intended to destroy Iran's overall military capacity. Iran then might acknowledge the limited nature of the Israeli attack by limiting its own response. Then again, it might not. Leaders in Tehran might not even see such a tactic as limited, or they might be subject to domestic pressures to respond in a big way.

Something larger shows up in this discussion. Historically, Israel had escalation dominance in the Middle East. Whatever an opponent might do, Israel could confidently come back and match it, and raise the stakes. This gave Israel the ability to calculate how much punishment to inflict. Escalation was dominated by Israel.

To understand escalation dominance, it's instructive to go back to the Cuban missile crisis of 1962. The United States had escalation dominance in the Caribbean. If the crisis was confined to that region, the United States could trump any move by the Soviet Union. There was nothing the Soviet navy could do in the Caribbean, as it was too distant from its bases. That's one reason President Kennedy chose the blockade. If it had come to an invasion of Cuba, the United States could overpower any resistance by adding more force to the attack. Cuba was too far from the Soviet Union to get a big ground force there. If Moscow had tried to do this, the ships carrying the force could have been sunk by the U.S. Navy.

The Soviets could have responded outside of the Caribbean, however. They could have put pressure on Berlin or in some other part of Europe. Here the stakes were more evenly matched. The United States had escalation dominance in the Caribbean but not in Europe. Expansion of the Cuban missile crisis out of the Caribbean to Europe would have dramatically increased the severity of the crisis, because it would have shifted its location from a region where the United States held the big stick, in the Caribbean, to a region where it didn't, in Europe.

Israel has had escalation dominance in the pre-nuclear Middle East. In a nuclear Middle East it no longer does. That's why Iran getting the bomb is such a big deal. It completely changes the game. And it's why a nuclear Middle East is such a worrisome threat to Israel and to American influence in the region. No wonder Israel is so intent on preventing it from happening.

Suppose Israel attacks and Iran responds in a big way, by firing missiles at U.S. bases in the Middle East, at Israel, and by laying sea mines and attacking ships in the Persian Gulf. This response would be large enough to draw the United States into the conflict. Think for a moment about the domestic politics of this branch point in the United States. The United States would be forced into a war to protect Israel in a war that Israel started. There would be a significant body of opinion that Israel's policy was to manipulate the United States into the war all along. Perhaps U.S. public opinion would automatically swing wholeheartedly to Israel. But not necessarily. Israel might be hung out to dry, even if the United States joined the war against Iran. There are many ways for the United States to do this. The most obvious one is for Washington to slow down the resupply of weapons to Israel. That was done in the 1973 war, when President Nixon wanted to pressure Israel into giving back the Sinai at the end of that conflict.

U.S. restraint in support of Israel is more likely under two conditions: when Israel is seen as starting the war and if the war drags on for a long time. When Israel is attacked, as it was in 1973, Americans see Israel as defending itself and punishing the aggressor. When Israel is seen as the aggressor, all bets are off.

Long wars are always a problem for Israel and for the United States, because domestic politics kick in and the talk turns to costs— human, financial, political. A short war is over before this can happen. But the key feature of a long war is that the plans for making a conflict short have been proven not to work. Planners then turn to ideas that were originally discarded in favor of shorter, cleaner options. A long war in the Middle East would ratchet up its intensity, in casualties, types of weapons used, and targets attacked. Its geographic scope would likely be much greater. Israel might feel the need to strike targets in Syria, Lebanon, or even Egypt. Each of these constitutes a major upward jump in escalation. Iran, for its part, could expand the war to the Persian Gulf, Iraq, and Afghanistan, and with terrorist attacks almost anywhere.

From the U.S. perspective, a long war that intensifies and widens geographically is a grave danger, yet it barely surfaces in most discussions of attacking Iran. Some commentators speak as if the whole matter will be over in thirty days if Israel attacks Iran. But that is only one possible consequence of this branch point, and it may not be a particularly likely one. Consider Vietnam or Iraq. Both were thought to be short wars when they began. Both turned out to be very long.

There is something especially dangerous about long wars. At each step along the way, each party takes what seems to be sensible, short-term decisions given the information they have at the moment. But the accumulated impact of these individually sensible steps may be a protracted war with escalation spirals that take on a momentum of their own. This is because, when a country gets into a long war, it builds up a sunk cost, the number of lives already lost and the damage already sustained. To quit means to say that these were expended for nothing. These escalation dynamics can become more powerful than the political disputes that caused the war in the first place. This factor shaped the wars in Vietnam and Iraq, which dragged on for many years.

Even if Iran renounced its nuclear program after an Israeli attack, it would have to be policed for many years to come. Moreover, Iran would be in no mood to cooperate with IAEA inspectors because of the lives lost and damage sustained.

Another possibility is to occupy and politically transform Iran. Israel cannot possibly do this alone. Needless to say, the U.S. experience in Iraq and Afghanistan has reduced the American appetite for such an effort. An American invasion and occupation of Iran would require far greater resources and manpower than either Iraq or Afghanistan. Counterinsurgency and occupation are manpower intensive. The U.S. personnel demands for a campaign of this size would require serious consideration of a return to the draft.

Another type of escalation must be considered in thinking about an Israeli attack on Iran—compound escalation. Compound escalation involves starting a new conflict or crisis other than the original one. The Cuban missile crisis again provides an example. Had the Soviets responded to Kennedy by threatening Berlin it would have been an example of compound escalation. In the case of Israel attacking Iran, Iran could respond by attacking American bases in the Middle East, blocking shipping in the Persian Gulf, staging terrorist attacks in Europe, or starting a crisis in Iraq or Afghanistan. These would all be compound escalations because they bring in issues not directly related to Iran's nuclear program.

Compound escalations dramatically increase the stakes and often the intensity of conflict. This is because whole new issues are contested, for example, freedom of navigation in the Persian Gulf, energy security, and the American presence in the Middle East. If a U.S. Navy ship is sunk in the Persian Gulf, the United States may well be compelled by domestic opinion to respond with its own escalation against Iran.

A conflict that began on the limited issue of Iran's nuclear program would thereby be expanded to a war whose stakes had expanded to energy security, counterterrorism, and the U.S. presence in the region. This expansion would open up new dynamics and, in turn, would shape the behavior of the involved states. Israel could be expected to move on a number of issues that it is currently deterred from taking, such as expanding settlements in the West Bank, cleaning out southern Lebanon, and destroying the Syrian army. These are "unthinkable" today. But in a large war with Iran they would hardly be so.

Figure 5.1 summarizes the possible consequences of a war with Iran.

After weighing the alternatives, Israel may decide to go ahead with a strike. My own view, however, is that the discussion of this matter needs to be conducted at a higher level than is usually the case in both the United States and Israel. I find that many of the most important scenarios are not analyzed, or are dismissed as "unlikely." Most especially, this includes the prospect of a big, long war that gets out of control in the sense of compound escalations that bring in issues unrelated to Iran's acquisition of the bomb. In either case, attack or no attack, we are approaching a branch point in the Middle East. Two very different worlds will follow from the decisions that will be made. My own judgment is that careful consideration of the possible scenarios works against attacking Iran's facilities. This makes it important to think about the branch that follows when Iran gets the bomb.

FIGURE 5.1

POSSIBLE CONSEQUENCES OF A WAR WITH IRAN

- Requirement for periodic restrikes of Iran every few months or years for the indefinite future
- Israel invades and occupies southern Lebanon to clear out Hezbollah
- Arab attacks on Israeli settlements in the West Bank
- Full alert and preparations for launch of Syrian chemical rockets
- Israeli preemption of Syrian WMD sites
- Opportunistic, additional expansion of Israeli settlements in the West Bank
- Iran destabilizing governments in Bahrain, the United Arab Emirates, Jordan, and Saudi Arabia using terrorism and/or working with domestic political factions
- Homegrown suicide-bomber attacks inside Israel
- Iran foments disorder in Iraq and Afghanistan, undercutting any positive gains from ten years of U.S. efforts to build stable governments there
- Alert of Iran's chemical rockets
- Sharp increase in oil prices as Iran attacks shipping
- Increases in terrorism in Europe
- Increased use of targeted killings by all sides
- Greatly increased empowerment of political Islam centered on anti-Jewish and anti-American themes
- Pushing Egypt and other countries toward nationalism directed at Israel and the United States, and weakening the movement for democracy in Arab Spring countries

HOW A NUCLEAR CONTEXT CHANGES THE MIDDLE EAST

Assume that Israel doesn't attack Iran. Iran gets the bomb and, almost certainly, all kinds of sanctions are placed on it.

Nuclear weapons will change the context of the Middle East from a region with identifiable ceilings on the amount of violence to one with potentially limitless violence and indefinite, ambiguous lines separating the degrees of violence. Political and military moves will depend on estimates of where things might go if their intensity were to increase. In broad terms, risk management will replace cost-benefit calculations.

Even low-level conflicts that at present are not seen as especially dangerous will be viewed in a different context. This could lead to more caution in decision making. All actors may be wary of starting a big crisis that could take them to places that they don't want to go. Especially in the early period of a nuclear Middle East, there might be extra risk aversion.

On the other hand, there may be an immediate nuclear crisis. If sanctions press too hard on Iran, it will have to respond, for its own domestic political reasons.

There is also the likelihood that other countries will try to get their own deterrents. Saudi Arabia stands out here. The United States will try to stop this development, of course, but—given Saudi wealth and the international nuclear market—success can hardly be guaranteed.

Then there are all the old issues that plague the Middle East and have not gone away. Israeli settlements, Gaza, Hezbollah, and Lebanon will still exist as issues—but they will look different in a nuclear context.

The important point is that a nuclear Middle East does much more than increase the size of the bombs that can be used. Focusing only on the highest degrees of warfare, nuclear strikes and counter-strikes, misses the wider spectrum of conflict, much of which will probably occur at a far lower level of intensity on the escalation ladder, well short of nuclear attacks. It is this lower region of intensity and escalation that has received little attention.

But it is critical for a number of reasons. The path to nuclear war in the Middle East comes from mishandling these lower-level conflicts and crises, much more so than it does from the mullahs deciding one day to press the button. There will be a premium on crisis management skills. For this reason, the early years of a nuclear Middle East are likely to be especially dangerous, as each side feels out the other over limits and restraints. Red lines that have evolved over many decades in the Middle East may not be adequate, either because they do not deal with the new nuclear context or because they do not cover the many new destabilizing possibilities.

The first nuclear crisis could take on transcendent importance for the same reason the 1948 Berlin crisis did in the first nuclear age. Norms of what is and is not permissible without causing major escalation will be determined. The first crisis could set a pattern for a long time to come.

To see how much difference a nuclear context makes, the "prenuclear" situation in the region needs to be understood. Quotes are used to acknowledge the fiction that the region was not, in fact, prenuclear at all.

In the 1950s, when Prime Minister David Ben-Gurion analyzed the challenges facing Israel, he saw implacable Arab resistance to its existence. Israel wasn't going to change this attitude through diplomacy and goodwill. So the question was how Israel could survive in this hostile environment.

Ben-Gurion's strategic insight was that a war wouldn't achieve the goal of securing Israel's existence. An Israeli victory, no matter how decisive, wouldn't suddenly persuade Arabs to accept it. Ben-Gurion believed it would take *repeated* conflicts to get the Arabs to change. Call it operant conditioning. An individual modifies his behavior, but not necessarily his feelings. In Ben-Gurion's view, the

Arabs would experience repeated "unpleasantness," which would serve to modify their behavior—if not their hatred for Israel. Three conventional wars were fought after independence, in 1956, 1967, and 1973. Usually these wars are studied individually. But it's their sequential and accumulated impact that matters. The wars operantly conditioned Israel's Arab neighbors, even if they didn't change their attitudes toward Israel.

Following the 1973 war, there was a beginning, if grudging, de facto acceptance of Israel's existence by some Arab countries. They changed their behavior, if not their feelings. Egypt, Jordan, and Syria stand out. Each is a little different, but after 1973 none attacked Israel as it had before.

Israel carried out operant conditioning by inflicting lopsided damage on the Arabs. Ten-to-one, even one-hundred-to-one damage exchange ratios were common. These are numbers describing the destruction of the Egyptian air force in 1967, and they have also occurred in Gaza and Lebanon in recent years. The choice of how lopsided was entirely up to Israel because it had escalation dominance in the region. The types of weapons used, the rules of engagement, and the targets could be chosen to inflict light, medium, or heavy damage. Restraints did exist, but they were more moral and political than military and strategic.

Israel needed a qualitative technological edge in conventional weapons to follow this approach. Meat-grinder wars with large casualties wouldn't be sustainable. And Israel relied on U.S. support for this qualitative technological edge.

The Arab states understood this, even if some terrorist groups did not. They also understood the red lines that, if crossed, might trigger a lopsided attack on them. They were deterred from crossing these thresholds, and even from getting too close to them. Syria, for example, gave weapons and support to anti-Israeli groups. But not so much that it would draw Israeli air strikes on Damascus.

Israeli strategy evolved around these red lines. Israel could have crossed the Syrian border with air or ground forces many times. The Syrians, the Israelis, and the Americans all recognized that breaching the border would constitute a major escalation. In the 2006 Lebanon War, Israeli warplanes buzzed the summer home of Syrian president Bashar al-Assad. This communicated what might come next, a strike on Damascus, if Assad increased support for Hezbollah with more deadly weapons. It signaled the bargain: don't go too far or you'll regret it.

Israel's nuclear weapons were also a deterrent to threats from outside the region. In his 1991 book *The Samson Option*, Seymour Hersh says that Israel targeted cities in southern Russia with nuclear weapons. The Israeli fear was that the Soviet Union might act to destroy Israel's nuclear force, or that Moscow might provide some deadly new weapon to the Arabs. Israel's nuclear forces were also a hedge against an Arab military breakthrough, a last-ditch threat to force them to pull back or face the ultimate consequence.

Israel's strategic posture, the mix of paramilitary, intelligence, conventional, and nuclear forces, was designed for three distinct classes of danger. The paramilitary and intelligence forces mainly handled internal security and dangers from the occupied territories. They could call on the other military services for help. Conventional forces handled Arab attacks. The nuclear forces were to deter the Soviet Union and, later, chemical and biological attacks on Israel.

Israel's nuclear forces, it should be observed from this discussion, didn't have very much to do. They weren't hardened because the Arabs didn't have any weapons that could destroy them. They did need to be concealed from satellites. If a leaked Pentagon satellite picture showed up in the press, it could force the United States to distance itself from Israel. Or, as Henry Kissinger feared in 1969, it could lead Moscow to give a nuclear guarantee to Damascus or Cairo. But Israel's nuclear forces didn't have much to do other than to stay secret and offstage.

It wasn't like the United States during the cold war, when America had to go through all kinds of efforts to create nuclear forces that had the ability to defend allies and at the same time reassure them. America's forces, and Soviet forces, also had political and strategic significance. If one side appeared to have more nuclear weapons than the other, a perception of imbalance was thought to follow. This is one of the reasons behind the superpowers' enormous nuclear buildup.

Israeli strategists did not have to think about many political and military requirements for its nuclear forces. After the 1979 peace treaty with Egypt, the prospect of a conventional attack on Israel was eclipsed by other threats, so even the Arab breakthrough scenario became less important.

This Israeli approach worked reasonably well until the region's military geography changed. The "outer threats," Iraq and Iran, had been too far from Israel to worry much about. But, in the 1980s, Saddam Hussein had nuclear and WMD programs. He also had missiles that could reach Israel.

In the first Gulf War, in 1991, Saddam fired thirty-nine Scuds into Israel, all with conventional or inert warheads. They did little damage. But this isn't what mattered. A once remote enemy, Iraq, had struck Tel Aviv. Israeli leaders understood that Saddam's rockets might have contained sarin gas or anthrax spores. These missile attacks fell into a strategic gray zone lacking conventions. If Iraq had fired a chemical missile at Tel Aviv, that would have qualified as crossing the line, and Israel probably would have retaliated with either nuclear or chemical missiles. If Iraq had sent an army toward Israel, that would have triggered a conventional response.

But firing long-range conventional rockets fell into a gray zone that hadn't been considered by Israeli leaders. Existing norms didn't cover it. This is worth emphasizing. Even in 1991, the extant conventions of the day didn't cover all of the cases. What happened next is what happened in the cold war. Israel improvised on the spot.

Israeli leaders had good reason not to retaliate against Iraq in 1991. The Israelis wanted to avoid an escalation spiral, and to avoid splitting the U.S.-led alliance waging war on Saddam. They also feared that a retaliation against Iraq might lead to Saddam actually using chemical weapons against them.

The psychological effect of Saddam's missile attack against Israel far outweighed the insignificant damage it caused. Moshe Arens, Israel's defense minister during the 1991 Gulf War, described his feelings.

> The precautions Israel took—the preparation of sealed rooms, the distribution of gas masks—were very unpleasant. During the war little Israeli children were walking around with little brown boxes at their sides that contained the gas mask kit they were prepared to put on their faces the minute the alarm was sounded. Whenever an alarm was sounded—which happened almost every day during the war—people ran for shelters, ran for sealed rooms, and put on their gas masks.
>
> Those Scud missiles were a somewhat upgraded version of the German V2 rockets from World War II. The Germans fired these rockets against Britain toward the end of the war and caused very considerable damage. There was no way of intercepting them. We did not know how to shoot down a ballistic missile that comes at us at supersonic speeds.

The references to gas, and the rocket's genesis, the Nazi V-2, are noteworthy. Saddam's primitive missiles did little damage. But they marked the beginning of fundamental change in the Middle East.

The new risk map of a nuclear Middle East looks quite different from the pre-nuclear one.

Most significantly, the highest degrees of violence can come from countries in the region, not like in the old days when only the Soviet Union posed such a threat. This is indicated by nuclear and chemical devastation attacks in Figure 5.2.

The dividing thresholds that regulated conflict in the Middle East fade into a gray zone of ambiguity because they are only beginning to take shape.

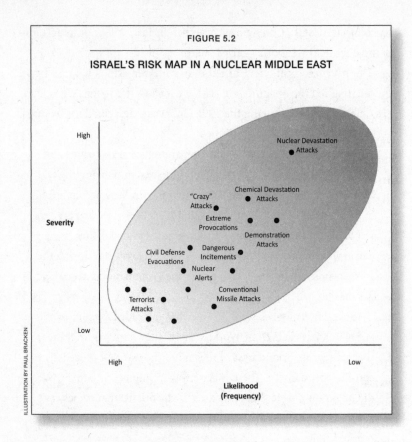

FIGURE 5.2

ISRAEL'S RISK MAP IN A NUCLEAR MIDDLE EAST

STRATEGIES FOR A NUCLEAR IRAN

It is surprising how little thought has been given to what Iran might do with nuclear weapons. Some people argue that the mullahs will hit the button immediately to wipe out Israel. The other prominent argument is that Iran will be deterred from doing anything with the bomb. These two possibilities are somehow thought to be the only possibilities for a nuclear Iran.

But there are many more possible cases than these two. In my view, both are unlikely, yet the debate about a nuclear Iran cycles back and forth between these two particular alternatives.

A failure to seriously think through strategies for a nuclear Iran is an example of a wider failing in the way people think about the second nuclear age: not considering how small nuclear forces could be used. In part, this failing comes about because there is a general attitude that giving any credibility to the idea that nuclear weapons have uses is wrongheaded. Another reason for not thinking about small nuclear forces is the American strategic experience. Nuclear arsenals in the cold war were so vast that there was never much need to think about small forces, those of fewer than one hundred weapons.

There are several strategies for Iran that need to be considered in any assessment of a nuclear Middle East because Iran's choices will have a great deal to do with war and peace in the region. It's also important to devise a list of possible Iranian strategies because we need to think about the alternatives to the simpleminded cases of "immediately hit every button" and "deterrence will always prevail."

It is useful to exclude some strategies at the outset because they are unlikely or infeasible. Iran cannot possibly develop a nuclear war–fighting strategy similar to those of the United States and the Soviet Union in the cold war. The Iranians lack the wealth, experience, and technology to do so. Iran cannot build space-based early warning satellites, rapid retargeting computers to reassign weapons, or reconnaissance satellites to locate Israeli nuclear forces during a war. It just isn't possible.

The inability to deploy a high-tech nuclear force may focus the attention of Iran's leaders and their staffs to areas of innovation that are more suitable to Iran's situation. Asymmetric strategies against superior American forces show up repeatedly in Iranian thinking— naval swarming tactics to harass U.S. Navy ships in the Persian Gulf, giving advanced weapons to Hezbollah, and terrorism. Asymmetric nuclear strategy innovation would be a logical next step.

A list of strategies for a nuclear Iran is shown in Figure 5.3. The list is in no particular order, but every item on it is feasible for Iran within the next decade. Nothing on the list requires sophisticated technology. This is a key point because there is often an unwarranted assumption that because a country does not have access to the latest technology it must necessarily also have a primitive strategy.

FIGURE 5.3

STRATEGIES FOR A NUCLEAR IRAN

- A minimum deterrent
- A defensive deterrent
- An offensive deterrent
- A strategy of extreme provocations
- Keep the nuclear pot boiling
- Nuclear weapons as political currency

A Minimum Deterrent

A small, survivable force of ten to twenty atomic bombs built to deter Israel and the United States from attacking Iran would constitute what is called a minimum deterrent. A minimum deterrent is just that. It is the smallest force that deters an opponent from attacking you. Adding more weapons is considered wasteful because the military and political payoff is zero once this minimum threshold of weapons is reached.

The number of weapons needed to deter Israel from attacking comes from Israel's compact urban geography. Most of its population lives on the coastal plain. Iran doesn't need more than a few weapons to destroy it.

But Iran has other enemies who must be deterred, not just Israel. An ability to destroy three or four U.S. bases in the region and to strike at Saudi Arabia are also needed for Iran under the minimum deterrent strategy. Counting on some losses and launch failures, the number comes to about twenty nuclear weapons.

I can't say whether Iran will embrace a minimum deterrent or not. What I can say is that minimum deterrence is the overwhelming favorite of the United States, meaning, given that Iran goes nuclear, this strategy is the one widely believed in America to be what Iran will choose. It is the least bad alternative, from the American perspective. This is for two reasons. First, a minimum deterrent shows Iranian restraint. Iran would recognize that there isn't much to be achieved from building more atomic weapons, and this alone would signal that these weapons don't gain the Iranian government very much. The other reason this strategy is imputed to Iran in U.S. strategic circles is that it's the easiest one to think about. Other alternatives don't have to be considered, nor do various uses of nuclear weapons that would raise more troubling problems.

Every conference that I attend in the United States about a nuclear Iran has someone arguing that "Iran will only have a minimum deterrent," but significantly I find no such view when I go to conferences in Israel. The United States and Israel, already disagreeing about when Iran will get an atomic bomb, are going to disagree even more about strategy when Iran does get it.

Another feature of a minimum deterrent is that its performance is high—until a crisis or shock hits. Most of the time it works just fine, in the sense that it deters Israel and the United States from attacking. For every day they don't attack, people can point to Iran's deterrent and say, "See, it's working." But the performance of a minimum deterrent needs to be assessed in conditions of crisis, war, and provocation. In other words, it needs to be tested under stress conditions.

Iran is likely to see this point. Every country that has ever gotten the bomb has. It isn't a particularly subtle point. A nuclear strategy needs to be considered both in peacetime and during stressful conditions. A strategy that looks very good in peacetime may look very poor in a crisis.

A Defensive Deterrent

Stress testing a small nuclear force is likely to lead to a larger force even if the strategic purpose of the force was originally to serve as a minimum deterrent. This is because small nuclear arsenals lend themselves to paranoid assessments of their vulnerability. Even if a small force is considered desirable, its small size means that an enemy might easily destroy it. Both Israel and the United States have the ability to do so, using conventional weapons, if they know where Iran's nuclear weapons are located. But even if they do not know where Iran's weapons are kept, Iran's leaders are likely to lean to suspicions that they do.

A defensive deterrent is the result. It is a minimum deterrent with an insurance policy of a larger force, thirty to forty atomic weapons. A defensive deterrent has the added advantage that it further discourages the United States and Israel from pushing Iran around too much.

The United States and Israel would do nearly anything to replace the government in Iran to prevent it from getting the bomb. Sanctions, cyberattacks, targeted killings, sabotage. But, once Iran has atomic weapons, the American calculus changes. Call it the theory of the obsolescent policy. An Iran without the bomb will be sanctioned, its scientists killed, and its officials arrested if they travel outside the country. Money will be channeled to dissident groups, opportunistic army officers, and civil society groups.

But if Iran gets the bomb, this policy looks a lot different. It is obsolete. The fear then is that an unstable Iran will have nuclear arms falling into the hands of the radicals, such as junior officers in the revolutionary guards. Or the fear will be that a disintegrating Iran will give the bomb to Hezbollah or some other group. This is where a bigger nuclear force has an impact. The defensive deterrent, larger than the minimum deterrent, means that government disintegration could produce a much bigger disaster from the perspective of the

United States. The larger force thus increases deterrence of provocative interventions against Iran because, even if they succeed in over-
throwing the government, they could have the effect of losing
control of nuclear arms to the crazies. This may make it especially
appealing to Iran because it has had a paranoid streak about the
United States, going back much further than the 1979 revolution to
the overthrow of Prime Minister Mohammad Mossadegh in 1953. A
pure minimum deterrent may not be sufficient, given Iran's experience with the United States. The deterrent may have to be considerably larger for Iran to have any confidence in it.

An Offensive Deterrent

In the first nuclear age, the belief was that nuclear weapons were horrible but that they still had defensive uses. The concept that the bomb
could be used for offensive purposes didn't get much attention. Both
superpowers saw the bomb as a defensive weapon, as a way to deter
the other side.

But deterrents can be offensive as well as defensive. One needs to
go back to the 1930s to find an example of this. Adolf Hitler used
German military power this way. In the 1930s, Hitler didn't threaten
to wipe out Britain and France with his military. Rather, he marched
into the demilitarized Rhineland, made political demands, and
destabilized Austria and Czechoslovakia with terrorism and Nazi
thugs. He postured his military so that if Britain or France acted to
stop him in any of these places they would receive a massive counter-
blow. It was a deterrent used for offensive purposes. In modern terminology, Hitler had a second-strike strategy: it deterred an allied
response to his provocations. He dared them to strike the first blow
on Germany while he moved into one country after another.

An offensive deterrent is what Israel's strategists think Iran will
establish. When Israelis say that strategists in the United States don't
understand the Middle East, this is what they mean.

An offensive deterrent strategy is what Iran used in the game changer war game in chapter 1. Insights can be gleaned from games and scenarios to describe what an offensive strategy for a nuclear Iran could look like. Figure 5.4 shows some of the possibilities.

FIGURE 5.4

OFFENSIVE WAYS FOR IRAN TO USE NUCLEAR WEAPONS

- Go on nuclear alert by dispersing mobile missiles, conducting nuclear tests, announcing airborne alerts
- Provide subnational groups with advanced conventional weapons, "smart IEDs" (Improvised Explosive Devices), cluster bombs, missiles, anti-ship missiles
- Support spectacular but deniable acts of terrorism
- Nuclear spoofing, with war games, practice launches, civil defense exercises
- Declare a launch on warning policy
- Provide nuclear technologies to other countries, such as Egypt or Syria

---

None of the items on the list in Figure 5.4 requires Iran to actually fire a nuclear weapon. Indeed, it could be said that nuclear deterrence was holding strong because Iran wasn't firing atomic weapons at anyone.

I have little doubt that the planners in Iran will come up with an even more creative list. If we ask why Iran hasn't done these things already, the answer is clear. They would provoke American attack. But this is exactly where a nuclear context changes strategy. Strikes to punish a nuclear Iran are going to look a lot different than strikes against a nonnuclear Iran.

A Strategy of Extreme Provocations

Iran may follow a strategy of extreme provocations once it has a stock of atomic bombs. This approach takes the offensive deterrent strategy and intensifies it to create nuclear crises. Sometimes this is called strategy by crisis. The goal is to increase the sense of danger in Israel and the United States by focusing their attention on where things might go if a crisis or disagreement escalates.

Needless to say, this strategy is exceedingly dangerous. Staging a Cuban missile crisis for the purpose of getting a political edge is not something that can go on repeatedly. At some point countries will react. In 1939, even Britain and France acted to declare war on Germany. But if Iran needs to distract attention from domestic problems, there may be no better way than to stage a nuclear crisis with Israel.

Keep the Nuclear Pot Boiling

One way to avoid the dangers of extreme provocations is to dial back their intensity. I call this "keeping the nuclear pot boiling." This is what the Soviets did in the early part of the cold war. They pressed in one area after another, in Berlin, Cuba, and Laos, while using a fiery nuclear rhetoric.

Suppose Iran announces that because of Israel's threatening behavior it is moving to a launch on warning policy. Special radars are purchased from Russia for this purpose. Israel launches an intelligence satellite in a routine move and Iran fires a missile with a dummy warhead from one of its hardened silos a few minutes afterward, using a signal from spies inside Israel who witness the launch. The story is leaked to the media by Iran's intelligence service. This would cause an international uproar, of course. But it could easily be justified by Iran on the basis that it was a matter of deterrence. The test launch by Iran would remind Israel that it was under the nuclear gun.

The idea behind keeping the nuclear pot boiling would be to maintain tension with Israel, but to keep these tensions under control. There is a continuum of intensity, which will define a new spectrum of Middle East drama. "Keeping the nuclear pot boiling" is a conscious choice for Iran to increase nuclear tensions in the Middle East at low levels of intensity, rather than the medium-high intensity of an extreme provocation strategy. If strategic or political conditions change, Iran could always pursue more intense and dangerous strategies, such as one of extreme provocations. This capacity would itself be an element in undermining Israel's escalation dominance.

Nuclear Weapons as Political Currency

Nuclear weapons as political currency describes the situation where Iran doesn't have a nuclear strategy in the military sense, but rather views its bomb entirely in political terms. Little or no thought would be given to the targets it would fire at, its crisis management tactics, and its strategic purposes. The bomb would be used entirely as a political device, domestically and internationally.

It may strike some readers as implausible that a country would develop nuclear weapons and give little thought as to how they would use them. But it is not surprising at all. In the late 1940s the United States did this. There were official targeting plans, but they had nothing to do with political reality, as the 1948 Berlin crisis showed. The bomb was seen almost entirely in political terms.

Iran could use the bomb to expose Israel's nuclear weapons by offering to sign the NPT as a nuclear weapons state. The offer would not be serious—the United States would never accept it—but it would draw attention to Israel's nuclear forces. Iran could also use the bomb to offer itself as the natural leader of the Islamic world. This, I suspect, wouldn't work either, but that isn't the point. It would draw attention to Iran, and that's all that matters. This strategy could lead to Iran neglecting some important details of its ownership of nuclear weapons, and in this respect could open it to vulnerabilities and sloppy performance if an actual crisis did arise.

ISRAEL'S NUCLEAR STRATEGY

Israel will have to respond to a nuclear Middle East. For the first time Israel will face a nuclear opponent in the region. What difference does this make?

Israel's nuclear deterrent was built for a world where nuclear arms were kept in the background. They were not asked to carry a heavy strategic burden like U.S. nuclear forces were in the cold war, at least, if you believe as I do that the chance of a Soviet attack on Israel was always a remote possibility. Now Israel will need to think through its deterrent, what it is used for and what form it should take.

In a nuclear Middle East there will be an enlarged role for Israeli nuclear forces. One list of requirements is shown in Figure 5.5. It is approximately ordered by the importance of the objective. I say approximate because it is difficult to make sharp distinctions in priority between certain cases.

This chart sets forth one priority list for Israel's nuclear forces. Other analysts may reorder the list, moving some items higher or lower. Or they may add or subtract items. Regardless of objections to this particular list, it is essential that leaders think through the issues it raises. There are many new requirements for Israel's nuclear forces, and depending on which ones are chosen to emphasize, there will be a considerable impact on Iran, the United States, and other countries.

Many of the items on this list are new, in that Israel's nuclear forces didn't require that they be considered all that seriously. Other items on the list were only theoretical possibilities. In a nuclear Middle East, they no longer are.

Israel's nuclear posture has to handle the big things, those at the top of the list. If it can't do that, the other uses of nuclear weapons won't matter much. Moreover, there are limits to what nuclear weapons

---

FIGURE 5.5

REQUIREMENTS FOR ISRAEL'S NUCLEAR WEAPONS

- Deter a devastation nuclear attack
- Deter a devastation chemical attack
- Deter a limited nuclear attack (for example, aimed only at Haifa or Dimona)
- Draw the United States into a crisis
- Deter a "hysterical" Iranian nuclear response after an Israeli-controlled conventional strike on Iran (for example, on its nuclear complex or Republican Guard forces)
- Deter extreme nuclear provocations by Iran
- Fire nuclear warning or demonstration shots to "introduce" nuclear weapons into the Middle East
- Deter nuclear proliferation in the region
- Convey an image of Israeli invincibility
- Deter conventional missile attacks
- Deter militia and terrorist attacks on Israel

---

can do, and it is important to identify these. The last item is included to make this point, that Israel's nuclear weapons probably will have little role in deterring terrorist attacks.

Clearly, Israel cannot have soft nuclear forces that are easy to take out via an Iranian missile attack. If Israel continues to rely on aircraft and missiles, it will be vulnerable to Iranian nuclear attack. Some new strategic mixture of sea-based and ground-based forces is needed. What cannot be emphasized strongly enough is that this new posture will have several functions; it will not be solely to deter an Iranian devastation attack. It will have to be evaluated in terms of its performance in escalation control and at lower levels of war and crisis.

Israel's deterrent is likely to be considerably more complex, more dispersed, and more noticeable than its current one. The command-

and-control system will be especially vulnerable, as the links connecting political leadership to the forces are the weakest part of the system.

There are many possible responses here. The Israelis could deploy more mobile missiles in the Negev Desert. Or they could move part of the deterrent to sea, aboard ships and/or submarines. A maritime force could be made up of sea-launched ballistic missiles, cruise missiles, or, cheaper still, nuclear missiles on barges protected by the Israeli navy.

Israel is already shifting some of its nuclear force to sea in the form of cruise missiles, and perhaps other kinds of missiles, aboard submarines. The submarines are diesel powered and built in Germany with the full consent of the German government. This shift will give Israel's nuclear force a far larger geographic footprint that will be a lot more noticeable, politically speaking, than the nuclear force it has had in the past. It's worth highlighting some features of a submarine-based nuclear force. The United States went this route in the cold war. But it can be very expensive for a small country like Israel.

Here we see a problem for a small, secondary power like Israel. It is very risky to have fewer than three submarines for carrying nuclear missiles. With two, an accident might halve the survivable deterrent. Submarines do have accidents, even those carrying nuclear warheads. Three subs at sea would seem to be the absolute minimum prudent number.

But to have three submarines on patrol, about seven to nine are needed. This is because submarines are always breaking down, need preventive maintenance, and require crew changes. It's a pretty expensive proposition. Moreover, German submarines are designed for short patrols with the submarines out of port for a minimum duration. They are not like American-made subs, which are built for long-haul deployments under stressful conditions. The possibility exists of significant mechanical and other kinds of technical problems, aggravated by the fact that Israel doesn't really have its own submarine industry. It will be reliant on outsiders for maintenance and repair, and this dependence raises the political profile and the political risk for Israel.

There are ways to reduce the number of subs, but they come with greater risk. For example, some subs could be kept in port, to be flushed to sea if tensions rose. But the problem is that the missile flight times in the region are only about ten minutes. A sub couldn't get out of port fast enough.

Ideally, Israel would also like to keep a nuclear-weapons submarine in the Arabian Sea, to retaliate against Iran from nearly all azimuths. The problem is the Suez Canal. When Hosni Mubarak ran Egypt, he let an Israeli submarine use the canal, one that was widely rumored to carry nuclear weapons aboard. This permission was apparently a signal to Iran of where Egypt stood. It's hard to see how Israel can count on Egypt allowing such transit in the future. The region's political changes factor into the deterrent equation.

Another challenge is that it would be almost impossible to keep Israel's new deterrent out of sight; Google Earth pictures of Israeli submarine bases would be on every news site in the world. And this new visibility can be used to criticize Israel. It can also be used to show the graphic differences in U.S. nonproliferation policy, with the United States and Germany winking at Israel's expanding nuclear force while cracking down on others.

Israel's nuclear profile is likely to increase on the production and R&D side, as well as on the deployment side. You can't just take an old nuclear warhead built for a jet and stick it into a cruise missile and put it to sea. It doesn't work that way. The environmental conditions (salt air, rolling seas) are different from keeping a warhead in a cool bunker somewhere. There will have to be a lot of testing and technical innovation in Israel's labs to make the transition to a more survivable force.

Israel has other political objectives beyond deterring Iran from a devastation attack, and, like it or not, nuclear weapons make a difference. One is to draw the United States into any nuclear crisis. For all the talk about the solid character of U.S.-Israeli ties, the history of the relationship is fraught with distrust. The United States has long worried that Israel will take some surprise action. Israel has long worried that the United States will be slow to react in a crisis, for the purpose of pressuring them into some kind of accommodation. Trust issues, which have always been difficult, will be even more so in a nuclear context.

Israel has long said that it will not be the first to introduce nuclear weapons into the Middle East. But what exactly does this mean? One way to introduce nuclear weapons is simply to announce that you have them.

But saying this may not be enough. Especially now that everyone knows Israel has the bomb. It doesn't have the political shock effect it once did. One Israeli response is to "introduce" the bomb by exploding one of them 100,000 feet over Tehran. Everyone would see it. Windows would shatter. But the damage would be low.

Or Israel could attack some conspicuous military target in Iran with nuclear weapons. An Iranian Revolutionary Guard base is destroyed by a nuclear weapon. The message follows: "Call off what you're doing or it's going to get worse." My view is that this is how Israel's nuclear war plans are structured. They almost have to be. There has to be a range of options available to dramatically "introduce" nuclear weapons. The words are chosen carefully, for drama may be a big part of this. Dramatic effect, on Iran and on the United States, is needed to communicate just how serious things are. What Israel shoots at here is less important than the objective—to shock Iran and get the Americans involved.

This is pretty unpleasant stuff to think about. Unthinkable, you might say. It could lead to an apocalypse worthy of the Book of Revelation, which, after all, was written for this part of the world.

STRATEGIC INTERACTIONS IN A NUCLEAR MIDDLE EAST

This discussion has two important conclusions. First, strategic interactions are building up in the nuclear Middle East. It's not only the particular strategies of Iran or Israel or the United States that matter. Powerful interactions are creating a regional nuclear system. One side's strategies and weapons interact with those of the other side. These interactions are intensifying, and show up not only in weapons but also in enlarged surveillance technologies (spies, satellites, radars, reconnaissance airplanes), conventional forces, and chemical weapons. The coupling among these systems is increasing. In July 2012 Syria moved some if its chemical weapons to prevent them from falling into the hands of insurgents as disorder spread throughout the country. But the increased reconnaissance ability of Israel and the United States was also a factor behind the move. Syria faced a decision: move these weapons or lose them in a preemptive attack, at which point the regime would lose its most important deterrent. The Syrian WMD dispersal underscored the strategic interactions developing in the region.

The tightening of interactions between Israel and Iran is also increasing. Israel gets a new satellite system. Iran deploys a mix of missile types giving it greater flexibility. But the larger dynamic, that a regional nuclear system is building up in the Middle East, is even more important.

A second conclusion is that these interactions are becoming too large to confine to the region. Europe and South Asia are becoming tightly linked to the regional nuclear system in the Middle East. This is because Iran can reach Europe or India with its missiles. The United States has already responded to this threat with a missile defense system to protect Europe. And Israel is working with India on satellite intelligence for early warning of Iranian dispersal of its mobile rockets. In addition, Israel launches satellites from an Indian space center forty miles north of Chennai, on India's eastern coast.

Consider Iran's emerging strategic posture, as shown in Figure 5.6, as an example of increasing strategic interactions in the region.

FIGURE 5.6

IRAN'S EMERGING STRATEGIC POSTURE

- Mobile missiles
- Fixed missiles in silos
- A hardened nuclear production complex
- A dispersed nuclear production complex
- Asymmetric conventional tactics (maritime swarming)
- Support for terrorism
- Financial and technical support for Hezbollah and others
- Split command and control

In building this posture, Iran saw what happened to Iraq under Saddam Hussein. Saddam started a nuclear-weapons program that was destroyed by Israel in 1981. Iran's hardened and dispersed nuclear production complex was built so that it wouldn't undergo the same fate. Iraq's reactor was a single-point target, a geographically compact nuclear complex, built aboveground. It was easily destroyed by Israel. If Iran had any doubts about building vulnerable nuclear plants, Israel's 2007 attack on the Syrian plutonium reactor surely erased them.

But Iran's nuclear complex has another strategic purpose that goes beyond making it hard to destroy. It is now so large, in so many locations, that destroying it would require massive and repeated air strikes, thereby increasing the scale and the self-deterrence of an attack. Collateral damage and airplane losses would be high. The size and spread of Iran's nuclear facilities contributes to deterrence by removing the option of a surgical strike. Israel launched 14 airplanes in the attack on Iraq's reactor in 1981, but launching 114 airplanes over a greater distance to hit dispersed targets in Iran drives up the chance of catastrophic failure. If the mission is detected before it reaches its target, it will have to be aborted. This will be impossible to keep secret and will be a spectacular fiasco. If surprise is maintained and a strike proceeds, Israeli pilots may be captured. Or Israel may drop bombs on the wrong targets, such as a hospital or school. The operation required is so large that the chances of something going wrong increase geometrically.

Iran bought missiles and established a missile industry in the country. Missiles have been installed in fixed silos and on mobile launchers, to give maximum flexibility. Mobile missiles are harder for an enemy to target, but they take many hours to move and set up, and they cannot be fired while on the move. Fixed-silo-based missiles are more vulnerable, but they can be instantly launched. Presumably, this is to have a retaliatory capability, 24/7, when mobile missiles were moving but not yet set up.

I do not know if Iran has a launch on warning capability for these silo-based missiles. But it's hard to believe that this tactic won't occur to Iranian planners. Any history of the cold war will show that it was considered. Launch on warning is a policy that can be easily announced and improvised in short order. There isn't any special technology needed for it, only some radars, missiles, and a telephone or radio link between them. The more imperfect the radars, the more unpredictable it makes Iran. And an unpredictable Iran will produce the North Korea effect—U.S. forces don't stage provocative military exercises against Pyongyang because the regime is just too erratic. This may be a goal of Iran—to develop a reputation of unpredictability.

Concerning launch on warning, it should be noted that there is an existing convention that makes it attractive for Iran. When Israel launches satellites from Israeli territory it fires them west, that is, over the Mediterranean. This places an added energy burden on the missiles because the earth's rotation goes the other way, from west to east. The reason Israel fires missiles only west from its territory is to avoid provoking its neighbors in the Middle East so they do not interpret a space launch as an actual missile attack on them.

This convention means that not many missiles ever fly out of Israel going east. So if a flight of missiles from Israel did show up on Iranian radars, they might well interpret it as an attack. A launch on warning declaration by Iran could deter this; at least it would give serious pause to Israel. In the first nuclear age, most of the talk about launch on warning was just that—talk. No one was crazy enough to put launch on warning into effect, although they could have done so. It was a nuclear head game. Unpredictability was the intended goal— "Can we really be sure the Soviets won't go into a launch on warning mode?" This might apply to Iran as well.

The Iranians want to keep their enemies off guard, uncertain as to what they'll do next. There is already a great deal of this in Iran's playbook. Swarming scores of small, fast attack boats around U.S. Navy ships and split command and control between the Revolutionary Guards and the regular Iranian army make Iran unpredictable. Suppose an Iranian Revolutionary Guard speedboat scores a lucky hit on a U.S. ship in the Persian Gulf. Iran's command-and-control system makes it hard to figure out who, exactly, was in charge—that is, who ordered the attack. Was it intentional? Or was it a local commander acting on his own?

Israel's response to Iran's missiles shows how the strategic dynamics are tightening. Israel has spy satellite programs that were greatly expanded in 1988. An obvious question is why Israel wouldn't just rely on the much more capable U.S. spy satellites and work with U.S. intelligence.

The answer is pretty obvious. The United States could turn off the intelligence flow at any time to pressure Israel to change policy, or to degrade Israel's targeting accuracy. In 2011, Israel announced that its new spy satellites will have near real-time communications ability back to Israel. Existing Israeli satellites fly over Iran and take pictures and listen in to what's going on, but they have to wait until they pass over Israel to download the information. Their orbits pass over home ground stations every ninety minutes. The new satellites instead will transmit the information to a communications satellite for immediate download to Israel.

Why, exactly, does Israel need an independent satellite intelligence program? One reason is to determine if Iran is dispersing its mobile missiles—and not having to wait ninety minutes to get the answer. Once these missiles are out the door, they're much harder to locate. Israel needs to know when this is happening, not to wait to hear about it from the United States or from CNN. Israel has several requirements for timely warning. Civil defense plans call for evacuations and in-place sheltering. This demands timely information on the dispersal status of Iran's missiles, to get the message out to the public. The current Israeli civil defense system uses public announcements over TV and radio and also uses mass e-mails and automated messages sent to cell phones and mobile devices. Israel, moreover, also needs to protect its high command, the handful of officials authorized to launch nuclear missiles and airplanes. The high command needs to be evacuated to secret wartime locations. Otherwise Israel would face a decapitation strike.

CONCLUSIONS

The Middle East is about to go through a major branch point that will shape its future for decades to come. While no one can accurately predict which branch will be taken, whether Israel will attack Iran or not, the Middle East is moving into a nuclear context.

A nuclear system of interacting actors and systems is well under way in the Middle East. It is common to focus on individual countries when discussing strategy, but the larger issue is the formation of this dynamic system of mutually coupled actors. Each acts to achieve its own objectives, but in so doing creates a larger structure. Whether anyone understands this structure under conditions of stress, as opposed to its peacetime performance, is seriously open to doubt.

Strategy in this nuclear context extends to using atomic weapons in ways that are not confined to the highest levels of violence. The problem isn't Israel and Iran hurling atomic bombs at each other—at least not only that—nor is it whether deterrence will work in a nuclear Middle East. These are only two of a much richer set of strategic dynamics in the region.

The reason these dynamics matter, and why they must be considered in a more sober way than they have been, is that they can lead to extraordinarily dangerous interactions, arms races, and loss of control. The nuclear interactions can spawn far more severe dangers than the old dynamics of the region and could swamp the politics that have previously shaped conflict there. A nuclear context will change the calculations of all parties about even small conflicts that in the past have been accepted or ignored. It will create a new array of strategic opportunities for countries, militias, and groups.

The politics of the Middle East have long since spilled over to the rest of the world, as 9/11 and many other examples show. Now the military dynamics are spilling outside of the region. Whether it is North Korea supplying a nuclear reactor to Syria, Israel working with India to launch spy satellites, or Iran fielding rockets that can reach Europe, the military dynamics alone are getting difficult to confine to the region. They are reaching a level of geographic scale and intensity that may well swamp the confident predictions that the Middle East has always been troubled and that not much has changed. Such a viewpoint seriously underestimates the dangers of a nuclear Middle East.

· 6 ·

SOUTH ASIA

In the five years from 2006 to 2011, Pakistan doubled the number of its atomic bombs, making it the fastest-growing nuclear power in the world. In addition, plutonium reactors are now under construction to produce the fissile material for scores of new nuclear weapons, most likely tactical nuclear weapons Pakistan will deploy on ships and battlefield weapons. Over this same period, India has deployed a nuclear triad of bombers, missiles, and a submarine capable of firing nuclear weapons.

Looking at the arms race in South Asia is like looking at an impressionist painting. If you look at it from ten inches away you see the details but not the large structure of the whole thing. Step back ten feet and it looks different. The pattern stands out, the relationship of one part of the canvas to another becomes clear. Focusing on immediate issues in South Asia that dominate the news cycle—a diplomatic initiative, a bombing in Pakistan, a new Indian jet—is like this. It misses the slower rhythms and the interplay of the different parts of the South Asian nuclear system.

Only by looking at South Asia in ten-year increments does the larger picture become clear. South Asian dynamics have taken on a powerful nuclear context that is reshaping each side's strategy. This is enlarged with naval forces and long-range rockets. And it is so complex that, in order to understand it, one must divide the dynamics into a number of interconnected subsystems. These include political decision making, intelligence, command and control, advanced conventional weapons, information warfare, and strategic innovation—meaning innovation adapted for a nuclear environment. There isn't just one factor that's driving the arms race in South Asia, but rather several factors. Integrating these factors is difficult, and our tools are imperfect. But it is absolutely necessary to do so. Scenarios are one valuable way to integrate these subsystems into a larger strategic canvas. Failing to consider these subsystems and their impact on nuclear stability is akin to looking at the painting from ten inches away—it misses the most important aspects of the work, and hence the most dangerous elements in it.

THE ARMS RACE IN SOUTH ASIA

A nuclear arms race broke out in South Asia in 1998, when Pakistan and India tested atomic weapons—ending a long self-imposed moratorium. Like the arms race between the United States and the Soviet Union, this one has important economic features. India is barely racing at all, hardly breaking a sweat. India's GDP grew on average 7 percent annually, despite a world recession, between 2005 and 2011. This newfound wealth gave India the ability to pursue a broad military modernization without hurting the economy. Pakistan's economic position is much more desperate, and it has increasingly relied on nuclear weapons as it falls further behind India. It has built a much larger nuclear force than anyone anticipated, now estimated at 110 to 120 bombs.

South Asia is going through what can be called the first bounce of the nuclear ball, an arms buildup. This is a time when both sides are getting the bomb. The focus is on acquiring fissile material and producing weapons. This drives Pakistan's plutonium mills and India's nuclear deal with the United States.

The second bounce of the ball may not be like the first. It may see intense crises and shocks—aggravated by the enlarged nuclear forces. So it would be a mistake to take the current environment as the environment of the future. Like the first nuclear age, the second will be dynamic. Different ten-year periods are likely to see different problems and different shocks.

India has not responded to Pakistan's buildup with more nuclear weapons—at least not yet—but this may be coming. New Delhi has mainly responded with strategy innovation, improved intelligence, missiles, and a triad of nuclear forces.

An important example of India's strategy innovation involves new ways of using conventional forces in a nuclear environment. Called "Cold Start," it calls for the prompt mobilization of fast-moving battle groups made up of armor, helicopters, and mechanized forces to thrust deep into Pakistan as punishment for a Pakistani attack or a terrorist outrage.

Cold Start's subnuclear option recognizes the nuclear threshold as central to which way any conflict will go. The concept is to fight below the nuclear threshold, if possible. But Cold Start has a nuclear element, too. Should Pakistan fire nuclear weapons at this Indian force, India can escalate with nuclear strikes of its own. India's gamble is that Pakistan will not escalate to nuclear use in response to such a conventional attack.

Cold Start has a number of fascinating features. It shows how both countries have shifted from conventional war fighting to escalation strategies. I do not believe that this was a matter of conscious choice by either country. Rather, it is an emergent property of the nuclear system in South Asia. India and Pakistan have little choice but to play the game this way, short of a sweeping arms control or disarmament initiative.

Escalation as a strategy has come into being not because anyone wanted it to but from the mutual interaction of both sides having nuclear weapons. While escalation strategies have always existed in South Asia, they are now front and center. This is a fundamental change from the conventional attrition strategies of previous wars.

Cold Start also shows that the dynamics in the region go beyond nuclear weapons in the narrow sense. There is no rigid arms race in the sense that each side matches the other in atomic bombs. If it were like this, it would actually be easier to control. But the arms race is more complicated because it involves parallel changes in key subsystems, and these have their own momentum.

If the arms race in South Asia were limited to nuclear weapons, which is the way many observers look at it, it would be one thing. But the competition is broadening, with India tightening linkages among intelligence, command and control, cyberwar, and strategy innovations like Cold Start. For example, for India the "front end" of Cold Start is better intelligence to determine exactly what Pakistan has done and the state of its conventional and nuclear forces. India has invested heavily in satellites, radars, signals intelligence, and reconnaissance to give its commanders an accurate picture of what Pakistan is up to.

This intelligence system, in turn, is linked to a rapid mobilization of Indian army and air forces in the Cold Start battle groups. Any delay in mobilization would undermine the entire strategy of counterescalation against Pakistan. The tightening linkage of intelligence to mobilization means that large Indian battle groups will be surging toward the India-Pakistan border, probably crossing it, as Pakistan's nuclear weapons are readied for use. It isn't a reassuring picture.

Cold Start is controversial for this reason. The United States, in particular, has tried to discourage India away from it because it looks like a fast way to produce a nuclear war in South Asia. I wouldn't be surprised if India changed the name Cold Start, because it connotes going to war quickly, from a cold start. But though the name may change, the strategic concept probably won't, because India has to come to grips with the nuclear realities of South Asia in some way and because its army and air force want to play a role in the defense of India—even in a nuclear context.

Pakistan's buildup has had a more nuclear emphasis than India's, yet even here there are critical subsystems that are tightly integrated. One subsystem is Pakistan's nuclear-weapons factories. Several plutonium reactors are under construction at Khushab, near Rawalpindi, to produce the fissile material for an enlarged nuclear force, far beyond what Pakistan already has. The plutonium program has rapidly accelerated in the past few years, undoubtedly helped by U.S. aid diverted from Afghanistan and intended for antiterrorism and anti-Taliban efforts in Afghanistan and Iraq.

Historically, Pakistan has relied on uranium for its bombs, so the addition of plutonium is significant. Why the change? One reason is that it takes less plutonium to make a bomb. There is more bang for the buck. Another reason is that plutonium is easier to mold into the irregular forms needed for tactical nuclear warheads for short-range army missiles, cruise missiles, and anti-ship missiles.

Pakistan is building not just more nuclear weapons but a variety of weapons for land, sea, and air—battlefield missiles, nuclear cruise missiles aboard ships, and possibly atomic demolition weapons, which are small and light enough to be given to individual commandos or terrorists for detonation inside India. The United States and the Soviet Union deployed these during the cold war.

India, for its part, has about eighty nuclear weapons. Both nations have boosted fission weapons, one step away from a hydrogen bomb, and very likely have standby hydrogen bomb tests ready to fire on a few weeks' notice should political conditions change. Each tried to test an H-bomb in 1998, but apparently neither attempt worked. A self-imposed test moratorium has been in effect since then. Neither side wishes to upset relations with the United States but it is likely that each could fire a test H-bomb in short order.

A noteworthy feature of this arms race is that India, a regional power on the subcontinent, is also a major power in the world. Pakistan builds up because of India. But India builds up because of Pakistan and China. Anything India does has to be considered through these two lenses.

India's long-range missile, the Agni, has a range of 2,100 miles. However, in April 2012 India successfully tested a new 3,000-mile version of the Agni, giving India the ability to reach China's northern cities, including Beijing and Shanghai. India thus joined an exclusive club of countries that have an ICBM. It's hard to imagine that India doesn't have a nuclear warhead planned for the Agni, because it would be pointless to have a missile to land merely a high-explosive bomb on a distant city. It's also difficult to believe that plans for a MIRV'd nuclear warhead for the Agni are not under way. MIRVs put several warheads on a single missile, and each can be fired at a separate target. They are much more threatening, and destabilizing, than single-warhead ICBMs. The United States and the Soviet Union MIRV'd their missiles in the cold war. For India, a MIRV'd ICBM capability would announce to the world that it was as technologically advanced as China.

Both India and Pakistan often flight-test their missiles. You've probably seen reports in the news saying that Pakistan or India has tested another missile, but you've likely not thought much about it. The tests are actually quite revealing. There may be political signaling going on here; each side often tests to show displeasure at something the other is doing.

But it isn't all politics, by any means. From a physics point of view, a nuclear missile requires a small, lightweight warhead. A missile flies a lot faster than an airplane, and it goes through turns whose g-forces could pull apart a poorly designed warhead. Saddam Hussein learned this lesson the hard way in 1991, when many of his Scuds disintegrated on the way to Israel. The reason for so many tests in South Asia is to measure the speed, acceleration, and stresses on the missile and its payload.

The flight tests show that each side has serious programs to put nuclear warheads on their missiles, and to ensure that the whole package—missile and warhead—actually fires. This isn't any symbolic or political display. Each country is climbing a learning curve to field an effective nuclear force.

India, far more than Pakistan, invests in spy satellites, reconnaissance aircraft, drones, early warning radars, and electronic intelligence. India is building an early warning capability, to tell it when Pakistan is preparing to launch or when it has already done so. In the first nuclear age the superpowers built early warning systems to alert them to an atomic attack in progress. Some elements were put in the polar north of Canada. Others were put in space, to detect hot missile plumes.

India has a large program under way to harness information technology (IT) to support its intelligence and early warning efforts. The launch of the Agni missile in April 2012 that gave India an ICBM capability received a great deal of attention around the world. One week later India launched a new radar intelligence satellite. It received little attention, yet it provides insight into the future direction of Indian defense. The Indian radar satellite carried advanced sensors aboard called synthetic aperture radar (SAR). SAR provides the ability to "see" through cloud cover and also at night. Further, India has deployed a related technology on its fleet of intelligence and reconnaissance aircraft, as well as aboard the satellite, called active electronically scanned array (AESA) radars. AESA radars spread their transmissions over many frequencies, providing microdetail of various target characteristics, such as what they look like in different conditions, for example in day and at night. They also have lower power on each wavelength—meaning that the object of attention is less likely to know it is being "painted" with a radar signal. In other words, India can look at targets inside Pakistan without Pakistan knowing that it's being scrutinized. This technology is also called low probability of intercept (LPI) radar because the target has a low likelihood of intercepting the radar signal, and thus being alerted to the fact that it is being targeted.

What's going on here? These technologies have uses for remote sensing for environmental and agricultural purposes, but they also have important strategic uses. They are ideal for selecting particular targets from a broader class of targets by using the enhanced micro-details provided by the radars. In addition, they do not tip off the enemy that he is being scrutinized. If Pakistan knew India was mounting a greatly increased reconnaissance effort in a crisis, Islamabad might get nervous that the information collected was being gathered to increase the precision of an attack. In short, India is developing IT systems that are ideal for detailed, stealthy target identification. The targets could be Pakistan's army, ships, terrorists trying to enter India, or mobile nuclear weapons. Indeed, following the November 2008 terrorist attack on Mumbai, India accelerated its deployment of these surveillance technologies.

India collects detailed, high-resolution information about targets in Pakistan and, presumably, China. If Pakistan moves a missile, a warhead, a ship—India wants to know about it. The increasing number of Indian intelligence platforms with these technologies on them, airplanes, ships, and satellites, suggests frequent updating of the information. The pictures aren't just detailed and stealthy, they are also current.

India obtains these technologies from homegrown programs and from foreign defense companies. Israel has a space launch agreement with India, as already mentioned, for intelligence satellites.

But there is a more prosaic reason for India's advantage. As the IT industry globally moves to wireless systems in LANs, Wi-Fi networks, and mobile telephones, the technologies used in them are becoming mass produced and better in quality. Moreover, they produce a very large amount of data, which require intensive processing. These trends play to India's considerable strengths in commercial IT.

Pakistan is far behind India in this kind of early warning. The notorious ISI, Pakistan's intelligence service, has been consumed by politics and opportunism for decades, and its technical performance has lagged as a result.

Pakistan does have spies and some modern warning systems. But Pakistan must rely on others, especially China, for an accurate, up-to-date intelligence picture of the world around it. Because it is so technically unsophisticated, Pakistan may be vulnerable to deception, something that could be an important consideration in a crisis.

FUTURE DIRECTIONS FOR THE ARMS RACE

As to where the arms race in South Asia is headed, there are several different possibilities. There is a tendency for many analysts to use the past and simply extrapolate into the future. But this straight-lining of past trends into the future can be misleading. India is a much richer country than it was in the past, and much of this wealth comes from technological and business innovations.

India's military in the past was a gigantic, inefficient, sluggish infantry with bloated headquarters and support staffs. New Delhi might use its newfound wealth to properly fund this old military force. In this case, it would buy state-of-the-art tanks, artillery, and aircraft, backed up with a minimum nuclear deterrent.

There are more dynamic possibilities, however. India could choose a different path, closer in kind to the modernization of its IT sector. There is considerable evidence that this is now taking place. India is shifting its capital from "old" programs to "new" ones, including nuclear weapons, missiles, submarines, intelligence, stealth, cyberwar, and satellites.

The reason for thinking this shift will accelerate is that India already has a large edge over Pakistan in the old military programs.

Investing more capital in them gives decreasing marginal returns. The best opportunities for India are in the new program areas, especially in a nuclear context and with respect to China.

Cyberwar could be especially important for India. India has a world-class IT industry, which can be used for military purposes. Leading Indian IT companies such as Wipro and Infosys have revolutionized world business with their innovations. The impact of Indian IT is to do more efficiently what a company already does, but in addition to fundamentally change how it does it.

It is hard to imagine that the IT industry won't be a more significant part of India's military modernization, as information warfare has become such an important piece of modern military power. It could be exploited in many ways, ranging from better early warning of attack, to anti-command-and-control strikes on Pakistan, and to responding to Chinese information warfare. Other defense technologies, like stealth and precision strike, are also likely to be attractive to India.

India is also acquiring a great deal of advanced military technology from the West. In 2010 India agreed to buy stealth fighters from Russia and in 2012 signed a deal to buy the French Rafale fighter. One of the key reasons behind these deals was Russian and French willingness to do what the United States was unwilling to agree to—transfer technology to India. In addition, the French Rafale was selected because it comes in a model that can be landed on an aircraft carrier. India probably wants a carrier to show its flag around the Indian Ocean and because China is developing an aircraft carrier.

It is true that the Indian defense and armaments bureaucracy has historically been one of the most sclerotic, corrupt, and least innovative of any in the world, but India is changing. Multinational companies are investing wholesale in India. Indian IT companies rapidly climb the learning curve to enter new global industries, seemingly overnight.

There are two models of Indian military modernization, then, which lead in very different directions. In one, India sticks with modernizing at the weapons level, getting modern tanks and airplanes. In the alternative model, India builds systems for quick reaction, precision strike, information warfare, stealth, and a more flexible nuclear force.

This alternative model has an important implication worth describing. In the first nuclear age, conventional forces were considered "good" and nuclear forces "bad." The idea was that conventional forces served as a shock absorber against nuclear escalation. At least, that's the way it was thought about back then. In Europe, for example, NATO's defenses were built to meet Soviet conventional attack with a purely conventional defense.

But the pattern showing up in South Asia is not so simple. Conventional precision strikes can take out nuclear targets. Cyberattacks can paralyze nuclear command and control as much as a bomb can. The clear lines separating conventional and nuclear war are blurring in South Asia.

NUCLEAR WEAPONS AND PAKISTAN'S DETERIORATING POSITION

Pakistan is in an unenviable and even impossible position: it is losing the arms race with India. Worse for Pakistan, India has an economy so much larger than Pakistan's that it is winning this race easily. Moreover, India is nationalistic, nuclear, and has a global role in economics and politics.

Pakistan lags in almost all areas of modern conflict except one: nuclear weapons. And that is the problem. Pakistan may be forced to use nuclear weapons to try to restore a balance with India. If this were to happen, and recent trends like Pakistan's buildup show that it is, the subcontinent will become a thicket of nuclear weapons.

What else can Pakistan do? Its GDP is only about 10 percent of

India's. This is about what Japan's GDP was compared to the United States in 1941. Pakistan has little of the technology needed to counterbalance India. Pakistan's civil society and government have notorious problems that prevent economic modernization.

So Pakistan faces a lopsided imbalance in military power. At some point Pakistan's generals have to consider that India will take advantage of its bigger economy and bigger military. The problem for Pakistan is how to restore strategic credibility so that India doesn't exploit this growing advantage.

One answer, from Pakistan's perspective, is with nuclear weapons. Figure 6.1 lists the ways that Pakistan could try to counterbalance India using the bomb.

Each of these is a possibility for Pakistan. All are within Pakistan's technological competence. The first item on the list, that "there is no problem," is included for completeness. It asserts that all Pakistan needs is a small number of nuclear weapons to deter India. Thirty bombs might do the trick. Aside from complete disarmament, this minimum deterrence approach is the preferred U.S. strategy for Pakistan, and the United States has argued at length that Pakistan should adopt it.

Let's expand this point a bit more. Academic conferences are often held around the theme of avoiding nuclear war in South Asia. Pakistani military and civilian experts are invited to the United States for these meetings. All kinds of issues are discussed, from guarding nuclear weapons to measures to build confidence ("let's agree not to go on alert in a crisis" or "don't put nuclear bombs on missiles, keep them separate from each other"). These meetings never convince the Pakistanis very much, and I sometimes wonder whether they do more harm than good. They have a tone to them that suggests that Pakistani planners are a bit dimwitted and are in need of U.S. help to educate them about nuclear deterrence. This tone turns off the Pakistanis, who are actually pretty savvy on nuclear deterrence. My concern is that the Pakistanis walk away feeling that the

FIGURE 6.1

WAYS PAKISTAN COULD BALANCE INDIA
USING NUCLEAR WEAPONS

- There is no balancing problem. Deterrence works!
- Acquire hair-trigger weapons—fast-reacting weapons, quick-launch missiles, jets on runway alert
- Rely on irrational determination. Remind India of Kargil, and Mumbai, by backing extremist groups who do "crazy" things
- Rely on massiveness by building a far larger nuclear arsenal
- Rely on scare tactics: high-yield weapons, ground bursting, radioactive fallout
- Threaten limited attacks. Three to five nuclear shots to demonstrate that Pakistan will go nuclear first; or give tactical (battlefield) nuclear weapons to field commanders
- Warn of escalation and the risk of eruption
- Warn of a loss of control, have slapdash command and control, and "nonaccidental" accidents
- Warn that its back is to the wall and it can't afford *not* to fulfill its threats to go to nuclear war

United States doesn't understand their problem—facing a big India that is rapidly modernizing and certain to outrace them.

It should be noted that the other extreme of minimum deterrence, nuclear war fighting, isn't on this list. Nuclear war fighting is a strategy with gigantic arsenals with phased strike options and sophisticated technology, things like warning satellites, retargeting computers, and hardened command and control. I cannot believe Pakistan can do this. It would be expensive and technologically far out of its reach.

Pakistan might try other approaches on the list. It could shift to a quick-reacting nuclear force. Marrying nuclear warheads to missiles and jets and having them ready to go on short notice is an example.

A variation of this is the third item on the list. Pakistan has used irrational strategies in the past, backing terrorist attacks on India and supporting the Taliban. This might convince others that it could be tried in the nuclear field, too. It says, "Look, we've behaved in crazy ways in the past so you have to think we might do it again. We aren't really crazy, of course, but we also don't think everything through in advance."

Pakistan could build so many weapons that India couldn't be sure of destroying them all in a first strike. A variation is to rely on frightful strategies. Pakistan could leak secret plans indicating that it had large-yield weapons, set for ground bursting, with maximum radioactive fallout on India. There are even ways to lace an H-bomb to make the radiation more deadly and long lasting, for example, by salting cobalt into some of them. Cobalt's radioactive isotopes, with a half-life of five years, would devastate vast regions of India.

Pakistan could also plan demonstration nuclear attacks, much like Israel. This move could exploit the grave concerns over Pakistan's ability to control its nuclear force by manipulating this very anxiety. Sloppy command and control has its uses, especially if one believes, as many Indians do, that Pakistan would never rationally reach a decision to fire its weapons. War by accident, or from some command-and-control glitch, could be especially convincing given the past performance of Pakistan's armed forces.

COMMAND AND CONTROL

Presidents George W. Bush and Barack Obama have gone out of their way to say that Pakistan's nuclear weapons are safe, that they're "under control." Why have two presidents issued reassuring statements?

There are no comparable announcements about Israel's weapons, or China's. No cold war president said that Soviet nuclear weapons were under control either.

An obvious concern is the danger of Pakistan's bombs falling into terrorist or jihadist hands. There are militant groups that would love to get their hands on these things.

Yet the two presidents were doing something beyond addressing this concern. They were trying to shape perceptions in India, in Pakistan, and in the United States. It is in fact a nuclear head game. But unlike cold war head games, this one was intended to assure audiences not of risk but of safety, that everything is okay in the command and control of Pakistan's nuclear forces.

Imagine if a president said the opposite. "We've looked at Pakistan's nuclear command-and-control system and we don't think it's really safe." "We think Pakistan might lose control of the bombs to terrorists or to groups like Laskhar-e-Toiba; or that someone might sell the weapons the way A. Q. Khan did; or that a 'mad major' in the Pakistani army could start World War III." Saying such things wouldn't be politic, to say the least. It would inflame fears all over and thereby make the problem worse. Congress would call hearings. The Pentagon would have to come up with some sort of a plan in response.

And India would get very nervous. If Pakistan is vulnerable to attack from terrorists, India, or anyone else, then the deterrent value of its nuclear arsenal evaporates. In a crisis, it makes India lean to attacking earlier rather than later. No U.S. president wants India to think this way. So the president says, "Pakistan's nuclear weapons are secure."

Of course they're not. Those who watch this sort of thing do not believe that Pakistan's nuclear weapons are safe. In a cable released by whistleblower WikiLeaks, a French diplomat told U.S. officials in September 2009 that the French government was "not sure that the Pakistani nuclear deterrent is secure," especially "with the frequent movement of nuclear weapons by the Pakistani military." The less secure Pakistan's force is, the more the United States has to say that it is secure.

Pakistan is playing a nuclear head game, too. I think the official Pakistani command-and-control system is designed more to influence outsiders than it is to control nuclear weapons. Consider how it started. In 2000, two years after Pakistan tested its first atomic weapons, and when Americans in the strategic community and Congress were concerned about the security of its arsenal, Islamabad announced the establishment of a national command authority (NCA). Pakistan's NCA is responsible for protecting, moving, and firing nuclear weapons. The announced version describes a deliberative group of senior leaders responsible for guardianship of the arsenal.

It's worth exploring Pakistan's NCA in detail, to show just how unworkable and unrealistic it is. The terminology itself is revealing. Pakistan chose the name NCA because that was the same term used by the United States in the cold war for its top-level control of nuclear weapons. The Pakistanis meant the term to be familiar, and therefore reassuring, to an American audience.

Pakistan's NCA is composed of the prime minister (as chair); the minister of defense (vice chair); the ministers of foreign affairs, interior, and finance; the chairman of the Joint Chiefs; the director of the army's Strategic Plans Division; and the service commanders of the army, navy, and air force. That's ten people.

Now, picture this NCA at work—in a bunker with flickering lights, shaken by explosions—calmly discussing Pakistan's next move. The conversation might go something like this:

"Okay, let's see where we are," says the prime minister. "We think two atom bombs have destroyed our army in Kashmir. We've just learned that there's radar warning of rockets coming in, and we're not sure if they're nukes or high explosives. They'll hit us in four minutes, so we'll soon see. I've asked my good friend the defense

minister to poke his head out the bunker door to see if he spots a mushroom cloud. He'll get back to us right away, I'm sure."

The prime minister then adds, "We have to be very careful here, we don't want to make a move that might let some terrorist get their hands on one of our nukes. If that happened the international community's confidence in our stewardship of nuclear weapons would go down, and we wouldn't want that. You all remember how mad the Americans were after the A. Q. Khan flap."

The prime minister then says, "Let me get a sense of the meeting before we take a formal vote. I think that's a good way to proceed unless anyone objects. Let's start with my respected colleague, the minister of finance. What do you think we should do?" The finance minister begins a PowerPoint presentation his staff has put together on the crisis and its impact on the economy.

It strains credulity to think that such a meeting could ever take place. Think of the confusion inside the U.S. government on 9/11, after four airplane attacks. Chaos ruled, even with good communication, high trust among the principals, and loyalty between civilian and military leaders. And no mushroom clouds.

Pakistan has none of these things. Add poor communications, extraordinary secrecy, and little experience in nuclear crises. Add that the missile flight time from India to Pakistan is anywhere from four to nine minutes.

One more detail. If Pakistan's NCA ever did meet like this, one Indian high-explosive bomb could wipe it out, destroying the group that is supposed to order retaliation. In other words, one bomb could take out Pakistan's deterrent. Common sense points to the conclusion that it probably doesn't work this way.

You begin to see the absurdity. So why has Pakistan announced in such tedious detail how the system (ostensibly) works? The reason is that Pakistan needs to reassure the United States to keep the foreign aid flowing and to reassure India, so New Delhi doesn't get an itchy trigger finger.

If the declared NCA system doesn't work as announced, then what does work? Pakistan almost certainly has a secret alternate command-and-control system. The official NCA is a facade, meant to reassure outsiders that the nuclear weapons are safe.

But it has another rationale, too. It's the cover story for a deception plan about the real command-and-control system. It's intended to deny outsiders an understanding of how the real one works. Like Patton's phony army pointed at the Pas de Calais to throw Hitler off the track of the Normandy invasion, Pakistan has something else in mind.

There are good reasons to believe in the existence of such a hidden system. Both superpowers had them in the cold war. One atomic bomb on the White House or the Kremlin wasn't going to take out the force, let me assure you.

I cannot believe Pakistan has overlooked this, either. I don't care about cultural differences, or top-secret assurances between some Pakistani deputy minister and his American counterpart. All command-and-control systems face a coercive reality. If authority is given to a single command center, vulnerability to a decapitation strike increases. At the other extreme, every major in the Pakistani army could be given the authority to fire a nuclear weapon. That's not a good idea, for obvious reasons. A trade-off between these two extremes is what every nuclear country faces. There's no getting around it.

Common sense points to linking this trade-off to the level of threat. In peacetime, when there is little chance of war, the command system will be tightly centralized. Only the top people can make things happen. In a crisis, it'll decentralize.

There are other factors at work here that are peculiar to South Asia, and which worsen the command-and-control problem. In the

United States, the Constitution and civilian control over the military is unquestioned. Pakistan isn't like this. The government changes every few years, back and forth between the army and civilians. Coups and rigged elections are not uncommon. South Asia's history is also replete with assassinations: Indira Gandhi, Rajiv Gandhi, Benazir Bhutto, the attack on India's parliament, routine assassinations in Pakistan. Going after the strategic apex is part of the region's history.

Pakistan has to recognize something else, too. The U.S. strikes on Saddam Hussein's headquarters in 2003, against the Taliban in Afghanistan and Pakistan, in Libya, and the killing of Osama bin Laden were all attacks on the brain of the enemy. Headquarters was the target. These attacks had something else in common. The United States has built up significant know-how for executing strikes on the strategic apex. There was an enormous, specialized intelligence effort. Captured papers, mobile phones, radio intercepts, computers, and close eyeball surveillance of targets preceded the attacks. Advanced stealth drones monitored Osama bin Laden's compound months before the attack in order to see the pattern of movement. This information was integrated with satellite intercepts of Pakistani communications. All of this intelligence was closely woven into the response cycle of whatever weapon that was used. A cruise missile fired from a sub, special forces on helicopters, an air strike—all were repeatedly practiced.

There are some newer considerations as well. Sophisticated cyberattacks on Iran's centrifuges have been reported in the press. China's cyberattacks on U.S. military computers, blinding them or overloading and infecting computers with viruses, are routinely reported in the news.

It would be hard for Pakistan to miss all of these things and what they point to: its own nuclear command-and-control system as a target.

Pakistan's chief rival, India, has an advanced IT industry, so it isn't a big step for it to develop cyberattacks. India is moving toward stealth aircraft that are hard to see on radar. Pakistan might dismiss all of this, but this is not likely.

Islamabad faces threats to its command and control from many actors, and from different types of attack. It might be attacked from India, the United States, terrorists, fundamentalists, or even Pakistani army colonels. Depending on how cynical one is, another "attack" could come from Pakistani civilians, that is, from a democratic government trying to discharge its duties. Historically, civilian governments have had little control over the military or the nuclear weapons. The Pakistani army would like to keep it that way.

It's hard to believe that planners in Pakistan take the facade command-and-control system seriously. It fits the peacetime political reality of assuring outsiders that they don't have to worry. But that's not the environment in which it will be called on to perform. Pakistan surely knows this. And so does India.

BULLET TO THE HEAD—A SCENARIO OF A SOUTH ASIAN NUCLEAR CRISIS

What might a serious nuclear crisis in South Asia look like? Let's address this with a composite scenario that incorporates the above discussion with my knowledge of command and control and with what several observers and studies argue are serious risks. The scenario is offered as a systems integration device; it pulls together critical subsystems (nuclear weapons, intelligence, command and control, political decision making) to illustrate some key points.

> India has two plans for war with Pakistan. The first is a conventional air-and-missile attack on Pakistan's nuclear forces. The second plan calls for a nuclear attack on Pakistan's nuclear forces. The nuclear plan has a much higher chance of disarming Pakistan but results in enormous collateral damage.

*War games played in New Delhi concluded that, in the event of
a conventional attack, Pakistan is likely to strike back at Indian
cities with nuclear weapons. However, because of its high security
classification, few civilians saw the results of these games. Most
Indian political leaders didn't think about these matters in any
case.*

*Against this Indian planning context, an intense crisis erupts in
Kashmir. At the same time, there are demonstrations in Pakistan
directed at the army for jobs and greater political freedom. Pakistan uses lethal force against the demonstrators and raises the tensions in Kashmir. Pakistan moves three divisions forward. India
protests this action.*

*Unknown to almost all Indian political leaders, however, there
is a top-secret annex that goes beyond the two Indian plans. It
is known only to the prime minister and a few generals. Even the
defense minister isn't clued in.*

*In the crisis, the Indian prime minister calls a meeting to discuss
the secret annex, which calls for a nighttime conventional missile
strike on the homes of top Pakistani generals, along with an attack
on the nuclear command-and-control headquarters. Information
to support this attack has been culled by a secret Indian intelligence unit that has penetrated Pakistan's mobile phone system,
hacked into computers and e-mail, and shadowed senior officials
associated with the nuclear forces. India has mapped out Pakistan's nuclear command-and-control system in considerable detail.*

*The night attack on Pakistan is intended to decapitate the mili-
tary high command and thereby prevent it from ordering the mat-
ing of atomic warheads to missiles and airplanes. The anticipated
chaos in communications, movement, and disrupted authority
will buy time for Indian follow-on precision conventional strikes
on the immobilized Pakistani nuclear forces. Another even more
secret annex details a massive cyberwar attack on Pakistan to*

make it impossible for communications and computer systems to work. When Pakistan turns on its computers, all anyone will see is an error message.

India aims to catch Pakistan asleep, decapitate the government, and paralyze retaliation. The Indian prime minister never believed he would be in a situation where this plan would be seriously considered. He had authorized it only for contingency planning purposes. But now the situation has changed, and the risks of a Pakistani attack look real enough for him to treat the plan with deadly seriousness.

The cyberwar annex also contained a deception plan. Indian counterintelligence had carefully scripted messages to plant in Pakistan to lull the leadership into complacency. The intent was to make the Pakistani high command think there was no reason to move nuclear warheads onto missiles and jets. Fake messages were created for the special communications network used by Indian officials, which was known to be tapped by Pakistan's ISI and perhaps by other intelligence services. An Indian deputy minister is instructed to call a close colleague using a phone line known to be tapped, to say, "We must watch developments in Pakistan carefully. But I heard it directly from the prime minister this morning that we are to take no actions—not even alerting measures—for fear it will inflame the situation." This message and others, of course, are phony covers for actual Indian preparations.

The intent of the deception plan is to deceive Pakistan into maintaining a peacetime posture, with bombs in a small number of locations. It is also to mislead the United States into thinking that India was not going to attack. The Indian bet is that America would do anything to defuse a nuclear crisis, and would pressure Pakistan to stay cool.

In the crisis, the United States pleads with Pakistan not to heighten tensions by alerting its nuclear force. The CIA tells the *president that Pakistan hasn't gone on nuclear alert, and neither has India. Indeed, it reports that India is going out of its way to de-escalate the crisis. The Indian ambassador in Washington agrees with the American request for calm. He is unaware of the secret annex and deception plan.*

Then China detects Indian preparations for the strike from a new signals intelligence satellite. Beijing launches a photo satellite that finds India preparing conventional forces, including stealthy cruise missiles, and passes an urgent message through a secret back channel to Islamabad. The message includes before and after photographs taken by Chinese satellites showing the forward movement of Indian missiles, planes, and ships. Beijing calls on Washington to restrain India's reckless behavior, which is bringing South Asia to the brink of nuclear catastrophe.

For years, U.S. advice to Pakistan has been that Taliban insurgents are Pakistan's real enemy. The Pakistani military, seeing the pictures from China, concludes that the United States is complicit in the setup, to deceive Pakistan into complacency as a joint Indian-American attack is launched. That this isn't the case hardly matters, because of the level of distrust and paranoia inside Pakistan.

Pakistan seals off the U.S. embassy compound in Islamabad and raids secret U.S. intelligence posts throughout the country, with deadly force. Several American intelligence officers are killed, shot while trying to destroy communications equipment. Pakistan's special forces, which the United States had been covertly funding to guard the atomic arsenal from terrorists, surround the U.S. embassy. All communications and electricity to the embassy are cut off. Powerful radio jamming signals disrupt outward communications.

Pakistan's fear is that American agents are cueing strikes on its atomic forces. Islamabad further believes (incorrectly) that this information is being transferred to Indian intelligence. The U.S. ambassador tries to reach the prime minister of Pakistan to tell him that there is no U.S.-Indian cooperation. But he is unable to get through. The Pakistani prime minister is in a secret location for fear of being killed in an Indian attack.

Pakistan goes on a full nuclear alert that astonishes U.S. intelligence. U.S. satellites "see" so many units (jets, missile launchers, fueling trucks, fake radio and cell phone messages) accompanied by a flood of other confusing signals. Nothing like this has ever been observed before.

Pakistan has a hidden command-and-control system. It has long existed, to be stood up only at a time of national emergency. It was designed to confuse outside powers about the location and readiness of Pakistan's nuclear forces.

The CIA tells the president that U.S. intelligence has, for all practical purposes, been shut down in Pakistan. The United States doesn't know for sure where any atomic weapons are, if they're moving, or even Pakistan's stage of alert. The CIA adds that, given what has happened, it would be prudent to assume that Pakistan's bombs have been married to the missiles and airplanes for prompt firing, and that backdoor command links that bypass the formal NCA system are likely in existence to ensure that the "go" order gets through to those who need it.

The Indians ask the United States for joint military action against Pakistan. The word nuclear *isn't mentioned. The United States feels that it would be "shooting in the dark," and says so. New Delhi counters that it is not the United States but India that faces the imminent threat, and that even if the crisis subsides, the result will be a Pakistan in nuclear hysteria for years to come.*

This scenario raises several very important issues. One issue is that nuclear weapons cannot be considered in isolation from other critical subsystems such as intelligence, command and control, information warfare, and precision conventional attack. There is a tendency to look only at the number of bombs each side has. But the biggest sources of instability likely come from the mutual interaction of these critical subsystems.

Then there's China. The scenario illustrates a multiplayer game, with Pakistan, India, the United States, and China. It posits the realistic possibility that in the next ten years China will have a more effective space-based reconnaissance system. Satellites, better signals intelligence, and all the rest are within China's grasp. It won't be as good as what the United States has. But it will be good enough to make China a potentially significant player in a nuclear crisis in South Asia. As near as I can tell, there has been little thought given to what this might mean. This is an enormous difference from the cold war, when America had to worry about what only one opponent, the Soviets, saw. The hotline, embassy communications, and conventions about limiting the intensity of operations were designed for a two-player game. In the future, the United States needs to think through the information requirements for a multiplayer game.

In this scenario, India responds not with a nuclear attack, but with a conventional or at least a nonnuclear attack. Cyberattacks, stealth, precision strike are combined to try to take out Pakistan's nuclear arms. What this shows is that the notion that conventional weapons are good, and nuclear weapons bad, is a lot more complicated in the second nuclear age than it was in the first. It isn't that one is better than the other but that both are tangled up in new and different ways.

Finally, and what is likely to be most controversial, is the Indian strategy of attacking Pakistan's command and control. The scenario name, "Bullet to the Head," is descriptive. Some people might argue that India would never do this. They may be right. India has no desire to get into a war with Pakistan. But Indian planners are likely to consider this option, because if they must go to war it may be the best one around.

Pakistan almost certainly thinks that India will consider this option, and that's enough to kick-start some dangerous dynamics.

Pakistan may shift to some of the strategies discussed earlier, such as marrying nuclear warheads with missiles in advance or putting its force on quick reaction alert.

In the cold war, there were bullet-to-the-head strategies that went like this: "The superpowers have so many nuclear weapons that it's impossible to destroy them one by one. A 'retail' strategy of destroying the enemy's missiles one at a time is thus utterly hopeless, so a 'wholesale' strategy has to be considered. If you can get off only one big nuclear salvo, aim part of it at the enemy's head." This thinking entailed early nuclear strikes on Moscow or Washington, as both sides came up with this concept. Other command centers, like communications facilities, were targeted, too. Such an attack might stun the other side as it sorted out what had happened. This might provide enough time to destroy the enemy's missiles before they were fired.

I am not defending this strategy, nor am I arguing that it would have worked. But I am saying that since it came up in the first nuclear age, bullet-to-the-head strategies will likely come up in the second nuclear age, too, but with some key differences. The biggest difference is that the arsenal sizes of the second nuclear age are small compared to the cold war. A bullet-to-the-head strategy might actually work if only fifty to one hundred weapons had to be destroyed by the follow-on attacks.

Another difference is that efforts to destroy command and control and nuclear targets could use cyberattacks and conventional weapons. Stealth and precision strike have changed the game a lot from the cold war days. They offer opportunities to paralyze an opponent that didn't exist in the first nuclear age.

CONCLUSION

Beneath a veneer of nuclear deterrence and a facade command-and-control system, some very dangerous dynamics are building up in South Asia. For the past decade, there has been little creative thought given to them. Instead the focus has been, understandably, on the first bounce of the ball in South Asia, the nuclear and missile buildup.

The fiction that Pakistan is building only a minimum deterrent and that India is investing in stabilizing conventional forces is difficult to sustain with each passing year. It misframes the problem. We are overdue in considering a wider range of scenarios and a better appreciation of the way new military technologies such as information warfare, stealth, and precision strike shape the dynamics on the subcontinent.

EAST ASIA

East Asia brings together the two most important powers in the world, the United States and China. Whether these two countries develop a cooperative or a competitive strategic relationship will, to a great extent, determine how many of the challenges of the second nuclear age are managed. It is virtually impossible for the United States to solve these problems alone, as the old Western coalition of France, Britain, and Germany led by America is badly fraying in influence.

In East Asia there are regional problems, too—North Korea in particular—which are greatly influenced by U.S.-China relations. The approach taken here is to focus on the region, North Korea and East Asia, and to work upward to analyze the strategic interactions of the United States and China in the global multipolar nuclear system, later, in chapter 9.

NORTH KOREA

North Korea is a small, weak nuclear state with a clever political strategy for using its weapons. Its military and nuclear forces are extremely primitive, but North Korea shows what a country can do with a dozen or so bombs.

To see just how clever its strategy is, go back to 2006. On July 4 of that year North Korea conducted missile tests with dummy warheads. These involved:

- Multiple firings, seven in total
- Two of which were launched within minutes of the takeoff of the space shuttle *Discovery* in Florida
- The missiles covered a wide geographic azimuth (toward the United States, Japan, South Korea)
- With missiles of short and long ranges

Commentators focused on the symbolism of July 4, Independence Day in the United States. Others focused on the failure of the long-range missile, the Taepo-Dong 2, which conked out after forty seconds.

While legitimate, these views overlook something important. The tests showed that North Korea could fire a salvo of missile shots in a short period of time. The seven launches coincided with the number of nuclear weapons credited to North Korea by the media at that time.

That two of the launches occurred minutes after the takeoff of the space shuttle, which was televised on international channels, suggests that North Korea used the shuttle launch to trigger its launches. The shuttle was used as a simulated U.S. preemptive missile strike. In the cold war both sides did this. The United States timed missile launches from Vandenberg Air Force Base in California to coincide with Soviet launches from its Pacific test range. When U.S. spy satellites picked up the fiery plumes of Soviet rockets, word was flashed to fire missiles from Vandenberg. This fantastic process took only a few minutes. The Soviets then watched U.S. missiles fire some ten minutes after theirs took off, and well before they splashed down in the Pacific.

The U.S. exercise wasn't conducted to test whether the missiles worked. At least, not only that. It had a strategic purpose. The U.S. tests simulated a launch on warning capability, and it was approved by the White House. The message was to let Moscow know that it couldn't attack the United States without provoking a response. It said to the Soviets: "We can launch our missiles before your missiles even touch down. Don't even think about doing something you'll regret."

North Korea was playing the same game. It didn't have space satellites, of course. But it did receive news of the shuttle launch via CNN and that was good enough. There's ingenuity at work here. Pyongyang can't match anyone in technology, yet alone the United States, so it makes do. The message sent was that a U.S. attack on North Korea would trigger an immediate attack on South Korea and Japan. This hostage strategy says to the United States: "Don't even think about doing something your allies will regret." That the United States and its allies would win hardly matters, because the damage North Korea could inflict would be enormous, not only because of its nuclear warheads but also because of its chemical weapons. As we know from the earlier discussion of the Middle East and South Asia, it's hard to pick out the nuclear missiles from those loaded with nerve agents or conventional warheads.

Not bad for a backward country that is like a starving rat—with nuclear teeth. A corrupt and crazy regime that can't produce food or energy, but it can build atomic bombs and a strategy for using them.

Let's look at the political side of North Korea's strategy. The regime would face extinction in the event of a war, not just defeat. This cannot be overemphasized. The North Korean leadership knows that on the long list of tyrannical regimes in the world, it is number one. This is a regime far worse than those of Saddam Hussein or Muammar Qaddafi. North Korean officials surely won't be given a safe exit out of a disaster. Rather, they will be put on trial and hung. They face the scenario where there is no tomorrow for them. The ruling Kim family knows this. The new head of state, Kim Jong-un, who came to power in 2011 after the death of his father, Kim Jong-il, is in an untenable position. Too much reform and the regime will collapse, and he and his family will be put on trial or killed. Too little reform and the people will continue to starve.

Yet the Kim regime survives, at least so far. The reason is because it receives foreign aid from China, the United States, South Korea, and Japan, much of it disguised as UN humanitarian relief. North Korea is propped up with this aid.

Anyone who says that nuclear weapons aren't usable should take a look at North Korea. Nuclear weapons are used every single day to extort food and oil from the rest of the world to keep the regime going. This is the key to its "nuclear strategy." What North Korea has done is to link its national existence to those of South Korea and Japan, through a strategy that makes internal weakness a deterrent. The fragility of North Korea's position—in food and energy, poverty, political legitimacy—perversely becomes a strength when linked to WMD and an army capable of destroying a good part of South Korea, even if it is ultimately defeated.

North Korea's strategy is to use WMD to connect its internal weakness with external pressures. It's like the plunger on an explosive. Pushing the plunger—cutting off food and energy—will produce an explosion in North Korea. But if outsiders push it, it will cause an explosion that takes them down, too. Outsiders had better not pressure North Korea to implode, then, or they will cause it to explode—all over them. Another way of saying this is that North Korea threatens to blow its brains out all over northeast Asia's living room. It'll create such a mess that its adversaries will stand back from pressing very hard. Who can blame them?

The North Korea case once again shows that the vocabulary of the cold war doesn't correspond to the new realities of the second nuclear age. To label North Korea's strategy a "minimum deterrent" because it has only a dozen bombs doesn't do it justice. It doesn't begin to adequately describe the transcendent madness of what North

Korea has built. "Suicide in your neighbor's living room" is a better description. There was nothing like this strategy in the cold war.

The United States could blockade North Korean ports and enforce a no-fly zone. China could seal their common border. The reason for not taking these actions isn't that they are militarily difficult. It's that, by starving the population, the result is a greater chance of a WMD attack on South Korea and Japan.

Turning weakness into strength is a hallmark of Korean strategic culture. It was used against Japan in World War II. It's a very Korean way of fighting more powerful enemies. Just think of little Korea, surviving for a thousand years, surrounded by the giants Russia, China, and Japan. North Korea has taken this culture and updated it for a nuclear environment.

There is no benefit for China, South Korea, Japan, or the United States that is worth the risk of pressing North Korea too hard. What these powers want is stability. North Korean strategy takes advantage of this and turns it against the outside world, almost daring its adversaries to press harder.

It's a psychological strategy. But it is institutionalized with a hard-edged military that has nuclear and chemical weapons. What rational American leader would ever play chicken with North Korea, knowing that Pyongyang can launch a nuclear or chemical salvo before it can be stopped by American air strikes? Everything reinforces American self-deterrence. When faced with killing tens of thousands of North Koreans, because of the scale required in a preemption, what American president is likely to order such an attack?

North Korea heavily depends on China for this strategy to succeed. When relations with Seoul and Washington get so bad that they cut back on aid, Beijing picks up the slack. The Americans and South Koreans know this, and so do the Chinese. An understanding has developed, but it's hardly something China welcomes. Rather, Beijing feels that there is no better alternative. If the Chinese were to pull the plug on economic aid, it might set off the nuclear powder keg that is North Korea.

Still, it's a very dangerous game, and there's no guarantee that it can go on indefinitely. Pyongyang has to stoke tensions to convince outsiders that it just might pull the trigger if pressed too hard. This is probably what was behind the attacks on South Korea in 2010. These attacks also showed the fine distinctions of thresholds and conventions that have developed.

On March 26, 2010, North Korea torpedoed a South Korean frigate, the *Cheonan*, killing forty-six sailors. The *Cheonan* was in international waters. Eight months later North Korea fired some 170 artillery rounds at South Korea's Yeonpyeong Island in the Yellow Sea, killing four villagers. There are fine distinctions in the two incidents worth noting. The *Cheonan* was a military target. This is less provocative than attacking a civilian village. The Yeonpyeong Island incident was a clear jump in escalation over the torpedoing of the *Cheonan*.

But even here, North Korea decided to attack a village on an isolated island. The worst that could happen was damage confined to the island. Attacking a mainland town on the DMZ (Demilitarized Zone) would have been a greater provocation and it would be more difficult to confine the damage. Suppose a Boy Scout troop was camping in the area, or a South Korean battalion was on a march. Seoul might interpret it as the start of an all-out attack. South Korea might mobilize reserves and surge troops to the DMZ. That, in turn, could lead to a full North Korean mobilization, something that has not happened since the end of the Korean War in 1953.

The whole affair might get out of hand. North Korea wants to stoke tensions, but I don't believe it wants war. Even in crazy North Korea there's a logic to escalation—namely, that it's limited. There are thresholds the regime is willing to cross (attack a ship or an isolated island village), and others that it's not willing to cross.

None of this is to say that escalation won't get out of hand, or that North Korea won't miscalculate—only that there's a long history of distinguishable degrees of escalation intensity. In 1968 North Korea seized a U.S. intelligence ship, the USS *Pueblo*. Later that year it sent assassins into Seoul to try to kill South Korea's president. North Korean commandos murdered several high-ranking South Korean officials at a diplomatic meeting in Burma in 1983. There have been airplane bombings, border incidents, and incidents at sea.

So North Korean provocations aren't new. What is new is the nuclear context. The estimates of where things could go have become much more sobering. Traditional military balance assessments have to take escalation risks into account as never before.

It's a good idea for the U.S. government, and others, to make a closer, analytical study of escalation and de-escalation. They need to understand the fine distinctions that, like it or not, shape the dynamics on the Korean peninsula. North Korea has changed the rules of the game, turning it into a competition in managing risks, rather than a problem of maintaining a conventional military balance, as in the past. But North Korea isn't the only place in East Asia where the bomb is becoming more important.

CHINA AND NUCLEAR WEAPONS

Historically, China showed little interest in the sophisticated nuclear strategies of the superpowers. Until the early 1990s, Beijing had only about twenty ICBMs. They were the only weapons that could reach the United States. Reportedly, warheads were not even attached to the missiles. It would have taken anywhere from twenty-four to ninety-six hours, depending on whose estimates one believed, to arm them.

China didn't seem to care as much about using nuclear weapons as military instruments as the United States and the Soviet Union did. Beijing was invariably said to have a minimum deterrent. On the surface this is certainly how it looked. Twenty missiles, not ready to fire, not even armed. China also had a declared policy not to be the first to use nuclear weapons.

But China's political use of the bomb dwarfed any military use. The American strategic vocabulary, with its overwhelming focus on deterrence, is geared to discounting political and strategic uses of the bomb. To call what China had a minimum deterrent glosses over its main purpose and its actual use.

China used its nuclear force without regard for silo kill probabilities or Western deterrent logic. If China had not been a nuclear power, it never could have played the political role Beijing's leaders wanted. How could a nonnuclear China have teamed up with the United States in the 1970s and 1980s to counter the Soviet Union? China became a virtual member of NATO. Indeed, China was more important than most NATO members when it came to deterring the Soviets from rocking the boat in Europe. The whole basis of this role required that China be a nuclear power.

The experience of China also shows that the mere existence of nuclear weapons creates possibilities that wouldn't exist without them. Even if a country hasn't incorporated these possibilities into its strategy—even if it hasn't thought about them—they can still have a considerable impact. Once China had nuclear weapons, other countries had to change their calculations. They had to consider "what next?" scenarios—even if Chinese leaders never did.

It's quite amazing, really. As an example, a U.S. planning scenario was developed to use tactical nuclear weapons against a Chinese army if it intervened in Vietnam in the 1960s. The plans were drawn up by the Joint Chiefs of Staff and the Pacific Command. In my first job after college I worked at a consulting firm that worked for the Pentagon. I came across a war game of the plan, a Chinese intervention in Vietnam that threatened to destroy the U.S. Army there. It was a repeat of what had happened in Korea in 1950. In this game the navy sailed its carriers right up to the Vietnamese coast to bomb the Chinese army, at enormous risk to itself, because the "North Vietnamese" pilots were actually Chinese with modern aircraft who hit the carriers right and left. But the game never got to the

United States using tactical nuclear weapons. Instead, the United States was willing to accept a strategic collapse in Vietnam, and the sinking of its aircraft carriers, rather than go nuclear.

At this time China had a nuclear force that was not much larger than North Korea's is today. Yet in the game the United States wasn't about to launch a nuclear strike that stood a high chance of success against the Chinese army. The Americans had to calculate what a big war with China would bring. The mere existence of China's nuclear force, as small as it was, amplified the escalation risks for decision makers in Washington.

A nuclear China seriously inhibited the United States in Vietnam. The Johnson-McNamara strategy of incremental escalation came from the desire to avoid a major war with China, one that after 1964 could have gone nuclear. It wasn't the bomb alone that did this. But a nonnuclear China would have been treated far differently by the United States. The first and second nuclear ages cannot be understood as contests between nuclear missile batteries that happen to have countries stuck to them. This misses the most important dynamics associated with these weapons.

Let's look at another example. This one shows the dynamics of a three-way game, so it's especially relevant for the second nuclear age. To counter the Soviet Union, President Nixon wanted to strengthen ties with Beijing. This was the reason for his visit to China in 1972. But the question was open as to exactly how to bolster China as a military power. The answer that he and his national security adviser, Henry Kissinger, came up with was to provide the Chinese with intelligence on Soviet forces in Asia. The concept was called "information transfer." It's likely to be a key strategic concept in the second nuclear age, too, because it's a way for an advanced country to use its information advantages to quickly increase the military power of a less advanced country.

In 1972, there was a big information asymmetry between China and the Soviet Union. The Soviets had excellent intelligence on the

Chinese, but the Chinese had almost nothing on the Soviets. Beijing just didn't have the satellites and advanced signals interception. So President Nixon decided to give the Chinese strategic information to close the gap. It bolstered China's military capability virtually overnight.

During Nixon's trip to China in February 1972, the president took Prime Minister Zhou Enlai aside and told him:

> As I look at the situation with respect to China, as we mentioned yesterday, the Soviet Union has more forces on the Sino-Soviet borders than it has arrayed against the Western Alliance. Now, I think that, as the Prime Minister knows, I have asked Dr. Kissinger to provide a briefing to whomever the Prime Minister designates on very sensitive material, what we know to be totally reliable on both the position of the Soviet forces versus China and also the general nuclear balance. I suggest that if the Prime Minister could designate, in addition to people on the civilian side, someone such as the Vice Chairman for Military Affairs [Yeh Chien-ying, Vice Chairman of the Military Affairs Mission of the Chinese Communist Party], I believe it would be extremely interesting for him. The meeting place should be highly secret, however, if this could be arranged.

The information transfer occurred the next morning, on February 23, 1972. This meeting wasn't a chat about diplomatic niceties. Glowing statements about U.S.-China relations and other platitudes were reserved for the banquet. This was a transfer of strategic information: useful to China for targeting, for military deployments, and in peacetime for planning defense budgets. It was information China could never have gotten on its own. For the Chinese to know which Soviet weapons were nuclear, and which weren't, was invaluable.

Kissinger provided maps and photographs of Soviet deployments and weapons to his Chinese counterpart. To appreciate the level of detail, it's worth looking at part of the declassified top secret transcript of the meeting. The recipient was Vice Chairman Yeh, of the People's Military Affairs Mission:

KISSINGER: Now, as long as we are speaking of tactical weapons, there are three others that are missiles, that are not aircraft. There is one tactical weapon to which we give the name of "FROG" that has a range of 155 miles. It's on a track; it's mobile. The newest version of it has wheels and most of it is in the newest version. The old version has a range of 155 miles, and the new version has a range of about 311 miles. This can have both a conventional and a nuclear warhead. And if it has a nuclear warhead it can range from 3 kilotons to 20 kilotons in the old version and 40 to 90 kilotons in the new version. This is what the old version looks like (*shows picture*). This is what the new version looks like (*shows picture*).

YEH (*in English*): Rocket.

KISSINGER: The way these are assigned is each division has four launchers. That means that in the Far East military district there are 76 to 84. In the Trans-baikal military district there are 28 or 32. In Mongolia there are 12. In the Central Asian military district there are 28. Or a total of 144 to 156 are in these four districts. Then in the Siberian military district there are 28. In the Turkestan military district there are 18. Then in the Far East military district, farther back than can reach you but available for reinforcement, are 9. In interior districts, east of the Urals, are 73. Or a total of 272–284.

Now let me turn to another tactical missile. It doesn't matter what we call it, because I don't even know what the name we give it means in English. It's a short-range ballistic missile which has a range of 160 nautical miles. This is more modern than the "FROG" and it has an accuracy of about a quarter of a mile. This is newer than the old version of the "FROG," but the new version of the "FROG" is newer than this. This can be used with conventional and nuclear warheads, but we think that all of these weapons I am giving you have nuclear warheads. This has tracks.

YEH: Two-stage or one-stage?

KISSINGER: One-stage.

YEH: And on the nuclear version, how many kilotons?

KISSINGER: From ten to 100. They have four different warheads, 10, 20, 40, or 100 kilotons, but we don't know which they have on which. In the Far East military district, of this type missile they have 12 to 18. In the Trans-baikal military district, they have six. In the Siberian military district they have six. In the Turkestan military district they also have six. There is a total of 30 to 36. We know the locations. All of these are nautical mile ranges. It's also true of the range we gave for the "FROG."

Let's understand what's going on here. The United States gives targeting information about another nuclear state, the Soviet Union, to a third nuclear power, China. The intent is to boost the strength of the weaker player. The United States hadn't wanted China to go nuclear in 1964, just as it hadn't wanted Israel to do so in 1966. America did not seek a multipolar nuclear world. That developed on its own. But the question arose: Given that countries owned these weapons, how should one manage the system to make it more stable?

The information transfer by President Nixon in 1972 wasn't a onetime event. In the late 1970s, I was involved with a project on this concept at the Hudson Institute, with Herman Kahn and Don Brennan. The question put to us was how to strengthen a perception in Moscow that the United States and China had strong nuclear ties that would get even stronger if there was a Soviet provocation. It was to reinforce thinking in Moscow that they had better not undertake any adventures in Eastern or Western Europe. The Hudson project came up with some fairly creative ideas. One was to simulate China's nuclear alerting signals in a way sure to be picked up by the Soviets

EAST ASIA   201

and to make it look like the signals emanated from China. An electronic package could be dropped into the Gobi Desert or some such remote place. The concept was that Moscow wouldn't want to escalate if it might trigger a major nuclear crisis. It was our view that the Soviets had been burned in the Cuban missile crisis fiasco of 1962, and that they wouldn't want to turn down this road again.

It can be debated whether Nixon and Kissinger's decision to transfer strategic information to China was the right one. Similarly, whether anyone should be analyzing ways to manipulate nuclear perceptions, as the Hudson effort explored, is also debatable.

They are one answer to the larger question of achieving nuclear stability when several countries have the bomb. The same question applies in the second nuclear age. Transfers of strategic information are one way to think about this important question. Transfer of information is especially important for the United States because it possesses the world's most advanced intelligence system. This question should be thought through *before* a crisis; tossing it at an unprepared president in the midst of a nuclear crisis is irresponsible, in my judgment. It has to be carefully planned ahead of time.

CHINA'S MODERNIZATION

China's ongoing military modernization is altering the balance of power in East Asia. This modernization uses advanced technologies, has a long geographic reach, and aligns with the strategic and economic conditions in China.

Among the most important developments are China's missiles. There are thousands of these, of many different ranges, and new deployments are under way. China's ballistic missiles, most of which are on mobile launchers, can reach all U.S. bases in the Pacific, from Kadena in Okinawa to Guam. An unusual feature of China's missiles is the use of horizontal tunnels to conceal their location and to move them around. The United States and the Soviet Union, in contrast, relied on vertical tunnels, called silos, for launching missiles. These vertical silos were holes in the ground reinforced with lots of concrete and were not connected one to the other. China has an interconnected horizontal tunnel system in which trucks carry the missiles, driving them to ports, vertical openings, for firing. Estimates are that China has over three thousand miles of tunnels for this purpose, and there may be a lot more than this.

A horizontal tunnel system is considerably more expensive to build. But it allows greater concealment of a missile's movements. It also makes the counting rules for arms control limits on missiles nearly impossible because satellites can't see underground. In the Soviet-American case this was solved with a simple counting rule: each silo counted as a missile launcher, even if it didn't actually contain a missile.

More important, the Chinese tunnel system shows a deep commitment to concealing information about deployments—both the number and location. It allows for rapid "pop-ups" timed to appear on an opponent's surveillance system, and it may have other features we do not know about.

Yet there is no doubt that China has a large number of missiles because these have been photographed. Many are deployed opposite Taiwan, and these missiles are kept in the open most likely so that they can be seen by U.S. intelligence. The large numbers make missile defense nearly impossible. Missile defense can work against small threats. It's expensive, but it still makes sense in certain cases. But large attacks saturate the defender's radars and computers with more targets than it can process. And the defender runs out of bullets.

China is also developing fast cruise missiles that travel three, four, or more times the speed of sound. This threat creates another nearly impossible defense problem. In theory, a Mach 3 cruise missile can be destroyed before it hits a U.S. Navy ship. But the smallest glitch in the defender's execution of shooting it down opens it to disaster. Moreover, an attacking cruise missile may have built-in countermeasures, such as chaff bursts to confuse the defender's radars. Or the cruise missile may execute avoidance maneuvers right before it hits its target, such as popping up or veering left or right. China possesses all of these technologies.

China's surveillance system is the key to the effectiveness of its missile force. Satellites, drones, signal interception, and spies are the front end of China's missile force because they locate the target that is to be destroyed. In the event of tensions, there is a good chance that China and the United States will interfere with each other's surveillance systems to degrade their performance. There will by a jockeying for information advantage, and likely cyberattacks to blind the other side.

China can already easily destroy a fixed target in the Pacific. GPS is enough for doing that, once the target's longitude and latitude are put into the missile's computer. Islands can't move, and they can't hide. They just sit there, year after year.

The United States is completely dependent on its bases in the Pacific. Japan, Hawaii, and Guam are the foundation of U.S. power there. There aren't any backups after these. Without bases, it's impossible for the United States to operate in the region.

China is building conventional warheads tailored to shut down these bases or to hold them hostage, while causing minimal collateral damage. Nuclear weapons aren't needed. Cluster warheads, for example, spread small bomblets over a wide area. Some have delayed action fuses that can fire at U.S. airplanes hours or days after they are spread. The effect is to force the United States to search a very wide area to sweep the bomblets in order to use the airfield. Fléchette warheads explode into thousands of small razor blade–like cutters. These can turn airplanes, buildings, or parts of ships in port (radios, sensors, radar) into mincemeat.

Mobile targets are much harder to destroy. These are navy ships, especially aircraft carriers. China's DF-21 missile, the so-called carrier killer, is fired into a general area where a carrier is thought to be located. China has long-distance over-the-horizon radars and satellites to get an approximate fix. Then, using sensors aboard drones, satellites, or ships, a terminal flight correction updates the missile's trajectory so it physically hits the ship. Hitting a ship at such a high speed causes quite a splat. It wouldn't even need a warhead. The kinetic energy, maybe just a titanium slug, would drive a hole through the vessel.

China also has diesel submarines. These are cheaper than nuclear subs, and quieter. This makes them hard to find. An aircraft carrier always travels with surface ships and submarines to protect it. There's already a cat and mouse game in the western Pacific. China tries to hug U.S. carriers in order to get close enough to sink them.

Hugging has already caused collisions and close calls between Chinese submarines and U.S. ships. In 2009, a Chinese submarine got tangled up in the sonar system of the USS *John McCain* near Subic Bay in the Philippines. In another incident that year, a navy intelligence ship used water hoses to douse the Chinese crew aboard a ship harassing it. The two ships were only twenty-five feet apart. If the cold war is any guide, there are likely many more incidents that are not announced by either government.

China also has a new generation of "brilliant" undersea mines with sensors that can track U.S. ships and fire a torpedo. These are like the mines in World War II movies, except that they have an IQ of about 140. And they don't require the ship to physically hit the mine. The torpedo gives the mines a range of many miles. China also has supercavitating torpedoes—rocket-propelled bombs enveloped in a frictionless gas bubble. They cut through the water at over 200 mph. A 5,000-pound torpedo hitting a ship at that speed would have a deadly impact, even without a warhead.

China also has stealth aircraft, anti-satellite weapons, and a highly developed cyberwar program. Some experts think China is among the most advanced in the world in these technologies. At a minimum, the United States needs to anticipate disruption to its command-and-control systems and the destruction of its satellites. China, further, could interfere with America's information infrastructure at home. Wall Street, power grids, phone networks, and local banking operations (like ATM withdrawals) could be disrupted.

Synergy of commercial with military technologies offers China a dynamic new landscape for innovation. China has leapfrogged over a generation of technology to challenge Western multinationals in global markets. It is now a global technology hub. The Chinese have among the most advanced technology research centers in the world. China's technology early on came from Western multinational companies, but China is now doing its own research and development.

What is so impressive is how quickly China has done this. Projects that would take years in the United States take months in China. GE, Motorola, Samsung, Google, IBM, Siemens, and Hitachi have major research and development centers in China because they need to stay up to date on the latest technology, and also to learn how to do things faster, such as bring products to market or adapt them to new conditions.

IBM, for example, has a large effort in China to develop smart grid technology. This is an IT-managed electric grid that senses changes in supply and demand and instantly responds by shifting loads. It is a very fast, agile system, because the switching speeds are so demanding in electricity. To develop this technology in the United States would take years. Regulations, added costs, and the shortage of engineers would slow it down. So IBM moved the project to China.

China shows this behavior in one field after another. Its mobile phone system is one of the most advanced in the world. It shows a mastery of digital network technology. Bullet trains travel at more than 200 mph. Chinese firms are challenging Western companies in global markets.

These technologies are not that different from what's useful in defense. Designing a system to track U.S. ships, feed the data to ballistic and cruise missiles, and update it with drones may not be easy. But it isn't any harder than smart electric power grids, digital phones, or high-speed trains. A country that in a little over a decade is challenging global markets in these sectors isn't likely to overlook their application to defense.

CHINA IS BECOMING MORE AGILE   •

China is rapidly modernizing its military. On this there is little debate. Where there is debate is over the purpose behind this modernization. Various answers are given by different analysts, often leading to abstract debates about China's grand strategy.

A different way of looking at China's military modernization is to recognize that it is undergoing a technological and organizational revolution. The portfolio of new systems and capabilities is wide ranging: stealth aircraft, information warfare, nuclear weapons, quiet submarines, an aircraft carrier, missiles, anti-satellite weapons. The list doesn't stop there. China has a considerable capacity for financial warfare, using its vast dollar holdings, its presence in all major financial markets, and its IT know-how.

The portfolio China is constructing is not yet finalized. There's a great deal of experimentation taking place. But the portfolio as a whole is having an important effect: it is making China's military more agile.

By agility I mean the ability to identify and seize opportunities and to move more quickly than rivals. This nimbleness is reflected in China's mobile missiles, a reactive air and sea response against the U.S. Navy, and information warfare. What all of these have in common is quick action.

Agility is important because the future is unpredictable. China doesn't know whether the United States will be a friend or an enemy. Likewise for Japan. Grand strategy is very hard to plan in an uncertain environment, because strategic conditions may change.

But while strategy can change on a dime, institutions cannot. They require years to develop a capability to take on new tasks. The more uncertain the future security environment is, the greater the premium on agility because it gives China an ability to respond quickly, adapt to change, and innovate to meet new challenges.

The Chinese military and the Chinese security establishment more broadly are getting more responsive, dexterous, and reflexive. The buzzing of U.S. ships and aircraft in the western Pacific, submarines trailing aircraft carriers and tracking them with radars and satellites, and moving missiles around underground tunnels all show it.

Agility can be measured at the platform level: targeting cycle times shrink; the frequency of cyberattacks grows; the amount of information between a missile and a radar increases to provide fine structure features of the target. Faster cruise missiles, submarines, and "invisible" stealth fighters reduce a defender's reaction time. These are the things that a U.S. ship commander worries about.

Agility also appears at a higher organizational level. Departments that were once largely independent of one another or coordinated through slow-moving bureaucratic channels now act in unison. Horizontal coordination is replacing the old vertical silos of China's military. The buzzing of U.S. ships and airplanes involves a horizontal coordination of China's radars, satellites, and drones with its air and naval forces, all working together.

China isn't building a big navy to counter the U.S. Navy. Rather, China is building a very different kind of "anti-navy" navy, designed to keep U.S. air and naval forces out of the western Pacific.

This anti-access system has several important consequences. It changes the conventions of strategic power in East Asia. For decades the U.S. Navy and Air Force could go anywhere in the Pacific they wanted to go. But getting near China now can lead to a counterresponse by Beijing that has to be taken into consideration. If the United States disregards increased Chinese agility, it may quickly find a swarm of intelligence and military forces on its fleet.

The political consequences of this have to be taken into account by Washington. China can raise the risk of an "incident," and of an unwanted escalation. China is important to the United States in so many areas, from handling North Korea to isolating Iran, that worsening relations because of a military incident could have a high cost.

Another way to think about China's enhanced agility is that it provides more rungs, more options, on China's escalation ladder. These added rungs are found at every level of escalation, including those that involve nuclear weapons. The possibilities China has for strategy innovation around these options is considerable.

Suppose the United States sails a carrier group to the western Pacific in a routine move. China puts the force in its electronic crosshairs. It is tracked in a way that lets the United States know that China is following it. Chinese drones come close to a U.S. aircraft carrier. The drone puts a laser on it. Sonar pings from Chinese submarines are picked up at the same time. A 200-mph torpedo zooms by, 3,000 feet on the starboard side. A smart mine registers a pickup and starts activating in a noisy way that is picked up by U.S. intelligence.

Next, Chinese stealth fighters surge from land bases. Mobile missiles start to move. All of this gets picked up by U.S. intelligence, too. The United States cannot ignore this. It can probe and test the Chinese defenses, but it has to acknowledge their existence.

Preparing for a strike on the U.S. fleet may not be what's motivating Chinese actions, at least not at the strategic level. What may be closer to the mark is Henry Kissinger's argument in his recent book *On China*. While Americans play chess, Kissinger says, the Chinese play go (*wei ch'i*). The two games are different. Chess is about maneuvering for a knockout blow. Go is about incremental gains. Small gains gradually accumulate, until one side has a decisive advantage. The United States tends to see recent Chinese moves from the knockout blow perspective. But China may have the more subtle go objective of making incremental gains in the western Pacific. The Chinese anti-access strategy doesn't have to work in the narrow military sense; it doesn't have to blast U.S. ships out of the water. China needs only what can be called a "not implausible threat" to deny access to the United States. This is a much lower performance standard than a knockout blow. China needs only to increase the risk to the United States that something could go wrong. This is much less demanding technologically as well. Although it can't be a complete sham capability, it needs only to shift American estimates of risk upward.

I have run crisis games on this topic. One thing that often happens is that the U.S. team decides that it doesn't want to take big risks just to prove a point about freedom of navigation. Putting the U.S. fleet forward could invite a big response by China. The United States would then face a counterescalation decision. Relations with China are too important to jeopardize with a military confrontation—one that could get out of hand. This escalation dynamic, even at low levels, has great political effect.

Perhaps strategic talks between the two governments could defuse the tensions that are building up. Rules of the road might be agreed upon. However, it is hard to believe that China would go to all the trouble of building this agile anti-access system and then sign away the gains from having it in an arms control agreement. Rules of the road are more likely to be determined by power realities developing in the western Pacific.

China's increased agility shifts risk to the United States. It's the United States that has to decide what geographic line in the Pacific to cross, with what size force. Historically, the Pacific has been an American lake. In the future, it could be a contested zone of rivalry.

CHINA'S NUCLEAR FORCES

China's nuclear forces make escalation of any kind much less attractive for the United States. Suppose in the naval flare-up discussed above, the United States does sharply escalate. It jams China's radars, blinds its satellites, and even shoots down fighters and drones that get too close to navy ships.

But then China goes on a nuclear alert. Its mobile ICBMs are moved. Submarines surge from port. Missiles against Taiwan are cued up. Other forces are mobilized. Everyone would hear the chambering of the round into the atomic shotgun. China could take these actions quickly, nimbly.

Call it *nuclear* agility. The Chinese could argue to themselves, and to the world, that taking these actions is prudent. If China doesn't go on nuclear alert, after all, their smaller nuclear deterrent could be vulnerable to American attack.

The United States, of course, is free to respond with a nuclear alert of its own. But such a U.S. action would badly miss the reality of the situation. China is a new rising power and would be given some leeway because it has a far smaller nuclear force. Going on its own nuclear alert doesn't do anything but cause problems for the United States. In particular, it doesn't reduce vulnerability because U.S. missiles are not vulnerable to begin with. The Chinese can't destroy U.S. ICBMs because they don't have enough weapons to do so. Barring some disastrous U.S. intelligence misestimate of how many missiles the Chinese have (which cannot be totally excluded), the United States going on alert would send a loud message to many countries that the United States was, once again, engaging in nuclear diplomacy. It would reverse years of nonproliferation efforts.

A nuclear crisis with China would be a catastrophe for U.S. antinuclear policies. America's policy of decoupling nuclear weapons from international affairs would go out the window. A nuclear crisis with China would give the lie to this narrative and would demonstrate to the world that these weapons were still very much part of great power interactions. The effect on Russia, India, and Japan would be enormous. They would feel a need to buttress their own nuclear deterrents or, in the case of Japan, reevaluate their whole defense strategy.

China's nuclear agility can turn a conventional crisis into a nuclear one. All Beijing has to do is order a few missile trucks and submarines around and say that it was forced into it by the vastly larger U.S. nuclear arsenal.

CONCLUSIONS

A new landscape of risk is taking shape in East Asia. The United States and China are feeling each other out. While different Chinese grand strategies are debated by American experts, it may be closer to the truth to say that technology, again, is outracing strategy. China's enlarged military portfolio is creating a more agile force, one that can spot what is going on around it, seize opportunities, and nimbly respond to counters. This represents quite a change from historical Chinese experience, which was geared toward absorbing enormous amounts of punishment without giving up.

The strategic impact of China's agility is not so much to tilt the military balance in its direction and away from the United States. Rather, it introduces new risks into the American decision-making calculus. These risks are military, in the example of unwanted naval escalations, and political as well. China could introduce nuclear weapons into a crisis merely by taking precautionary alerting measures. The political impact of this would be extraordinarily negative for the United States, more so than any negative impact it would have for China.

What this dynamic shows is the presence not only of a regional nuclear system in East Asia, but of a global one. Dynamics in East Asia could produce vast reverberations in the rest of the world.

PART THREE

THE WAY FORWARD

· 8 ·

HAVE WE FORGOTTEN TOO MUCH?

On August 29, 2007, the U.S. Air Force flew six nuclear cruise missiles from Minot Air Force Base in North Dakota to Barksdale Air Force Base in Louisiana. Moving a live warhead requires a lot of security. But in this instance the system broke down and the warheads were left unguarded for thirty-six hours. More serious, they weren't detached from the cruise missiles when bolted onto the B-52 for the flight. Separation of warheads from missiles is standard procedure. Flying live hydrogen bombs over U.S. cities is *not* the safest way to move these things. The secretary of the air force and the air force chief of staff were fired over the incident.

The Department of Defense asked former secretary of defense James R. Schlesinger to direct a study about the breakdown of procedures. The Schlesinger Report concluded that, yes, there were breakdowns in the proper handling of the weapons.

But it found a lot more. Nuclear weapons, the report said, were central to the cold war. Every aspect of them was taken seriously. But after the cold war ended, they had become far removed from the Pentagon's concerns. Few officials were paying attention to them any longer. The indifferent attitude filtered from the top all the way down to the field. Schlesinger put the breakdowns in a larger context: few were thinking about nuclear weapons at the top, and so it wasn't surprising that this kind of mistake was made at the bottom.

In the press conference releasing the report, Schlesinger suggested that a course on the basics of nuclear weapons be taught in the Pentagon to a generation of officers and civilians with little knowledge of them.

A STRATEGIC HOLIDAY

That a college primer—Nuclear Strategy 101—is needed in the Pentagon shows just how much attention to nuclear issues has declined. The primer is badly needed. Even the vocabulary and basic distinctions used to describe nuclear weapons is antiquated. How else could Israel, Pakistan, North Korea, and China be described as having "minimum deterrents"? Applying a cold war term to today's entirely different situation misses most of the important consequences of these weapons.

I would go further than Schlesinger. It isn't just the Pentagon that has taken a strategic holiday when it comes to the bomb. The Pentagon doesn't think about nuclear weapons because the country doesn't. The United States as a whole has taken a strategic holiday on all aspects of nuclear weapons. Whether it's deterrence, crisis management, or how others might use them, little thought is paid to anything nuclear.

Indifference would not be so serious if nuclear weapons were disappearing from the world. If the trend was toward their irrelevance, American benign neglect of nuclear issues might help speed it up. But the bomb isn't disappearing; it isn't fading into the background. More countries have the bomb and are modernizing their forces, and the bomb is deepening its grip on the Middle East, South Asia, and East Asia.

I am not calling for a giant shift to make nuclear weapons the centerpiece of American strategy. What I am saying is that the quality of thinking about nuclear weapons has reached a dangerously low level, in Washington and in the country. Unless there is a more meaningful understanding of these matters, the United States will miss obvious things and open itself to grave dangers.

In universities there is little knowledge of nuclear matters beyond a smattering of what's picked up from the news, cartoon distortions by advocacy groups, and television reruns of Hollywood's version of the cold war. Most university courses that include the bomb do so to show the excesses of the cold war. The bomb is an object of ridicule, mocked with lurid video clips of 1950s duck-and-cover civil defense drills and insane cold war plans.

The idea that the bomb played a useful role in the cold war, and that Israel, Pakistan, and North Korea are damn glad they have it today, gets no consideration.

Think tanks have not filled the gap, either. Most think tanks today bear only a faint resemblance to those of the past. Many of my former students now work in them. When I tell them that during the cold war the Rand Corporation had people like Herman Kahn, Albert Wohlstetter, and Daniel Ellsberg on staff—three very different characters—and Thomas Schelling and Henry Kissinger visiting in the summer, they are incredulous. When told that the Hudson Institute for many years kept a pacifist on its staff—to incorporate this perspective into their studies—they are stunned. My former students cannot imagine such a wide-ranging examination of U.S. policy taking place in today's think tanks.

Think tanks today have to fish where the fish are; they have to go where the money is. They have nearly all moved to Washington and they study terrorism, Afghanistan, and nation building. Next year the agenda may change, no doubt, directed by the White House, the Pentagon, and the headlines. But today's think tanks do not step back and look at important but not necessarily urgent issues, the ones there is no felt need to understand at the moment.

Most of all, today's think tanks don't bite the hand that feeds them. Rand was almost shut down by a furious Richard Nixon after the Pentagon Papers leaked. The Hudson Institute had to furlough its staff on several occasions after it criticized government policy. When Lyndon Johnson's Vietnam strategy was critiqued, Hudson immediately saw all of its defense contracts canceled. My former students working in today's think tanks cannot imagine their organizations acting like this.

The way Americans remember the cold war has a lot to do with the national decline in the quality of thinking about nuclear weapons. There is a structural amnesia when it comes to the bomb. What is remembered is a bad memory, associated with anticommunist hysteria and phony missile gaps. No one wants to be tagged with these associations, so there's little incentive to go beyond pious calls for disarmament and nonproliferation.

Some critics argue that current U.S. defense policy is still in the grip of so-called nuclear mandarins, old hawks clinging to outdated ideas. In this view, the mandarins oppose further reductions in U.S. nuclear forces and block arms control treaties.

The reality is exactly the opposite. The nuclear mandarins have long since died off. The overwhelming tone I find in the Pentagon on nuclear issues is near total indifference, just as the Schlesinger Report found. For the few officers who pursue the subject, it's a one-way path to a dead-end career.

The idea that the United States is clinging to nuclear weapons is absurd. The United States now has about five thousand weapons. This is sharply down, by 73 percent, since the end of the cold war. It's down 90 percent from cold war peaks.

The remaining weapons aren't being protected from greater cuts by nuclear mandarins. They're junk in the attic, old stuff built for a different era that should be thrown out. Everyone with any knowledge of the matter knows this. The nuclear force is run by a bureaucracy that doesn't really know what to do with it. What it does know is to guard it, try to avoid incidents, and not ask controversial questions.

No political leader in his right mind would ask this force to do something it hasn't practiced seriously in twenty years. No wonder there are safety lapses in the field. While a revolution in warfare has occurred in conventional forces, this revolution has completely bypassed the nuclear forces. They're strategic orphans, abandoned by indifference and willful avoidance.

Cleaning the junk out of the nuclear attic would lead to questions that no one wants to face. What should U.S. nuclear forces look like? How many should there be? Maybe the answer is 5,000, the current number. Maybe it's zero. Maybe it's 1,146. The United States has forgotten how to have a conversation about the question. More sophisticated questions are far beyond the bounds of current debate. What purposes does the nuclear force serve? How can the United States de-escalate a crisis in the Middle East? How can it communicate with another government in the chaos of a crisis? How might China give information to a third party to tip the strategic balance? These kinds of questions are far beyond the scope of today's discussion of nuclear weapons.

There is one notable exception to this strategic holiday. When it comes to nuclear nonproliferation, there is an army of experts. This topic gets enormous attention. Countless university programs and think tanks are devoted to it. It's okay to talk about ways of stopping the bomb's spread. But mention the word *nuclear* in any phrase that isn't immediately followed by the word *nonproliferation* (or *disarmament*) and the conversation ends. Exploring how other countries might use nuclear weapons is barely recognized in the United States as an imaginable topic of interest, so great is the focus on nonproliferation. The prevailing attitude in the United States is that the bomb is an outdated relic of the cold war and that it has no conceivable uses. The very idea that China, Israel, North Korea, India, or Iran will develop political and military strategies for using the bomb offends this sensibility.

Don't get me wrong, I think nonproliferation is important. I wish everyone would give up nuclear weapons. I wish the problems discussed in this book would disappear. But I wouldn't bet America's security on these things happening anytime soon.

If the world was moving toward eliminating nuclear weapons, there would be nothing wrong with pretending a little bit, exaggerating disarmament's momentum to nudge it along. Just as human rights violations are sometimes overlooked if a country is moving in the right direction, the United States could choose to ignore the bomb. But the only nuclear country on strategic holiday is the United States. Others are thinking long and hard about their nuclear forces, pouring billions into technical and strategic innovations.

The prevailing spirit in the United States appears to be that all it needs to do is keep plugging away at the NPT, get the UN to beef up sanctions on Iran, and cut U.S. nuclear arms further to demonstrate to the world that the bomb has no value. In other words, just keep on doing what America has been doing for twenty years and the problems will magically disappear.

Decisions are being made today with little connection to the nuclear reality in the world. If the United States continues to sleepwalk into the second nuclear age, it can expect one surprise after another. The question is whether this is a case of surprise sprung by an enemy or surprise that arises from our own failures of analysis and anticipation.

WILL "CONSERVATIVE" POLICIES BE ENOUGH IN THE SECOND NUCLEAR AGE?

The United States has followed what can be called conservative policies in the second nuclear age. This doesn't refer to "liberal" versus "conservative" in the usual fashion of American politics. Rather, it means conservative in the sense of using traditional, moderate, cautious policies that are reactive rather than proactive. Conservative policies avoid risk, tend to preserve the status quo, and shun methods that do not conform to international law and custom.

An example is America's handling of North Korea. North Korea tested the bomb, twice, and the United States demanded resumption of the six-party negotiations and imposed economic sanctions. These are perfectly respectable, legal actions. They respect the existence of North Korea and were invoked only after the regime tested its bombs.

The United States is a powerful country and there is a lot to be said for a conservative bias so as not to upset the international system. Conservative U.S. policies, after all, dampened the intensity of the cold war, too. They may have been the single most important reason why it didn't get (too) hot. So there is historical precedent and good reasons today for sticking with moderate policies.

But there are exceptions to these risk-avoiding, traditional policies. The invasion and occupation of Iraq in 2003, on the mistaken belief that Saddam Hussein had WMD, stands out. It surely wasn't a traditional, status quo–preserving action, for it overthrew a government by force. No one would use it as a model for responding to nuclear proliferation, either. That the largest U.S. "nonconservative" response was a foreign policy disaster hardly makes it exemplary for future policy.

Another nonconservative policy is much smaller than invading Iraq, but it may be quite significant. The cyberwar attacks on Iran's uranium enrichment machinery, widely believed to have been engineered by the United States or Israel, were certainly nontraditional. The computer virus attacks were the first-ever information warfare attack to destroy a target.

These two examples may mark a turning point in the way America approaches the second nuclear age. Each can be argued as a good or bad decision in itself, but together they may indicate a broader shift to greater risk taking.

Nearly everyone would prefer that the United States stick with policies that avoid risk, preserve the status quo, and have wide international support. But this may not be possible. The United States may be forced into more hazardous approaches.

In the cold war it took only two to tango, and both superpowers were overwhelmingly conservative when it came to anything nuclear. But the regional nuclear structures discussed in earlier chapters do not show a similar pattern. At any rate, there are enough danger signs in the Middle East, South Asia, and East Asia to raise serious doubts of assuming that conservative policies will prevail in all cases.

U.S. DOMESTIC POLITICS

Conservative policies have a key vulnerability. Domestic politics usually supports them—but only if they work. If regional nuclear crises flare up, or if a security disaster occurs, domestic politics will turn sharply in the other direction.

Nothing succeeds like success. Had the promise of the bomb disappearing from world affairs actually come about, then domestic politics in the United States would overwhelmingly support the centrist, status quo–preserving policies that made it happen.

But if the bomb doesn't disappear, if Israel gets into nuclear trouble, if Pakistan looks like it will spiral into atomic chaos, domestic politics may take a hard turn in favor of riskier U.S. policies. Actions formerly off the table will be back on it. Unthinkable options will get serious attention. And status quo–preserving moves will be abandoned.

One danger of too much nuclear denial, of too much U.S. restraint, is that it invites a sharp political turn if this approach fails. It's about more than Washington interest groups. A security disaster for Israel may cause a tidal wave of domestic reaction in the United States. Domestic politics could force large changes in policy in a very short period of time. The White House, the Congress, and the Pentagon may have to pivot in a hurry, and use much more assertive, risky steps to manage the problem. Coalitions for restraint may disappear overnight. Those who have discounted nuclear dangers may be discredited. The whole atmosphere will be politicized because the public won't understand how years of reassurances and calls for nuclear nonproliferation have led to such a disaster.

Recall the atmosphere after 9/11. There was a sharp turn in direction afterward. The 9/11 attacks showed that there were bad people out there, out to kill Americans, who needed to be stopped.

Now, add a nuclear context. Israel goes through a shattering nuclear crisis. Pakistan and India go to the brink. North Korea lashes out as the Kim regime totters. The American public's attitude will make 9/11 look like a polite disagreement on a Sunday morning talk show.

Yet there's a big difference between 9/11 and a nuclear disaster. A nuclear crisis isn't as time permissive. After 9/11 there were months available to think through the response. A nuclear catastrophe may require immediate decisions, especially if the enemy has a stock of unfired weapons. There may be little time for study committees. If prompt action isn't taken, the scale of catastrophe could climb to disastrous levels.

In the heat of public fury and fear, officials may pursue irresponsible moves that have not been adequately thought through. Reckless escalation—to show that something is being done—is possible. If three million lives are lost, the response will be much greater than if three thousand were, the approximate number killed on 9/11.

Whatever the international repercussions of a nuclear crisis, the domestic political reaction in the United States is likely to be of equal importance. If it looks like the United States is the next target, that a major ally has been threatened, or that an American nuclear guarantee isn't worth the paper it's printed on, the public will ask how and why this was allowed to come about.

Managing the second nuclear age will require great skill. But saying this actually says very little, since few people will argue against skill-ful management. What can be said is that the United States has for-gotten too much about nuclear weapons, and that there is a great deal of catching up to do. This is especially true when it comes to looking at how other countries could use them.

In addition, we need to think about nonconservative policies. New strategies that do not accept the status quo need to be analyzed, not banned from the discussion. U.S. strategies that are currently off the table should be articulated and seriously examined because the strategic environment may change. The present era is only the first bounce of the ball, as secondary nuclear powers get the bomb and stock up on missiles and related technologies. The second bounce of the ball could look quite different. Managing crises and wars and redesigning arms control at global and regional levels constitute the next set of challenges.

9

GLOBAL DYNAMICS

The regional nuclear dynamics of the Middle East, South Asia, and East Asia are part of a larger order that is now forming, a global nuclear system. It is not global in the sense that every nation wants atomic weapons, but rather in the sense of it being large scale with identifiable, interacting parts. Its large scale comes from cross-regional interactions and from the dynamics of the major nuclear powers with one another. The scale of this global system is so great and so complicated that it is necessary to break it down for conceptual purposes.

The large number of nuclear decision-making centers is quite different from the first nuclear age. Major powers with nuclear forces, secondary powers with nuclear forces, nonnuclear countries who try to go nuclear, and subnational groups are all strategically interlinked. The actors in this global system are connected through an interplay of conflict, cooperation, manipulation, collusion, and compromise. In practical terms, this means that managing the global nuclear order as if it were a series of independent nonproliferation problems is no longer workable. The NPT was devised for the world of the 1960s and 1970s, when technology and know-how were scarce, and where the two superpowers agreed to keep nuclear weapons out of their regional rivalries. New frameworks are needed for the second nuclear age, frameworks that put more emphasis on dynamics and instability, going beyond statics and containment, which lie at the heart of the NPT regime.

GLOBAL DYNAMICS

Not all of the dynamics and instabilities of this global system can be identified because they are still forming. Many surprises are in store, no doubt. It's like a brand-new casino that has just opened, where the glitches in the system haven't been worked out.

But some dynamics are apparent. Cross-regional linkages are increasing because of the transfer of sensitive technology and intelligence sharing. North Korea supplies Pakistan with data on its missile tests. India and Israel share satellite intelligence. China provides Pakistan with a nuclear weapon design.

Another dynamic is that the new military forces are too large to confine to a single region. They may be intended for regional security, but their impact stretches far beyond it. Nuclear weapons, missiles, submarines, and surveillance systems have a geographic reach that is much larger than the old military formations. Iran's missiles can reach targets in Europe, not just in Israel. Military programs in South Asia spill over to affect China, as Indian missiles are seen as threatening Beijing and, more broadly, as Indian technology takes on Asian-wide strategic significance. India is moving to a nuclear triad of airplanes, missiles, and submarines and may MIRV its long-range missiles. This clearly spills outside of the South Asia region.

Major powers play a dual role in this global nuclear system. They have to deal with one another on nuclear matters and manage the regions at the same time. Surprisingly little thought has been given to the mutual interactions among the major powers. This is partly due to the habit of conceiving nuclear strategy, arms control, and crisis management as a two-player problem. It is no longer a two-player problem, and most of the classic arms control approaches of the first nuclear age need to be redesigned for a multipolar world.

The greatest risk of nuclear escalation lies in the regions—the Middle East, South Asia, and East Asia. Instability in the cold war came from the superpower competition in the regions, but there were always sharp limits on nuclear interactions. The Cuban missile crisis was the exception that proved the rule.

The second nuclear age is in many ways the mirror image of the first in this regard. The greatest nuclear instability is in the regions, and there are limits on major-power nuclear interactions.

The first nuclear age can be thought of as a giant roulette wheel. It was spun many times throughout the cold war and sometimes the ball landed on a "crisis" between the Soviet Union and the United States. Usually it did not.

The casino of the second nuclear age has a different layout. There are three roulette wheels: for the Middle East, South Asia, and East Asia. These wheels are where the greatest risks of nuclear escalation are. Should a bad number come up, it's likely to be at one of these roulette tables. A local dealer, a person from one of the regions, spins the wheel. A crisis in North Korea may come. Or one in the Middle East. Maybe there's really bad luck, and crises in each come up at the same time.

Some analysts have argued that the greatest risk is in the Middle East, or that it is in South Asia or East Asia. But no one really knows, and in any case, the more important issue is that the house, the major powers, has lost control of the game compared to the first nuclear age. Their onetime monopoly on nuclear weapons is gone.

The casino of the second nuclear age has yet another roulette wheel that influences the odds of the three regional tables, even if it doesn't control them. This major-power roulette wheel requires high stakes to play. Russia, China, India, and the United States have large

GDPs and nuclear forces. Britain and France are allowed into this game through a sponsor's exemption because they were the victors in World War II. Major powers play to lower the odds of a bad number coming up among themselves. But they also try to gain from their place at the high roller table. As in any casino, there are show-offs and strategic calculators, each trying to make a statement and win what he can. Broadly speaking, however, there is a house rule that appears to apply to the high-roller table: to bet with your head, not over it. So the high-roller table doesn't see extreme nuclear risk taking. However, this could change, and in addition there could be very different assessments of what actually constitutes a high risk because the players are so different from one another.

The major powers also have to consider their dual roles. Each is influenced by a mixture of narrow self-interest and an appreciation that they have other responsibilities, especially in the regions. One complexity is that some of the major powers play roulette at more than one wheel. This is why it is difficult to predict the odds of what will happen. India plays at the South Asia regional wheel and at the high-roller wheel. China plays in East Asia, South Asia, and may play in the Middle East. The United States has interests in all of the roulette wheels.

There are many examples of these dual roles. Should Russia sell an enrichment plant to Iran, or will that make the Middle East too unstable? Should the United States sign a nuclear reactor deal with India, or will that undermine the NPT and stimulate Pakistan to greater nuclear weapons production? Should China give more atomic bomb technology to Pakistan, or will that destabilize South Asia?

The rules for playing dual roles are only beginning to be worked out. Many of the problems and inconsistencies have yet to be discovered. This casino has just opened, and many of its rules are not yet even written down—yet alone agreed upon by the players. Unlike the first nuclear age, the house itself is weaker in dictating and enforcing the rules because the major power monopoly on the bomb has broken down. Without clear rules to govern behavior, strategy, and limits on the size of bets, the stability of the house is open to question. Stability is understood as a situation where the casino operates and enforces the rules at all of its roulette wheels, and nothing too disastrous happens if a bad number comes up. It means that the house can endure a run of bad luck without breaking the bank.

Yet without accepted casino rules, no one can say for sure if the house is really stable. It might go out of business. Then regional betting could become totally unregulated, and even the high-roller wheel could see much riskier bets.

There are two big worries about this casino. One is that it is so new. The wheels have spun only a few times, so far. There isn't a lot of experience. If this casino operates long enough, the rules and the odds will be better understood, as they were in the first nuclear age. But to reach this point the roulette wheels will have to be spun many, many times. Most people find this to be a chilling possibility.

The other problem is that this isn't an ordinary roulette wheel. It is nuclear roulette. Someone may bet over his head and bring down the house. It doesn't take a long streak of bad luck to break the house as it would in a normal casino. A single spin can do it.

THE MAJOR NUCLEAR POWERS

The major powers with nuclear weapons—the United States, Russia, Britain, France, China, and India—haven't given them up, and there's little sign that they will. The theory behind the NPT was that the major powers would give up nuclear weapons at some point in the future. Not only has the bomb spread to secondary powers, but not a single major power has given it up, and, in addition, India has joined the nuclear club.

The global system that developed after the cold war is, to a great extent, a multipolar *nuclear* system. Having nuclear arms helps define a country as a major power. Looking back, it would be surprising if this had not developed. Any major power that gave up the bomb would decline in its relative standing. The notion that Russia or China would disarm after the end of the cold war was never a serious possibility. That India would want the bomb so that it wasn't kept out of the club of major powers is also hardly surprising.

The evolution of a multipolar nuclear order is quite natural. China used the bomb in the 1960s to break with the Soviet Union and, later, to achieve a degree of parity with the United States. India did, too, in the early 2000s. For India, negotiating with the United States on nuclear power and stability in South Asia required that it come in as an equal. This meant having the bomb. India wouldn't be much of a counter to China if it didn't have it. Today, India has become virtually a legitimate nuclear weapon state, whatever the NPT fiction says.

There's a clear difference in power between major and secondary powers in this order. If a major power such as Brazil or Japan wanted to go nuclear, there is nothing to stop it. In contrast, there are secondary powers that have wanted the bomb but haven't gotten it. South Korea and Taiwan tried, but the United States stopped them. Even South Africa, which had it, gave it up, though it was never a major power. The pressure to keep the bomb from Iran is enormous.

The dynamics among the major nuclear powers show several clear trends.

MAD Is Out

One of the most important trends is that nuclear weapons are not at the center of relations among major powers as they were during the cold war. Unlike the first nuclear age, the second does not make nuclear arms the bedrock of security for the major powers. This is good news for the world. The doctrine of "mutually assured destruction" (MAD)—the threat to destroy another's state and society—is completely out of fashion.

That MAD is out shows that major power relations are a lot better than in the first nuclear age. Since these are the most powerful countries in the world, this is good news.

Major powers are not building insane numbers of nuclear weapons, as they did during the cold war. The term *MAD* was coined by my former colleague Don Brennan at the Hudson Institute, and he meant it as a disparaging description of cold war U.S. strategy. MAD meant tens of thousands of nuclear weapons pointed at the Soviet Union. This fantastic number of bombs was considered a strategic end in itself, beyond any military utility. *Overkill* was the term used. The argument was that perceptions of nuclear striking power mattered. If the Soviets had appreciably more weapons than the United States, this numerical fact would weaken deterrence. Brennan called this thinking "MAD," which it was.

Look at the nuclear arms of the major powers. They have been sharply reduced, with huge cuts in the nuclear production infrastructure as well. In the United States, the specialized laboratories for nuclear weapons, Los Alamos and Livermore, now devote far more attention to environmental problems than to nuclear war. Russia's vast nuclear infrastructure has been dismantled, but this has created other problems, including former Soviet engineers selling their knowledge to Iran and North Korea. China is the most secretive of the major nuclear powers, and we don't have entirely good estimates of what is going on behind the scenes, or in the vast underground tunnels that have been built.

Most experts today can't immediately recall the number of bombs Russia has, or even how many the United States has. As to what current U.S. nuclear strategy toward Russia is, what replaces MAD, no one seems to know or care. It just doesn't appear to matter.

This is a fundamental change in how the major powers think about nuclear weapons.

The Higher Regions of Escalation May Be Blocked Off

Nuclear war between major powers has sharply declined in probability in the second nuclear age. The upper regions of the escalation ladder: limited nuclear attacks, controlled strikes, destruction of national command and control—the stuff of the cold war—are probably blocked off as well. Now that all the major nuclear powers have secured second-strike forces, the major powers have too much to lose by pursuing any of these goals. And, unlike the cold war, there is no big ideological struggle that is worth going to nuclear war over.

But it would go too far to conclude from this that nuclear war is impossible, or that nuclear weapons are drifting into irrelevance. As long as these weapons exist, they may be used. And, rather than fading from international relations, nuclear weapons have returned even among the major powers.

What is happening is that the nuclear dynamics among the major powers have shifted to lower levels of intensity. The top of the escalation ladder may offer options that are effectively sealed off for political and strategic reasons, but the lower and medium levels are by no means precluded. These lower levels need much more attention.

The locus of nuclear rivalry is shifting downward and so the threat to reintroduce nuclear weapons back into strategy is becoming more potent. There are many examples of this. In April 2007, President Vladimir Putin of Russia suspended his country's participation in the Conventional Forces in Europe Agreement, a cold war arms control treaty. He was angry at U.S. plans to establish missile defense bases in the Czech Republic and in Poland. Putin warned that an American deployment would reignite the arms race and he made references to the Cuban missile crisis.

The effect of Putin's threat was jarring. Support for the American missile defense effort declined, and later it was canceled altogether in 2010 by President Barack Obama.

Or consider China's 2007 anti-satellite test. The purpose of anti-

---

FIGURE 9.1

WAYS MAJOR POWERS COULD "USE" NUCLEAR WEAPONS

- Use cold war metaphors—"the United States is taking the world to a new Cuban missile crisis" [Russia, China]
- Express fear of upsetting "strategic stability" [Russia, China]
- Break an arms control agreement [Russia]
- Have a military officer make "unauthorized" provocative statements about using nuclear weapons [Russia, China]
- Have a cavalier attitude to selling nuclear technologies [China]
- Test an anti-satellite weapon [China]
- Have a white paper come up with the impolitic conclusion that nuclear weapons have a role in defense—and not just for deterrence [China, Russia]
- Suspend or revoke a previously declared pledge, for example, suspend "no first use" of nuclear weapons [Russia]
- Sail a ship or airplane presumed to carry nuclear weapons to an ally's base to underscore extended deterrence
- Go on a "partial" nuclear alert. Say that it was precautionary, compelled by the other side's dangerous actions
- Provocative tests: MIRVs, SLBM launches, airborne bomber alerts
- Test fire a hydrogen bomb

---

satellite weapons is to blind command and control. No doubt this was part of the reason for testing it, to see if it worked. But it also introduced a jolting note into U.S.-China relations, overshadowing talk about trade deals, currency values, and the problem of North

Korea. China was a major power and wanted to remind the United States that it was also a nuclear power.

Take another possibility. If India were to test a MIRV warhead for its long-range missiles, the ones that can reach targets in China, it would heighten global concerns that an arms race between two major powers was increasing. India would get considerable attention. There would be summit meetings with the United States and Russia, and perhaps with China attending. India's stature would rise even further above the region, outflanking Pakistan's efforts to promote its agenda.

There are many ways to use nuclear weapons at the lower and medium levels in the second nuclear age, as suggested in Figure 9.1. The figure lists those countries, in brackets, that have already undertaken the item listed.

The Chinese have used many items on the list. Their generals have said all kinds of things about the utility of nuclear weapons. China selling sensitive nuclear technology to Pakistan brings the bomb back to the stage, too, creating all kinds of problems for the United States.

The cumulative effect of actions that bring the bomb back in to international relations is to make the United States walk on eggshells. If the United States appears to be so averse to anything associated with nuclear weapons, then other countries will use this sensitivity whenever they need a counter to American pressure.

World War III?

Some commentators worry that World War III will erupt as a result of nuclear escalation in one of the regions. They draw on historical analogies, such as the Cuban missile crisis in 1962 or Sarajevo in 1914, to argue that a nuclear war could spread.

But a World War III arising out of the regions isn't very plausible. The major powers have different regional interests, certainly, but they are not so great as to lead to a nuclear war. Significant firebreaks exist between supporting a regional ally, on the one hand, and containing a regional war, on the other.

China isn't likely to give a nuclear blank check to Pakistan. Nor is Russia going to give one to Iran. China may back Pakistan; it may transfer strategic information about an Indian or U.S. alert. But go to nuclear war on Pakistan's behalf? That's an altogether different matter.

The problem, actually, lies in the other direction. Regional powers worry that they won't get backing from a major power. Taiwan, Israel, North Korea, and Pakistan worry that their struggles don't have the global significance that the Cuban missile crisis or Sarajevo did. They aren't "powder kegs," tinderboxes with explosive potential to drag the world into a terrible conflict. If they were, major powers would be sure to intervene on their behalf.

The nightmare of secondary powers is that if the regional powder keg blows up, the damage will be almost entirely inflicted on them. They fear that the major powers will provide rhetorical and moral support and not much else. Indeed, much of their nuclear strategy is less about blowing up enemy targets than it is about manipulating a major power to come in on their behalf.

Security disasters in the regions could arise from the empty or unwitting guarantees of major powers, assurances they have little intention of actually fulfilling. Major powers often have not thought through the responsibilities—and the obligations—they create with such pronouncements.

Accidental Nuclear War

Among the major powers the chance of an accidental nuclear war is vanishingly small. For some reason, a widespread view exists that even though the cold war is over, the United States and Russia keep thousands of nuclear weapons on hair-trigger alert, ready to launch at a moment's notice. If a computer chip fails, or a wayward weather rocket goes off course, Armageddon will follow.

This is nonsense. The problem is the opposite. These forces are almost never practiced in anything resembling realistic conditions. They are considered by the military as totally unusable for political and military reasons—so much so that they wish they didn't have to pay to guard them.

Ask yourself the following question. Would you design a system that gave launch authority to start a nuclear holocaust to a colonel, on the basis of the Pentagon's computers? These are computers supplied by the low-cost bid of a defense contractor. How about Russia's computers?

One of the controversies in the Iraq and Afghanistan wars has been the excessively strict rules of engagement put on U.S. forces. They follow more stringent rules than exist in many U.S. police departments. Yet the argument is made that their comrades back home can fire nuclear weapons based on a computer readout.

No one is that crazy. No president, in the United States or in Russia, is going to relinquish civilian control of the military on the most important issue of war and peace.

Forget about the hair trigger. I would describe the current U.S. command-and-control system for nuclear weapons in the following way. The wires connecting the "buttons" to the forces were cut after the end of the cold war. I'm speaking figuratively, obviously. The military completely accepts this. The connections would have to be restored, and practiced, to get a force that could fire.

In 2001 NORAD couldn't send up a single armed airplane to shoot down the 9/11 hijackers. That should give insight into the way complex organizations respond to unanticipated threats. If someone did order STRATCOM—the U.S. nuclear command—to launch the bomb, there would be disbelief on the other end of the telephone line, not robots responding automatically.

I believe the same holds true in Russia. Launching nuclear weapons on the basis of a radar blip is not something cynical Russian leaders are going to allow. They know better than anyone the unreliability of their people and their systems.

There's no need to keep forces on a hair trigger now. The United States or Russia could respond to an attack however they chose six days later, or six months later. The forces are not vulnerable to a knockout blow anymore.

The cold war was different, yes, but that was a long time ago. Emergency procedures for military action have all been revoked, and a generation of senior officers who have never experienced a nuclear crisis are now in charge.

There are great dangers of accidental war in Israel, Pakistan, and North Korea. But the hair-trigger myth for the United States needs to be put to rest. Saying to the world that the United States is on a nuclear hair trigger—when it couldn't be further from the truth—may reinforce the view that America is set to unleash nuclear hell at any moment. This is not a good image to project to the world.

Britain and France as Nuclear Powers

Britain and France have figured only slightly in the discussion so far. But they raise important questions of power and status—and both have nuclear weapons.

Both nations have dismantled much of their conventional military since 2000. The degree to which this has happened has been masked by focusing on defense as a share of GDP. The United States now spends about 4.5 percent of its GDP on defense. The NATO average is below 2 percent. But European expenditures are mainly used to prop up employment in their bloated aerospace and defense industries. They maintain huge research and development bureaucracies as a public works program.

Nuclear weapons are one of the few remaining symbols of hard power that Britain and France have. Giving them up would have significant implications not only for them but for the United States as well. It would drop the final curtain on the "1945 system" of an American-led order of the victors of World War II. Were Britain and France to give up the bomb, a sense of the passing of a European order would be further reinforced. America is very much part of that order.

But Britain and France have not only kept their nuclear deterrents, they have modernized them, even as they have dismantled their conventional forces. Britain keeps at least one nuclear-weapons submarine at sea at all times. France appears to have built an EMP warhead, a bomb whose radiation can knock out power grids and communications systems. These nuclear forces are very costly to build and maintain. Yet each country has been willing to shrink its army, navy, and air force while modernizing its nuclear weapons.

There are political reasons for this. The British and French want to hold on to their status as permanent members of the UN Security Council. If their military condition were fully understood, the idea that Britain and France should keep these seats, and their veto power, while India was excluded, would look even more absurd than it already does. That either country should be on the Security Council at all, while India, Brazil, Germany, and Japan are not, makes little sense in the twenty-first century. But nuclear weapons allow this charade to go on.

Britain, politically speaking, would hardly like to have France as the only nuclear power in Europe. Likewise for France, if the situation were reversed. Nuclear weapons thus give Britain and France more than they deserve in the UN, in Europe, and in the world. Once more, when critics say that nuclear weapons have no value, they fail to see that they are entwined with very important issues of status and power.

The British and French nuclear forces also raise issues about global power arrangements that the United States doesn't wish to see raised. For the United States, having Western European democracies on the UN Security Council is important. It counters China and Russia and makes it appear as if that body is the summit of world power. That this body also makes up the legitimate nuclear-weapons states under the NPT adds to the image.

Suppose India and Brazil joined the Security Council as permanent members with veto authority, replacing Britain and France. This would acknowledge a post-1945 international order. At the moment, Brazil does not appear to be seeking nuclear weapons. But it might make Brazil ask the logical question of why it is the only nonnuclear-weapons state in the group.

Moreover, the United States doesn't want to be the only democracy with the bomb. This would be the case if Britain and France gave up their deterrents. Yes, I know that India and Israel are democracies. But the two cases only prove my point. Would India and Israel substitute as nuclear allies for the United States in the same way as Britain and France? I don't think so, to say the least.

Japan

Japan raises deep questions about the emerging nuclear multipolar order. How long will the United States provide for Japan's defense? Can the current nuclear multipolar system accept a new member, a nuclear Japan?

For more than sixty years the United States has defended Japan. Japan pays for a good part of this. One reason behind this arrangement is that a nuclear Japan would be seen across Asia as destabilizing. It would remind Asians of Japan's barbaric behavior in the first half of the twentieth century.

China, in particular, has on many occasions urged the United States to stay in Japan, in order to stabilize the region. At least, this has been the line coming out of Beijing for the past thirty years.

But there are some significant changes under way that affect these arguments. One is China's buildup. At one time it was cheap for the United States to defend Japan. Neither China nor North Korea could reach across the water to attack Japan. This is no longer the case.

China's military modernization is going to make defending Japan a much more expensive proposition because the United States now has to counter a much more technologically advanced threat. As China grows militarily, the economic defense burden on the United States will become far larger than it is today. All the more so as China's modernization incorporates new nuclear capabilities, while the United States bans thinking about nuclear weapons in any of its responses.

Yet many American experts continue to argue that it is essential for the United States to play this role. Otherwise, they say, it's destabilizing.

World War II happened a long time ago, under a Japanese leadership that bears no resemblance to that in today's Japan. If Japan does decide to go nuclear, it would not automatically produce the dire results that many experts still cling to as an article of faith.

The United States would prefer that no new nations acquire nuclear weapons. But, given that the bomb has spread, some outcomes are worse than others. Many people assume that the spread of the bomb automatically leads to bad outcomes. Yet this is only true, strictly speaking, if the criterion used is nuclear nonproliferation. Other criteria would give a different result.

A nuclear China in the 1970s and 1980s was a good counter to the Soviet Union. A nuclear India, today, counters China. The purpose of security policy cannot only be to reduce the number of states with nuclear weapons. It should also be to make the world a safer place. The two goals are not necessarily the same, because some nuclear proliferation can be stabilizing.

Japan getting its own deterrent could be a stabilizing development. It would reduce the security burden falling on the United States and it would surround China with three nuclear powers, Russia, India, and Japan. What makes little sense is for the United States to promise the conventional protection of Japan in the face of China's across-the-board military buildup, which includes nuclear modernization.

If the United States can accept a nuclear China and a nuclear India, it can accept a nuclear Japan. A nuclear Japan that is conservative (in the sense of the term used earlier) and democratic could be a stabilizing force in the world. It is more likely to resemble Britain or France rather than Russia or China. Both Britain and France practice restraint on anything to do with nuclear arms.

A nuclear Japan would probably want a deterrent with a low political profile, as Britain and France have. Such a force likely would be sea-based. A submarine-based force gets nuclear weapons off the Japanese mainland. Japan could have continuous submarine patrols, a force that is "always on," so to speak—the rationale behind the British and French forces. This contrasts with surged/alerted nuclear postures, on mobile missiles, as China is building.

Any multipolar system has to allow for the possibility of new members. A nuclear multipolar system is no different. As new major powers arise, they may want the bomb—witness the rise of China and India. Trying to keep new members out of the major power circle didn't work in the case of China or India, and it isn't likely to work in the future either. Trying to restrict membership using a forty-year-old arms control treaty, the NPT, is even less likely to work.

In the particular case of Japan, treating its acquisition of nuclear weapons in apocalyptic terms, as if it means a massive rupture to the NPT regime or that it signals the return of a nuclear Tojo set to launch wars in Asia, is foolish. Any decision about going nuclear, clearly, is up to Japan. But hanging on to perspectives based on World War II and the cold war hardly shows an understanding of the emerging nuclear multipolar order that is taking shape.

Realignments

New entrants to the multipolar system of major powers is one possibility in the second nuclear age. Another is a realignment of the countries who are already in it. The defining feature of multiplayer games is coalitions, as different countries align with one another. It would be surprising if these coalitions were static. If history is any guide, they are more likely to be dynamic, to change over time.

Consider the United States and China. There have been repeated shifts in their alignment over the years. In the 1930s and 1940s, the United States sided with China against Japan. After World War II, the United States shifted when Mao Zedong took power. It sided with Japan against China in the cold war. In the 1970s and 1980s, the United States pivoted again. China sided with the United States against the Soviet Union. Next, after the collapse of the Soviet Union and the end of the cold war, there was another realignment, with the United States and Japan opposing China.

Over a period of eighty years, there have been four U.S. pivots in relations with China. Nuclear weapons played a significant role in all of the changes after 1945. The bomb wasn't the only reason for the change, but it surely influenced the calculations of the various parties.

China isn't the only example. In 1971, the United States tilted against India and toward Pakistan. The alliance between India and the Soviet Union and a war with Pakistan were responsible for this. U.S. opposition to India increased with its nuclear tests in 1998. Yet, by 2006, the United States had sided with India, to balance China. Nuclear matters played a key role here, too. Sanctions on India for its nuclear tests were lifted, U.S. nuclear reactors were sold to India, and joint military exercises were conducted between the two nations.

It isn't hard to imagine many possibilities for new realignments in the second nuclear age. Nuclear weapons will play a role, no doubt, because so many of the major powers have the bomb. There is a dramatic aspect to these weapons: they get the highest of attention from world leaders and the media. If the United States had sold an old destroyer to India in 2006, nobody would care. But sell a nuclear reactor to India and it gets global attention.

Forecasting realignments and coalitions is difficult. Perhaps the

United States and China will join forces again to tackle problems that neither can manage alone. Perhaps the United States and India will have a falling out. Perhaps Russia will become a friend of the United States as it was during World War II. These illustrations of potential realignment may be dismissed at the moment. But the history of multipolar systems is that the coalitions in them change periodically. Nuclear weapons could play a big role in the currency underwriting these realignments and for this reason make it even less likely that major powers will give up the bomb.

IMPLICATIONS

The big dangers in the second nuclear age are in the regions. But they are not the only places to worry about. The major powers will have a great deal to do with whether developments in the regions get better or worse. If they do not act cooperatively, it will be virtually impossible to sanction and isolate any country, such as Iran.

Moreover, relations among the major powers may not stay as pacific as they currently seem. If the major powers get drawn into regional conflicts, backing their local allies, it could mark a dangerous turn. Regional rivalries, unlike in the first nuclear age, will now have a strong nuclear element in them wherein the major powers don't control the atomic trigger. China and India are regional powers as well as major powers. China has serious disagreements with the United States, and, if these escalate, cooperation in other regions may suffer.

Russia, China, and India are modernizing their strategic forces, and this should give the United States pause on several fronts. These nations aren't buying the American argument that nuclear weapons have little value in the twenty-first century. Nuclear modernization provides Russia, China, and India with many more escalation options. Nuclear head games seem likely to be a big part of the second

nuclear age. Even low-intensity nuclear dynamics will have a disproportionate negative impact on the United States because it is the
leader of global antinuclear policies. This U.S. desire for a nonnuclear world gives America's opponents a reason to manipulate developments in the other direction, to show their independence, and to
shift competition to areas where they feel they have greater advantage.

10

A FIFTY-YEAR PROBLEM

The challenge of the second nuclear age is to manage an international order where rivalries increasingly take place in a nuclear context. This requires that reasonable goals be established as to the direction we would like the system to move toward, and it requires creative ways to manage the dangers along the way. Reasonable goals don't demand vast changes in human nature or international relations in a short period of time.

Parallels with the early years of the first nuclear age are instructive. In the late 1940s, there were calls for giving control of the bomb to the United Nations. Many critics argued that catastrophe would follow if this didn't happen. But the UN didn't get control of the bomb and no catastrophe occurred. There were many shocks in the cold war. But these shocks were managed in a way that did not lead to nuclear war or to a strategic disaster.

Nuclear shocks will occur in the second nuclear age, too. Unless these are skillfully managed, longer-term goals, however desirable, may not matter all that much. A perspective that combines long-term goals with better management along the way is absolutely crucial.

Herman Kahn pointed out that considering the cold war as "a fifty-year problem" provided badly needed perspective. Urgent problems of the moment looked different in a longer time frame. The immediate U.S. challenge in the cold war was to contain the Soviets. But over a fifty-year period that wasn't the general problem. A more fundamental consideration was to uphold U.S. values and not overstimulate the arms race to dangerous levels that could undermine the international order it was supposed to defend.

The challenge of the second nuclear age is to manage rivalries, now in a nuclear context, so that they don't get out of control, but also in a way that doesn't overload the regional and global systems with crises and arms races that they cannot absorb.

CURRENT POLICIES

It's surprising how few ideas are posited for managing the second nuclear age along these lines. The following list describes policies that either now exist or are most often proposed.

- *Preserve and tighten the NPT regime*, even in the face of violations and low morale among its supporters. While the NPT system has failings, it does isolate Iran, North Korea, and others. Most important, the NPT regime already exists, so it doesn't require new, creative thinking or new, difficult negotiations.
- *Containment.* If the status quo has to change (Iran tests a bomb), limit the scope of the changes by isolating the offending country from the international system.
- *Rollback.* Use sanctions, threats, and force (including preemption) to turn the clock back to a nonproliferated world.
- *Global zero.* Call for worldwide abolition of the bomb, but without specifying how or when this comes about. Political rhetoric is used to handle all problems.

Official U.S. policy is to preserve and tighten the NPT. At the same time, the policy seems to be gradually morphing into containment. The United States accepts in fact, if not in principle, that Pakistan, North Korea, and India have the bomb. Actually, in the case of India, there is a virtual acceptance of it as a legitimate nuclear power. Demands that India give up the bomb and sign the NPT haven't been heard in years.

In this respect, U.S. policy bears a resemblance to the cold war fiction that there were only two nuclear powers. Sticking with the NPT as the centerpiece of policy provides a story to use at international meetings and arms control conferences, and it placates certain activist groups.

There is considerable support for the NPT regime in government bureaucracies, the United States most of all, because it doesn't require creative or conceptual skills. The most useful feature of the NPT is that it already exists. The focus of government agencies can be devoted to the details of its implementation.

Negotiating a new NPT from scratch would be impossible as a practical matter. Just think what it would be like to negotiate a new treaty that allowed Israel or India in as nuclear-weapons states. It is much better to use the treaty that exists, even with its flaws.

If the NPT were wholly successful, there would be little need for other strategies, such as containment. Containment accepts that violators exist and provides ways to limit the harm they cause. North Korea's trade is monitored and, if appropriate, interdicted. Iran is sanctioned. Pakistan is handled diplomatically. Containment says that even if a country goes nuclear, it can be isolated from infecting others and it can be stopped from using its atomic weapons through deterrence.

Rollback is an altogether different strategy. It is a highly nonconservative approach with a shift from the current status quo, more risk taking, and more convention breaking.

The U.S. invasion of Iraq in 2003 was an example of rollback. The purpose of the war was to remove Saddam Hussein's WMD, and to use success in Iraq as a basis to challenge Iran. But, as Iraq didn't possess WMD, rollback has come to be seen as dangerous and counterproductive. However, this may change. In the event of some nuclear shock or disaster, rollback could again be taken seriously.

Global zero is a movement to use popular opposition to nuclear weapons to advance the cause of disarmament. Its ideas have received the support of many former senior U.S. officials, including Henry Kissinger, George Shultz, Sam Nunn, and Bill Perry. The focus is on the horrors of nuclear war. Sweeping changes to the international system are proposed, but how these are to come about is given scant consideration. Here, the problems of the second nuclear age are subordinated to political rhetoric.

Many people believe that the actual American policy is what might be called "soft acceptance." Nuclear proliferation is condemned, sanctioned, and denounced. Low-level risks are taken to stop it. A North Korean ship suspected of carrying missile parts might be turned back to port, for example. But, at bottom, such actions are taken more to convince the world, and perhaps to convince Americans, that the United States is taking vigorous action. Preventive actions are taken—but only up to a point.

Another significant feature of these policies is that all of them require the United States to do the heavy lifting. Other countries are asked for little more than their endorsement. Without the United States backing them, all of the policies would disappear in six months' time. The obligations, and risks, fall on America.

There exists one more policy, but it's one that almost no one supports, so it isn't included on the list. The United States could rely more on nuclear weapons. In the first nuclear age, U.S. nuclear weapons allowed for not having to build expensive conventional forces. But the United States won't get away on the cheap in the second nuclear age. Adding fifty ICBMs will have little positive effect on

Iran, China, North Korea, or Pakistan. If the goal were to destroy those countries, America already has plenty enough to do that. The U.S. strategic problem is different now, and it can't be solved with more nuclear weapons.

MANAGING THE SECOND NUCLEAR AGE

If the United States doesn't have a framework to manage the second nuclear age, the second nuclear age is going to manage the United States. Short-term pressures and crises will determine policy, rather than the other way around. Alternatives won't be clearly defined. More facts will be collected—about Iran's centrifuges, Pakistan's plutonium, and China's missiles—but there will be little comprehension of what these facts mean.

What's needed is a framework that offers more perspective and that uses strategic concepts to cut the job down to size. But such a framework is hard to devise. It is premature, yet at the same time overdue. We just don't know enough about the dynamics of the second nuclear age to say exactly how it should be managed. Yet it is overdue because the problems are increasing and a new global nuclear order is taking shape.

We cannot wait for a full-blown framework that will interpret events for us. But some pieces of that framework can be discerned. Each item discussed here makes important distinctions, and describes a dynamic, that is likely to be important in any fully worked-out theory. I make no apologies for the limited scope of these proposals. They are a starting point for a more productive discussion of some very big challenges.

Prolong the NPT Regime with a New Theory of Victory

The fictions of the NPT—that India, Israel, North Korea, and Pakistan are not nuclear states and that major powers will give up their weapons—serve a useful purpose. These fictions should be ved and extended. Even if they are seriously flawed, they have a fair amount of legitimacy, and until something better comes along it's all we've got.

However, the goal of nuclear nonproliferation needs a new theory of victory that acknowledges that some countries would be more dangerous than others when it comes to possessing the bomb. To some extent, this recognition is already taking place. India, as mentioned, is considered virtually a legitimate nuclear power because it is a democracy, committed to economic development, and cautious in its foreign policy. This doesn't describe Pakistan, to say the least. Israel is allowed in because of special circumstances, history, American backing, and because no one can think of any good way for Israel to give up the bomb. North Korea and Iran are definitely not legitimate nuclear-weapons states. Other secondary countries, Saudi Arabia and Algeria, should be stopped from getting the bomb, too.

Treating all countries the same is very democratic but it isn't terribly smart. A de facto double standard has built up. Like many fictions, this one has important stabilizing features. While I wouldn't expect Iran to ever accept this in principle, I can imagine Iran being compelled to accept it in fact.

The new theory of victory in the NPT should be to prevent the spread of the bomb to additional secondary powers. That should be the top priority because it recognizes the most dangerous situations, which are in the regions. This goal could be accomplished with U.S. leadership, military threats, economic sanctions, severing the country in question from international institutions, blockades, and no-fly zones.

The general principle suggested here would not treat new major power entrants to the nuclear club as if it were the end of the NPT. Japan or Brazil could go nuclear and I very much doubt that it would wreck the entire antinuclear system. It may be better if they did not go nuclear, but the reality is that if they want to get the bomb there is no practical way to stop them. However unfortunate it might be, there's still a large difference between a responsible major power getting the bomb and a secondary power doing so.

Limit the Intensity of the Dynamics

The intensity of competition is the single most important factor leading to nuclear crises and arms races. Let either go unchecked and the escalation spiral can take on a life of its own. Yet, remarkably, the degree of intensity of competition is omitted from most discussions of deterrence.

There is a graduated spectrum of intensity, ranging from peace all the way to nuclear war. Overlook this continuum, or confuse it with binary alternatives of peace and war, and you miss most of the important dynamics of the first and the second nuclear ages.

While the cold war was going on, no one had a good forecast of how it would end. Nonetheless, nearly everyone understood that it was important to limit its intensity. It wasn't sufficient to contain the Soviets. The dynamics along the way had to be dampened, too.

The intensity of competition needs to be limited in the second nuclear age as well. How to do this has gotten little attention in recent American strategic thinking.

The political basis for stability is very important in determining the degree of rivalry. Manage it downward and it will help defuse escalation. The Arab-Israeli dispute, Kashmir, the potential for the disintegration of North Korea—all are sources of instability and hardly disappear because they now take place in a nuclear context.

The major powers need to identify thresholds between differences they have with one another and those that could drag them into regional rivalries. A new dividing line should be established that delineates this. The United States and China can play cat and mouse in the western Pacific with their maritime forces. But neither country should let this spill over to unchecked support for their nuclear allies. That would be a truly dangerous development, so the dividing line needs to be recognized and strengthened.

A new convention among the major powers should be established. Rivalry should not spread outside of regional boundaries. Were China to respond to American moves in the Pacific by giving hydrogen bomb technology to Pakistan, it would be extremely dangerous. While no one can guarantee that a major power would not cross this line, doing so can be clearly marked as a dangerous escalation.

Variations of this convention point to other ideas. Regional allies of major powers may base a good part of their strategy on drawing them in. A convention that calls for major power cooperation in a regional nuclear crisis would be in the interests of all major powers because it would shield them from manipulation by their smaller nuclear allies.

Stay Conservative but Prepare Proactive Strategies

Strategies that are reactive, status-quo preserving, and risk avoiding are preferable to those that are not. The hope is that a second nuclear age will settle down, and that it can be managed with these kinds of policies.

But it might not. We need to think about what happens then. The advice is to act conservatively, but to think about what should be done if conservative policies fail to work. In those cases, strategies that take large risks, press the other side, and use military force have to be considered. One reason that counterescalation will be so important in the second nuclear age is that ignoring a provocation could produce repeats of it in the future. Yet counterescalation for the purpose of dampening intensity is a subject that receives little or no attention in the United States.

The United States also should try to manage a second nuclear age by trying to keep other countries on the reactive, risk-avoiding side of the ledger as well.

Conventions as Strategy

Conventions are another way to limit the intensity of nuclear dynamics. Having a convention doesn't mean the other side will respect it, only that they will notice it. Conventions make leaders think about what they are doing. They may induce caution.

Little thought has been given to what good conventions for a second nuclear age should look like.

Some examples of conventions could be:

- Secondary nuclear powers may not develop ICBMs
- No H-bomb tests
- Subnational groups may not have advanced weapons
- No nuclear alerts
- A regional nuclear crisis stays *in* the region

For example, an Iranian ICBM might draw a statement from Washington that it would not be tolerated. If Iran goes ahead anyway, the United States might destroy the missile on its launchpad with a conventional cruise missile, backed up with a promise to top whatever escalation Iran comes back with.

Hezbollah may receive arms from Iran, but the United States and others can interdict or sabotage them. This convention would also deter others from sending weapons secretly to Iran. France or Germany, for example, would not like to be discovered selling weapons to Hezbollah.

Stopping nuclear alerts is difficult, but if formal U.S. nuclear guarantees are issued, it would dramatically increase the gravity of the crisis, and that would be noticed.

Conventions nearly always work in peacetime, just as the *Titanic*'s watertight doors worked fine before hitting the iceberg. It is the performance in extreme situations that needs careful consideration.

If the United States doesn't think about them beforehand, many harmful conventions may develop on their own. Suppose Iran goes on a fearsome nuclear alert against Israel. After the Iranians have done so, it's very difficult to deter them from doing so again. It's a fait accompli. Trying to establish this convention afterward will be a lot more difficult once the precedent has been established.

Finally, conventions must be clear and simple. In the cold war, "no Soviet nuclear bases in the western hemisphere" was crystal clear. That was its beauty. With the diversity in today's world, the need for clarity is even greater.

The First Nuclear Crisis of the Second Nuclear Age

Crises can be, and have been, fulcrums for change in the international system. The Berlin crisis of 1948 and the Cuban missile crisis of 1962 were such turning points.

Crises in the second nuclear age need to be looked at this way, too. The degree to which they can leverage change could be much more important than the narrow stakes at issue. For this reason the United States needs to ask itself how it can exploit a nuclear crisis. The second nuclear age may have more crises, and stronger crisis rhythms, than the first, because there are more decision-making centers. So the exploitation of crises as pivots may be even more important than it was before.

Crisis exploitation and management is something of a lost art in the United States. This stems from the general distaste for anything nuclear. The tendency is to look at a crisis entirely as something to be managed away, to get out of a jam. But this is only one aspect of a crisis. There is also the need to make sure the precedents established don't undermine America's future bargaining position.

A first step to "using" crises is to recognize that they come in many different shapes, sizes, and locations. Developing a feel for the different types, through war games and scenarios, could go a long way to seeing emergent opportunities and to avoid thinking that crises are only about the stakes that caused them.

Make Plans to Stop Nuclear Murder

Mass murder is a feature of any fifty-year stretch of modern history. The two world wars saw poison gas, death camps, firebombing of cities, and atomic bombs. This pattern did not stop in 1945. Some 1.8 million people were murdered in the Cambodian killing fields in the 1970s. In 1994, 800,000 people were slaughtered in Rwanda in one hundred days. Ethnic cleansing in Bosnia-Herzegovina saw 150,000 killed in the 1990s. As many as 300,000 may have been killed in Sudan in recent years.

One reaction has been to establish a system of international institutions, courts, and agreements to punish those responsible. There have also been attempts at preventive measures, to avert disasters before they happen. Military intervention, no-fly and no-drive zones, and targeted killings of leaders directing the slaughter have all been used.

In light of this history, the prospect of nuclear mass murder must be faced. The above slaughters all took substantial time to perpetuate. Their duration ranged from one hundred days to several years. Now even a barely nuclear power could top these genocides in a day.

It is illogical to focus on slow-motion genocide yet ignore nuclear mass murder. This topic no doubt will generate a great deal of emotion and moral debate, but it needs to be put on the table. The United States could develop policies and plans that would make nuclear genocide less likely, or less catastrophic. It could do this by making certain announcements in advance. And it could prepare military plans to strike promptly in the event a nuclear genocide was conducted.

One question is whether to punish the guilty *after* the fact or to use preventive measures *before* something happens. Suppose North

Korea fires nuclear rockets at Seoul and Tokyo. A North Korea with twenty-five nuclear weapons could do more damage than all of the aerial bombings against German and Japanese cities in World War II.

One response would be to invade North Korea, arrest the country's leaders, and put them on trial for crimes against humanity. Upon conviction they would be hanged. The problem with this is that North Korea has more nuclear and chemical missiles. Common sense suggests it will use them under this policy because it will have nothing left to lose. The North Koreans could fire at more cities as an invasion was under way.

Another approach would be to prepare plans to rapidly disarm North Korea so that it couldn't fire its missiles. Ideally, it would be best to use only conventional weapons for this, but this may not be feasible in all cases, as the exact location of missiles may not be known. If North Korea fires nuclear weapons, and U.S. nuclear strikes were the only way to promptly limit further launches, then appropriate nuclear options should be drawn up to do so.

Nuclear attacks will kill many people, especially if North Korea locates some missiles in cities to use its citizens as a shield. Still, a U.S. attack with conventional and possibly nuclear weapons could greatly limit the damage to South Korea and Japan. It could prevent, or at least reduce, the scale of a nuclear genocide.

But this would only work if there were advance preparations and weapons to carry it out. It may require a "new look" nuclear force, rather than the current force, which is a leftover from the cold war. The current U.S. force was optimized for attack on Russian missile silos, not a messy contingency of pop-up targets and damage limitation.

Few people want to think about the United States firing nuclear weapons. But once it becomes apparent that North Korea (or another country) is about to fire, the problem will look starkly different. Yet it isn't possible to create an instant ability to do much if the problem hasn't been addressed beforehand. After the Rwandan massacre in 1994, many people said that the United States should have done something to prevent it. But little preparation had been done beforehand to allow such action.

The U.S. strategic posture, the combined conventional and nuclear forces that can attack another country's strategic weapons, needs to be analyzed not in terms of the political conditions and attitudes prevailing in peacetime, but in terms of what may happen in times of crisis.

Drill Down on Deterrence

Deterrence was a key concept in the first nuclear age and it will surely be so again in the second. But what is striking about American thinking on deterrence is the way it continues to rely on cold war classifications.

A three-way classification of deterrence in the cold war has become enshrined in American strategic thought.

1. Deterrence of a nuclear attack on the United States
2. Deterrence of nuclear attack on America's allies. This is called "extended deterrence"
3. Deterrence of a conventional attack on the United States or its overseas forces

The first case was the classic one of Soviet nuclear attack on the United States. The second was a nuclear attack on NATO or on another ally such as Japan. The third case was a conventional attack on NATO.

This three-way classification wasn't some academic theory. It drove hundreds of billions of dollars of weapons programs built for each category. War plans were structured around them. Separate command-and-control systems managed the different forces. Even communication and bargaining with the Soviets, in arms control and crisis management, relied on these classifications.

An entire class of weapons, called theater nuclear weapons, filled the gap between deterrence of a Soviet attack on the United States and deterrence of a conventional attack on Western Europe. More than seven thousand nuclear weapons were fielded in Europe to meet the deterrence demands of this second category.

This classification was also used in communications and bargaining. In meetings in Washington and Moscow, Soviet officials rejected the American categories as overly academic, theoretical distinctions that wouldn't be respected in wartime, or in any case, that they would never accept. Then the Soviets started to use the American lingo. A Soviet big shot spoke about U.S. "extended deterrence of Europe." A Soviet general would criticize the United States for deploying nuclear weapons to defend NATO. The key point is that the Soviets used American distinctions and vocabulary in their complaints. This acceptance of terms and concepts was a big psychological win for the United States. It showed that the Soviets understood American strategy.

Furthermore, the deterrence categories facilitated a conversation inside the U.S. bureaucracy about what it was doing. The army, the navy, the air force, the CIA, the Department of Defense, and the White House could talk to one another in a common framework and language. The categories may not have been perfect, but they were not grossly misleading. Not having them, or a suitable alternative, would have produced intellectual and organizational chaos inside the U.S. government.

I raise this to show the importance of the conceptual distinctions made in U.S. deterrence. It raises the question of whether current thinking about deterrence is doing the same job. It is not.

Even the cold war three-way classification left out important possibilities and was criticized for this at the time. Such criticism picked up an important gap in deterrence, a gap that is likely to be even more important in the second nuclear age.

The missing piece is that it didn't deal with the deterrence of extreme provocations. Don Brennan, my Hudson Institute colleague, gave groundbreaking thought to this problem. Even though he lost the argument, his ideas remain salient today.

Brennan argued for a four-way classification, namely deterrence of:

1. A nuclear attack on the United States
2. Extreme nuclear provocations
3. An extreme nonnuclear provocation
4. Other smaller provocations

He proposed organizing U.S. responses not just around nuclear or conventional attack but also around provocations. If these went unanswered, the chance of a huge security disaster increased. The Brennan concept was to organize forces, plans, alliances, and communications with the enemy around this scheme, rather than the three-way version. He did not advocate what the U.S. response should be for each category. But neither did the three-way categorization.

In the second nuclear age, the United States needs to get better at deterring nuclear provocations. Having the proper terminology and categories that communicate this is the first step. Yet nuclear provocation is a category that receives little attention. It doesn't even exist as a category in the U.S. vocabulary of deterrence. The cold war three-way scheme continues to be used more, I suspect, out of habit than anything else.

Deterrence of extreme provocations today would have to incorporate a wider range of threats than in the cold war. Iran using Hezbollah to attack Israel is a good example of what would have to be covered.

RETHINKING ARMS CONTROL

Arms control contributed greatly to dampening the extremes in the first nuclear age. The fact that the leaders of each superpower sat down and negotiated force levels and shared understandings told the world that these weapons were different and that they were not to be treated in the ordinary way.

But a great deal has happened since the summits of the cold war. The world has changed, but arms control hasn't. If you were to attend an arms control conference in 1975, or read a book or report written then, and somehow traveled in a time machine to today you would not notice any change. There is a continued fixation with the U.S.-Russia nuclear balance, the NPT, and sanctions on violators.

Arms control took the 1975 templates of the START, NPT, and ABM treaties and applied them to today's multipolar nuclear world. The United States withdrew from the ABM Treaty in 2002, in the face of widespread proliferation of ballistic missiles, yet even this action was bitterly opposed by the arms control community because it was said to undermine a central pillar of arms control. Had this treaty held, U.S. efforts to defend allies against missiles from Iran or North Korea would be illegal.

Rebranding Arms Control

Business schools study why companies go bankrupt. While there are always variations, decades of research on why they go bankrupt can be summarized in the following way: the business environment changes; the company doesn't change; the company goes bust.

Arms control is much like this. It once had a good business model, it solved real problems, and it had deep support in Congress, in academia, among the public, and even in the Pentagon. This has all but vanished.

Arms control is in desperate need of fresh ideas. It's like Sanka, an old, tired brand that is still around but in need of a makeover. I want to put the challenge to arms control in just this way. Without new energy and a new edginess, arms control's downward spiral into irrelevance will continue. Arms control is too important to allow this to happen.

Arms control started to lose influence in the 1980s, when its advocates lost certain arguments about the nuclear balance with the Soviets. The problem today, however, is that arms control is ignored—marginalized to the fringes of the strategic debate. Arms control advocates must recognize this or risk more irrelevance. It needs once again to become exciting, fresh, and pertinent. Without greater intellectual content behind it, no amount of public marketing by interest groups or social network tweeting is going to sell it to a disengaged public or to a deeply skeptical Congress.

Some history is needed. Arms control was conceived in the 1950s because some approach was needed to manage the arms race. The term *arms control* was invented as a fresh rethinking of disarmament. The term itself was coined to distinguish it from disarmament.

Disarmament had left a bad taste everywhere, becoming a forum for the worst kinds of sanctimonious hot air in the first half of the twentieth century. Countries banned war as a tool of international affairs in the Kellogg-Briand Pact of 1928. The signatories to this pact included the United States, France, Britain, Germany, Italy, and Japan! The 1930s, the League of Nations, and World War II showed where disarmament led.

The pattern started to repeat itself in the cold war. Soviet rhetoric called for "general and complete disarmament" and debased disarmament into a propaganda currency. Arms control was invented outside of the government by far-thinking individuals such as Don Brennan and Thomas Schelling. Brennan wrote the first book on the subject in 1961. It quickly took off because it realistically addressed a big problem, the arms race.

The formally stated purpose of arms control was to reduce the chance of war, or, if it couldn't do that, to reduce its destructiveness. Reducing the number of weapons might do that. Or it might not. In some cases *increasing* the number of nuclear weapons achieved this goal better. Arms control's purpose was not to decrease the number of atomic bombs but to make the world safer. These can be different goals.

An example: In the 1950s, there came a new generation of survivable missiles that added to the nuclear buildup because they increased the number of warheads. Disarmers hated the idea. Arms controllers loved it because these missiles made a first strike infeasible. The arms controllers won the argument, and in the early 1960s these Minuteman missiles were put in hardened underground silos. They significantly lowered the chance of nuclear war even as they increased the number of weapons.

Arms control carried its load—and more—in the cold war. More than anything else it communicated to the world that the bomb was a weapon apart from all others. That's exactly what is needed today.

Ideas for revitalizing the arms control brand, to give it a sense of energy, and to lower the chance of nuclear war have been few and far between in recent years. Yet it is an area of great promise. Some ideas for this follow.

No First Use—Guaranteed Second Use

One way to reenergize arms control would be with a U.S. declaration of no first use of nuclear weapons. The president would solemnly declare, "The United States will not be the first to use nuclear weapons under any circumstances."

This declaration would have a galvanizing impact. It would rebrand arms control as positive and exciting, and it would provide U.S. forces with a moral and political basis beyond a narrow military one. The United States would be in the position of taking the moral position that these weapons should never be used. The only possible use is to deter others from using them, or punishing those who do.

Politically, it would be debated worldwide, as other countries (not to mention U.S. government agencies) would be forced to analyze what the new policy meant for them. China, Japan, Russia, India, and every secondary nuclear state would have to think through its implications. That could be a very good thing, because it would force political leaders to take on vested bureaucratic interests in their own country.

There is a notable variant of no first use, however, that merits serious consideration. The idea is to append to a no-first-use declaration a U.S. promise of *guaranteed* second use. If any other country were to use the bomb—against the United States or anyone else—the United States would "guarantee second use" against them. Thus: "no first use—guaranteed second use."

This variant strengthens deterrence against anyone firing the bomb. It would apply to the entire world. North Korea, China, Pakistan, terrorists, even Israel.

The power of no first use, either alone or with guaranteed second use, lies in its blunt clarity. "No first use" means just that. It says the bomb is a weapon that should never be used. Yet it does not take the utopian leap, to getting rid of it, that is, to disarmament. Rather, it accepts the bomb's existence and tries to lessen its usability. This may be a halfway measure in some minds. But it's better to have a halfway measure that works than a full one that doesn't.

The United States has never embraced no first use, and so moving to such a policy would get enormous attention. In the cold war, no first use was rejected because it was thought to give an advantage to the Soviets, with their larger army in Europe. If the United States were to declare no first use of nuclear weapons, it was said, it might invite a conventional attack on NATO. I think this was wrong, but let's leave the cold war behind.

In recent years, no first use has been rejected because of a reluc-

264 THE SECOND NUCLEAR AGE

tance to give something up for nothing, and also for narrow military reasons.

But no first use doesn't give up anything. For all practical purposes, the United States has a de facto no-first-use policy today. I believe it's had a virtual no-first-use policy for a lot longer than that, probably since the mid-1960s. So nothing is given up that wasn't given up decades ago.

There is always the question of targets that can be destroyed only with a nuclear weapon. But is there a plausible scenario for the United States firing nuclear weapons first at these targets? Narrow tactical examples absent any consideration of political consequences are sometimes offered. "The Iranians have a bunker a thousand feet underground, they're about to fire, and none of our conventional weapons can dig it out." Fine. But let's consider a plausible scenario, as judged by political leaders in the White House, and the State and Defense Departments, not what a lieutenant colonel planning a tactical strike needs. Tactical planning is important, but it shouldn't decide national policy for breaking a taboo in effect since Nagasaki.

Having said this, I actually find very few lieutenant colonels who don't understand the point. No country benefits more from a tradition of non-use than the United States. Given its tremendous investment in conventional forces, and given the unique history of having used the bomb twice, the United States isn't going to go nuclear on account of a tactical expediency. I cannot imagine any North Korean or Iranian bunker that is so important that the United States would break a seven-decade taboo against nuclear use.

No first use, especially with guaranteed second use, contains a warning of enormous consequence. Because if someone does fire the bomb, the U.S. pledge not to use nuclear weapons is automatically suspended. Let's consider this. A secondary nuclear power would have to think that punishment would be vastly more likely if it fired its bomb. It would know with certainty that doing so would suspend

U.S. nuclear restraint. I like the guaranteed-second-use part because it makes the point even stronger. It's not that their use would allow the United States to consider hitting them. It would automatically invoke a pledge that the United States *would* hit them.

The United States needn't say that retaliation for nuclear use would be nuclear. Bear with me for a moment on the patois of nuclear diplomacy. Back in the 1950s, John Foster Dulles promised "massive retaliation" at "a time and place of our own choosing" if the Soviets attacked. He never used the word *nuclear*. That's what others thought he meant. "Guaranteed second use" doesn't contain the word *nuclear* either. It could work like Dulles's massive retaliation. It's hard to think of what massive retaliation, or guaranteed second use, would mean if it weren't nuclear. But that's for Iran, North Korea, and others to worry about.

There are several ways "no first use, guaranteed second use" could be implemented. It could be declared by the president in a speech. Or the guaranteed-second-use element of the declaration might be stated a week later in a speech by the secretary of defense elaborating on the president's remarks. Or, if appropriate, the declaration (in either version) could be prepared and kept in a White House safe. In a crisis in the Middle East or South Asia, the president goes on television to declare his concern with the rising tensions. He adds that the United States won't use nuclear weapons first, but if others did, that U.S. restraint would change.

A U.S. policy of no first use would apply to *everyone*. That is, if anyone goes nuclear, it suspends the U.S. pledge not to use the bomb, including on them. Strictly interpreted, if Israel went first, then Israel would bear the consequences. People will dream up all kinds of problems here. Does the pledge really apply to Israel? Would the United States ever really fire nuclear weapons at Tel Aviv? What about the use of other weapons of mass destruction by North Korea or Iran—is that covered? My suggestion on these questions is to not bring in the lawyers. If no first use morphs into the complexities of the START Treaty, and if it's written by the legal staffs at State and Defense, it misses the point. Just leave these questions unanswered.

Those who say that a U.S. no-first-use pledge is "just a bunch of words that no one would believe" are certainly not correct. Other countries would not see it that way. When President Nixon went to China in 1972, all that came out of the meeting was a "bunch of words" about global stability. The Soviets didn't see Nixon's visit as empty rhetoric, though. It shocked them, and it made them much more cautious. They had to go through a whole new assessment of their foreign and defense policies. It put them on the defensive. That wouldn't be a bad thing to happen for the new nuclear states.

No first use, either alone or with guaranteed second use, has as much to do with psychology and peacetime politics as it does with war. It would dampen nuclear provocations. Because "use," as in no first use, isn't strictly defined. A nuclear state would have to worry about what exactly the U.S. definition of *use* was. If they crossed certain thresholds, they might find out the hard way exactly what the United States meant. Again, this is a good thing to get them thinking about.

China and India already have no-first-use policies. Britain and France do not but, like the United States, they surely have de facto no-first-use policies. Russia has flirted with the idea. Thus, the United States would join other major powers in officially pledging no first use. This would have the added effect of coalescing major power nuclear doctrines away from war fighting and toward restraint. No first use would define what it meant to be a responsible major nuclear power.

It would be a useful convention for the second nuclear age for another reason, too. It would be significantly harder for other major powers to break their own pledges in a crisis. Suppose U.S. relations with China worsen. It would be much harder for Beijing to break the pledge of no first use. In academic conferences in China, its experts are always warning that China will do this. If there's a crisis, for example over Taiwan, and the United States does something untoward, China could declare no first use null and void. I have heard this ad nauseam in conference after conference.

But if the United States declared no first use, this looks much less prudent for China to do. Presumably, it would lead to a reciprocal suspension by the United States, and perhaps by others as well—such as India. Beijing would then face a dramatic, unprecedented political escalation of tensions. It would take the dispute to an entirely new level. Most likely, China doesn't want to go there.

A Great Power Arms Control System

From a fifty-year perspective, arms control looks much different from the way it looks on a day-to-day basis. Up close, it is all about Iran's centrifuges, the technicalities of verifying START, and getting North Korea back into the NPT. But over a longer time frame, it's hard to believe that with all the geopolitical changes taking place there won't be changes in arms control, too. This is already happening. Arms control is changing from a twentieth-century NPT regime into a twenty-first-century great power system. In the future, major nuclear powers will have much greater say over what defines arms control and what the arms control agenda is. The consequences of this have received only the barest attention.

I've used the term *great power* rather than *major power* to distinguish two groups of countries. The major powers are big countries in population and GDP, many with a nuclear deterrent. A great power arms control system is made up of those major powers who choose to work in a global framework to lower the chance of nuclear war or to limit the damage if it occurs. To give an example of the difference between the two groups, China (or another major power) might choose not to participate in a great power arms control system, but it would still be a major power with nuclear weapons.

A great power arms control system is in its earliest stages—but I would emphasize that it is forming. There's a convergence of policies among the United States, Russia, China, India, Britain, and France. Consider that among each of these countries:

- All have either official or de facto no-first-use policies
- Nuclear restraint has replaced MAD, launch on warning, and preemption
- Higher levels of nuclear escalation against one another have become practically "unthinkable"
- All are involved in negotiations about regional security involving secondary nuclear powers
- All have taken extraordinary measures against accidental launch with thick political controls on their armed forces
- All of the above have developed outside of the UN or NPT regimes

An "official" arms control system has developed. It gets the overwhelming amount of attention. The NPT is an obvious part of it. There is also START. But this official system is now so complex that it is difficult to accomplish new goals, or to take arms control to the next level.

Take START. It is a legacy of the bipolar cold war. And that is the problem. That the United States negotiates with Russia over nuclear world order is simply impossible to sustain with a straight face any longer. START doesn't have anything to do with the problems of the second nuclear age. The new START agreement runs to 365 pages and is designed to prevent a Russian surprise attack on U.S. missiles. It assumes a MAD-type world. Some people argue that START is a "model" for future arms control initiatives, that it eventually will apply to cover more countries. I suppose this treaty would run to thirty thousand pages and take thirty years to negotiate.

If there was ever an example of the environment changing, and arms control staying the same, START is it. It ignores the real problem of secondary nuclear powers altogether, while it focuses on the least likely scenario of nuclear war. I could write on an index card a treaty that would deter a Russian attack on U.S. missiles. The reason is the Russians don't have any interest in launching such an attack. Nor do they have the ability to do so, unless you believe in the validity of the wildly simplified missile exchange calculations that are trotted out to justify START. These calculations make the financial risk models used by firms like AIG and Lehman Brothers look positively rigorous and scientific in comparison. No one with a background in operations research or applied physics believes they reflect the realities of actually firing nuclear weapons.

While START solves a problem that isn't going to happen, the NPT fails to solve one that is. Israel, Pakistan, and North Korea have gone nuclear, with Iran likely to follow. There will be others as well. I see little prospect that the NPT can handle this. Even Mohamed ElBaradei, the Nobel laureate and former director general of the IAEA, has said that the NPT is a forty-year-old agreement designed for an era where few countries had the technology or opportunity to go nuclear. He calls for a thorough overhaul. That's fine. But it's different from saying the current NPT regime can handle the job.

This isn't a call for tossing aside START or the NPT. But it is a call to recognize fundamental changes in the global nuclear order.

There are problems with a great power arms control system. It wouldn't be "designed" by the United States, for one thing, which would diminish Washington's interest. It would acknowledge the evolution of nuclear multipolarity outside of the START and NPT frameworks, which are both closely tied to the 1945 system.

There's something exhilarating about the U.S. president and his Russian counterpart negotiating nuclear world order, toasting champagne glasses, and signing a thick, leather-bound treaty. The two countries love to do this, to have their leaders tackle the hard issues and demonstrate their commitment to world peace. It isn't surprising that the United States and Russia want to cling to these images. They highlight the exceptionalism of cold war summitry.

But it can't last. It's become a theater of the absurd as Pakistan doubles its arsenal, Israel deploys real-time satellites to spot Iran's missile alerts, and North Korea deploys a whole new class of uranium bombs. While this goes on, U.S. diplomats fly to Moscow for "urgent" negotiations about the rules for counting the number of nuclear weapon launchers.

A great power arms control regime could be beneficial for another reason. For more than fifty years, nearly all arms control initiatives have originated in the United States. This has led to a bland, uninspiring agenda. Greater diversity of intellectual capital would be a very good thing for arms control and for the world. That U.S. government agencies might have to come up with creative responses to other major powers' proposals may be exactly what is needed.

The measures offered here are only a beginning step for meeting the challenges of the second nuclear age. The big suggestions—seeing it as a fifty-year problem, managing regional crises, establishing conventions that lower the risk of war, and rethinking arms control— are useful headings for more thought and creativity. But without a more sober consideration of these suggestions the learning curve of the second nuclear age is likely to derive from harsh experience. Surely there is a better way of learning.

THE MATURING SECOND NUCLEAR AGE

The bomb has returned for a second act. And it has shown no sign of exiting the stage anytime soon.

While voluntary disarmament is always possible, doing so would place a country at a considerable disadvantage, politically and militarily. For Israel or Pakistan or North Korea to give up the bomb would have enormous consequences; they would have to rely on the promise of a major power for nuclear protection or on self-imposed restraint by its enemies. With the geopolitical landscape in flux, with the rise of new powers, and with political changes in the Arab world, voluntary disarmament is not a likely development.

In the first nuclear age there was a single overarching nuclear rivalry. It took only two to tango, so to speak, in order to moderate any provocations, limit the dynamics, and reduce the number of bombs through arms control. Today, the number of bombs is much reduced from cold war levels, but the number of rivalries that have taken on a nuclear context has increased. These rivalries, anchored in the regions but with global impact, have more deeply embedded the bomb in international affairs than was the case even during the cold war. And on top of the regional rivalries, there is now a multi-polar system of major powers, and it too has a nuclear element. No major power looks ready to voluntarily disarm, either.

The second nuclear age is already with us; it does no good to seek ways to prevent it from emerging. However, it will evolve in various ways. Over time the first nuclear age settled down, as conventions evolved that limited the intensity of the competition and as prudent decision making came into effect. This could well happen again. There are reasons to think so, because most countries do not want nuclear war.

But there are big dangers, especially in the transition years the world is now entering, as the international system tries to adjust to a new global order with multiple nuclear powers. In these transition years the factors of moderation are likely to be only incompletely developed, or they may not exist at all, because the stresses of the new environment have yet to be discovered or tested. At the same time, it may be a relatively calm gestation period, as the new powers build up their nuclear forces, missiles, and other systems. North Korea, Pakistan, and Iran are not too aggressive at present because they are at a vulnerable stage of their nuclear development. But as their forces mature, strategy innovations and nuclear head games could increase and so could the likelihood of a serious nuclear crisis.

The major nuclear powers are also maturing. All of them, except one, the United States, have modernized their forces for the twenty-first century, and they have positioned their forces strategically. I call these developments "the bomb backstage." The mobile missiles, submarines, bombers, and anti-satellite weapons of China, India, and Russia provide a silhouette visible behind the scenery of day-to-day politics. Sometimes we can hear what's going on, as when a big prop is dragged around backstage that gives off loud noises.

Exactly how far offstage this force is depends on the situation, of course. Yet it is always there. This is the key point. The bomb backstage can be moved closer to the audience's view by testing a missile or practicing an alert. It can nuclearize a dispute or turn a small crisis into something far more serious. The threat of bringing the nuclear force onto the visible stage has considerable strategic influence for these new nuclear powers, most especially in keeping the United States at bay.

Modifications to make the international system safer may come from grand designs, negotiations, conferences, and confidence-building measures. Treaties will have to expand in length and complexity to cover all the possibilities in this diverse world. This should stretch out negotiations for a very long time.

But changes to the international system may as likely come from crises, provocations, and perhaps nuclear wars. Israel may find nuclear threats against it intolerable or Pakistan may go into nuclear hysteria. The maturing of the second nuclear age may find itself on a fast track following one of these events.

An intense crisis or a nuclear war may prove to be so horrendous that the major powers will overcome their differences to punish the perpetrator, to make sure it never happens again. The shock of losing a country to nuclear attack, or of repeated nuclear crises that upset the international order, may spark the major powers into collective action. One question, then, is: How far will the major powers go? The retribution may focus on the offender, the country that broke the nuclear order, but it's also possible that the major powers may issue ultimatums to other secondary nuclear powers to hand over their arsenals in a forced disarmament. Disarming all countries with nuclear weapons who are judged to be irresponsible will look much more realistic following a nuclear disaster. That the major nuclear powers will possess the means to back up such an ultimatum is beyond question.

There is no guarantee that the international system can respond fast enough, or adjust to the degree required, to prevent a nuclear disaster. Technology greatly aggravates this problem. It not only increases the rate at which the bomb can spread, it can also create dangerous military imbalances. The rationale behind the arms buildup of the cold war was that falling behind might lead to political and military disadvantages that the other side could exploit. The balancing act, for the United States, was to prevent this—and, at the same time, not to overstimulate the arms race or unleash political forces it couldn't control.

This may be a lot more difficult now. Technology is more complex today, and it is far ahead of any strategy for directing it. National restraint and accepted norms of behavior are only at the earliest stages of development. The nuclear balance can be upset in ways it never could before, by conventional precision strike, cyberattack, stealthy drones, or a terrorist attack intended to purposefully cause an eruption. None of these items threatened the strategic balance in the cold war. Now they all exist. There are few accepted rules in place for limiting them, partly because they are still new. Yet virtually no thought has been given to the problems they pose.

Through a combination of prudence, and luck, the world made it through the first nuclear age without a nuclear disaster. Unless we prepare for the second nuclear age with a far more sober attitude, we may not be so lucky this time.

AFTERWORD TO THE PAPERBACK EDITION

In the months following the hardcover publication of *The Second Nuclear Age,* nuclear weapons have continued to roil international politics, reinforcing many of the arguments and observations made in this book. North Korea has tested another nuclear weapon and is actively engaged in efforts to miniaturize its bomb to fit on a missile. Iran has continued to expand its uranium enrichment program and has tested missiles with a range to hit Israel and much of Europe. India and Pakistan have also continued their missile programs, with India looking to field multiple-warhead launchers at some point in the future. China has escalated its territorial dispute with Japan over essentially worthless islands in the western Pacific and continues its across-the-board military modernization that is shifting the balance of power in Asia. Moreover, Russia and China have conducted their largest joint naval exercises ever, and have coordinated their policies on Iran and Syria to block the more ambitious U.S. efforts to change Syria's regime and stop Iran's nuclear program. Russia, for its part, has begun to field a wide array of new missiles and other nuclear-capable weapons.

These developments have sharp, clear signatures. Video clips of the shaking earth from North Korea's nuclear test, Iran's defiant speeches, and a Chinese cruise missile are vivid and frightening. But there are other developments that occur slowly, incrementally, that are harder to capture on video. In many ways these are more significant. In the Middle East, Israel has expanded its civil defense and its missile defenses. In South Korea, too, civil defense and missile defense have been expanded. That these programs are increasing is noteworthy because each has been associated over the years with antiquated cold war thinking. In the United States civil defense in particular was held out as an example of the excesses and paranoia of the cold war. Yet here they are in Israel and South Korea, a logical consequence of a nuclearizing Middle East and East Asia.

Missile defense has returned not only to the Middle East, but also to Europe and other parts of Asia. Experts are divided as to whether U.S. missile defense is aimed solely at Iran and North Korea, or in reality at Russia and China. In any case, Moscow and Beijing have vehemently objected, arguing that it undermines their nuclear deterrents.

The deeper point is that a multipolar nuclear system is taking shape before our eyes. Trying to fathom this system, to understand its global and regional parts, the crises that could develop, and its multiyear dynamics—because it isn't going away anytime soon—is admittedly complex. A world made up of one-on-one nuclear stand-offs (Israel versus Iran, Russia versus the United States, Pakistan versus India, etc.) is easier to think about as it sidesteps the messy interrelationships of a multiplayer game. Calling (yet again) for global disarmament is simpler still. Both of these frameworks, in addition, have exalted goals: reduce nuclear forces to the minimum required to deter attack; and move to "zero" nuclear weapons.

Trying to understand the crises and strategic dynamics of a maturing global nuclear order doesn't promise such grand outcomes. The goal is to shape—not replace—a multipolar nuclear system. But there's a saying on Wall Street that describes the current world situation. "You have to play the hand you're dealt, not the hand you wish you were dealt." This is useful to keep in mind when deciding which framework to use.

Here, recent developments may be usefully discussed in terms of multipolarity, tactical dynamics, and policy issues.

MULTIPOLARITY AND NUCLEAR WEAPONS

The world has continued to shift toward a multipolar order. It isn't just the rise of China, India, and others that's causing this. The U.S. economy is in trouble, and significant cuts in defense spending are underway. Acquisition of new weapons is postponed, forces are cut, and ambitions are lowered. There is little support today, for example, for using the U.S. military to build democracy in the Middle East.

A fundamental question of defense economics is emerging from these trends, namely, whether the United States can afford to protect key allies and regions, at least in the way it once did. It is useful to recall something often forgotten about the first nuclear age. Defense economics was a large reason the United States relied on nuclear weapons in the cold war. Having won World War II, then facing the Korean conflict, the United States was in no mood to match the Soviets and the Chinese on a division-for-division basis. Instead, the United States made a deal with the devil: it relied on nuclear weapons to contain the Soviet Union. It was no bluff; it was a Faustian bargain. These weapons could have gone off, ending civilization as we know it. This should be understood, because today other countries are going down the same road, embracing nuclear arms because they are cheaper than the alternatives.

Defense economics today needs to be understood in two ways: how the United States responds and how other countries respond to a multipolar order. For decades the United States has tried to eliminate nuclear weapons from the international system. Whether one likes to admit it or not, this would have given a lopsided advantage to the United States because of its technology edge in conventional forces. The response by North Korea, Pakistan, China, Iran, and other powers was quite natural. They decided to emphasize nuclear weapons to offset the American advantage.

Countries today face a choice of how much to rely on the United States for protection and for preserving international order. Japan relies on the U.S. nuclear deterrent for protection from North Korea and China. International order is different. Arms imbalances now developing between Japan and China could have large political consequences. As a result, Japanese domestic politics could move to include the extreme right, or there could be greater nationalism in Japan and China. Or it could lead to humiliations to Japan in its territorial disputes with China.

Both concerns were behind the recent U.S. pivot to Asia. Although new U.S. forces sent to Asia are small, they are intended to show serious commitment to fulfilling the American obligation to supply international order so that adverse political developments like these do not occur.

Developments in South Asia show another aspect of multipolarity and nuclear weapons. India is alarmed about Pakistan's atomic buildup, which continues apace with the likely deployment of tactical nuclear weapons in the near future. But India also has to consider how it fits into a multipolar nuclear system. India is not about to sign the nuclear nonproliferation treaty (NPT) for reasons that have nothing to do with Pakistan; other factors weighing on India include China's military buildup, concerns about America's defense cutbacks and the U.S. economy, and the potential for Sino-Japanese rivalry.

When India tested five atomic bombs in 1998, the United States led the charge to isolate India politically and economically to make New Delhi turn back its decision, and to sign the NPT as a non-nuclear weapon state. Consider the situation today. When was the last time anyone in the United States seriously called for India to sign the

NPT? India has now become an accepted member of the nuclear club, whatever the fiction of the NPT says. My discussions with Indian experts and government officials make the point even stronger. If India were to give up the bomb, New Delhi wouldn't be invited to arms control meetings the other major powers will someday hold. And India insists on having a seat at the table.

I am not raising an alarm about a huge nuclear arms race in Asia, something that I think is in many ways unlikely. I am saying that analyzing these issues in terms of a narrow deterrence calculus, Pakistan versus India, misses how the larger system also shapes India's choices.

Even the United States is beginning to recognize nuclear multipolarity. This marks quite a shift from the early aspirational goals of the Obama administration, for example, in the president's speech in Prague in April 2009. The Prague speech centered on a goal of a world free of nuclear weapons.

President Obama's more recent speech in Berlin, in June 2013, also dealt with nuclear weapons. He gave support to a world free of nuclear weapons, but he also included explicit recognition of complicating factors, issues ignored in the Prague address. Significantly, the Berlin address was accompanied by White House guidance to the Pentagon that "aligns U.S. nuclear posture to the 21st century security environment." Nuclear guidance documents like this one once were features of the cold war. President Carter, for instance, in 1980 issued his famous presidential directive PD-59, which was written after the Soviets invaded Afghanistan. In the years following the end of the cold war, such documents have been judged unseemly for the White House to put out. Usually a Pentagon official says something, and this is intended to de-emphasize the whole subject.

President Obama's nuclear guidance to the Pentagon also says that the United States is "focused on maintaining and improving strategic stability with both Russia and China." Given that the focus of the Berlin address was on deep cuts in the START agreement, the inclusion of China is quite significant, marking the first time that U.S. strategic arms control has gone outside of a U.S.-Russia framework. The U.S. recognition that the world consists of more than two nuclear powers is only the first step in a grudging American acceptance that a multipolar nuclear order has arrived.

TACTICAL DYNAMICS

By tactical dynamics I mean the actions, practices, and responses that can be used in a nuclear environment, where one or more countries have the bomb. The use of cyberwar, stealth, and drones are examples of such tactical dynamics. The United States, China, India, Pakistan, Russia, Israel, and North Korea have used some or all of these technologies. They have tactical military significance, obviously. But their significance in a *nuclear* environment hasn't received the attention it requires.

These technologies allow one side to accurately disrupt another's nuclear deterrent. Cyber attacks, for example, can blind radars and satellites, delaying a response. Drones can locate enemy nuclear weapons, even if they are moving around. Stealth, in aircraft and cruise missiles, cuts warning time to almost nothing.

Not since the early 1980s has it been possible to construct a theoretical scenario for a first strike on the nuclear forces of another country. Back then, a combination of the quick-reacting Pershing 2 missiles, accurate ICBMs and SLBMs, and missile defense (the Strategic Defense Initiative) made it possible, in theory, to take out the Soviet deterrent. Let's leave to another debate exactly how feasible this all was. I would only argue that Moscow took the threat very seriously in 1983, as discussed in chapter 3.

Now, in the twenty-first century, it is again possible to write this scenario. It isn't the United States attacking Russia that one should worry about; it's the regional nuclear powers in the Middle East, South Asia, and East Asia. Their nuclear forces are far smaller than those of the cold war, allowing for a much easier job of destroying them. Moreover, the new technologies like cyberwar, drones, and stealth can be tested in realistic conditions, a situation quite different from the scenarios of the early 1980s. These technologies can be perfected in the hunt for terrorists, and then aimed at other kinds of targets, like mobile missiles, jets on runway alert, and command-and-control centers.

Among other responses, these technologies could encourage regional powers to acquire more nuclear weapons than they otherwise would, so that some of their forces would survive. Or they could shift their forces to a hair-trigger level of readiness. This is a highly destabilizing development.

Recently, another tactical dynamic appeared that illustrated communication and bargaining with nuclear weapons in a three-way nuclear game. In March 2013 there was a crisis with North Korea over Pyongyang's repeated threats to attack South Korea and Japan. The United States flew two nuclear-capable stealth B-2 bombers from an air base in Missouri to participate in military exercises in South Korea. The B-2s dropped dummy bombs, but all of the press reports focused on the fact that these aircraft can drop nuclear weapons. Their Missouri base, in fact, is known to stock nuclear warheads of exactly the type the B-2 would drop.

A few days later, in early April, the United States canceled a test launch of an ICBM. Launches from California into a Pacific Ocean test zone are routinely undertaken to test missile reliability. This particular test was canceled because Washington did not want to escalate the crisis with North Korea.

But there was another consideration to canceling the missile test. A U.S. missile test during a crisis, here with North Korea, invites China to do the same thing. A crisis between China and Japan over a disputed island, for example, could lead to such a development. China conducts a "routine" ICBM test that comes down in the Pacific. The test ratchets up Beijing's pressure on the United States to stay out of the dispute. It effectively "nuclearizes" the crisis, making it more dramatic and dangerous. Were China to build an anti-carrier nuclear warhead, it would escalate the crisis even more, because the mere existence of such a weapon would inevitably affect U.S. calculations. Beijing wouldn't have to actually fire any nuclear weapons, only conduct a "routine" test, to gain a significant advantage.

Some experts have argued that signaling with the bomb is exactly the kind of tactical move that shouldn't be undertaken because it harkens back to the head games of the cold war. Yet here we are again, playing such games, this time in the second nuclear age. This time it's a three-way nuclear head game, involving the United States, China, and North Korea. It is an example of communications and bargaining that has to be managed in a multipolar nuclear system.

POLICY ISSUES

A striking feature of recent U.S. policy for dealing with the spread of the bomb is its slow, risk-avoiding, incremental character. Negotiations with Iran, for example, are held, adjourned, and resumed months later. Economic sanctions are imposed in a way that gives Tehran plenty of time to deal with them. Most important, Iran is given little reason to think that the United States will really attack it if it continues its enrichment efforts.

My purpose here is to not to criticize these policies, but to point out that more intense and assertive options exist, something advocates of the incremental approach fail to see or intentionally choose to overlook. It raises the question of whether U.S. negotiations are designed as much to not excite the situation at home, in the United States, as they are to stop Iran from getting the bomb.

Take the U.S. claim that in dealing with Iran "all options are on the table." There is a U.S. fear lurking behind this claim that more assertive policies would lead to inclusion of more options, ones that are currently far off the table. This is a reason for sticking to the current approach, to prevent these options from ever getting close to the table. Here are three U.S. options that most definitely are "not on the table" at present:

1. The option to develop a new nuclear warhead. The United States currently is extending the life of its aging nuclear weapons. But life extension is different from building a new warhead—it just allows the old weapon to last longer but doesn't give it any new features. Given that most U.S. nuclear weapons were built in the 1980s or earlier, this is an important distinction. A brand-new warhead, for example, might have advanced features allowing it to "talk" to intelligence sensors or to possess tailored special effects to destroy deep underground targets. Such new features are, at present, strictly ruled out.

2. The option to develop a new U.S. nuclear *force*, and not just a new warhead. Designing a new force is broader than building a new warhead, although it could include this. It might involve advanced delivery vehicles, such as hypersonic cruise missiles. New sensors, integration with intelligence systems, or super high reliability might require special fitting to ICBMs, bombers, and submarines. There is a great deal of talk, of course, about U.S. nuclear modernization, such as new submarines and bombers. But this isn't really modernization in the sense of the term used here. Current modernization plans are like fixing up a 1975 black-and-white TV you have in the attic: "We'll get the old thing down, replace the rabbit-ear antenna, picture tube, and vacuum tubes. It will cost a fortune, since nobody builds this stuff anymore. The old timers who used to do it have all retired." If we ask, "What about color, a flat panel display, cable ready, high definition, and Internet interfacing?" the answer is an emphatic "No!" The argument is that this would show that the United States believes nuclear weapons to

be useful—and that would be destabilizing. There is an added wish among some people that merely extending the life of the aging force will prove so expensive that it will lead to abandoning it altogether. Call this "disarmament through atrophy." Designing a new nuclear force would undercut this hope.

3. The option to actually use nuclear weapons. This option asks the question: Is it ever worthwhile for the United States to fire nuclear weapons first? Is it ever worthwhile to use them second? These questions raise deep political and moral issues, and are at present far off the table. If the answer to the first question is "no," that there are no contingencies where it is profitable for the United States to fire first, a no-first-use nuclear policy should be embraced. The United States would join China and India in having made such a formal declaration. The answer to the second question is a lot more complicated. Moral and political issues are front and center here. Because if the answer is "no," that the United States would not even fire second, then very significant questions need to be raised. Does this mean that North Korea, Iran, and Pakistan could fire nuclear weapons, kill millions of people, with the result that they would be subject only to a conventional retaliation by the United States? If this is so, it may be scant consolation to Japan, South Korea, India, and Israel. At a time when there is great interest in preventing Rwandan- and Serbian-like genocides, it is fantastic that "nuclear genocide" by states widely believed to be capable of it should escape nuclear punishment. It is an invitation for more countries to get the bomb, as Israel has already done, to ensure that any attacker receives *nuclear* punishment. Failing to use nuclear weapons, actually, may lead to a breakdown of order, because violators face no risk of nuclear punishment.

I emphasize that I am *not* advocating a new U.S. nuclear warhead, a new nuclear force, or first or second use of nuclear weapons. My point is different. It is to show that all options are *not* on the table, and that there are choices that the national discussion, at present, is woefully unprepared to have. Public fears about these possibilities are low. But following some nuclear disaster—a crisis or an actual nuclear strike—emotional reactions and fears will be high. Then, indeed, all options will be on the table. The problem is that it is better to think about these things now, not in an environment where dangerous, reckless actions stoke emotion and public fears that drive policy, instead of a more sober deliberation.

A NOTE ON SOURCES

1: GAME CHANGER

Games have many different purposes, something that is often misunderstood. The purpose of the games discussed in this chapter, both the historical games and the Middle East nuclear games, was to uncover issues and problems. For a discussion of the different purposes of gaming, see Garry D. Brewer and Martin Shubik, *The War Game: A Critique of Military Problem Solving* (Cambridge, Mass.: Harvard University Press, 1979); Martin Shubik, *Games for Society, Business, and War: Towards a Theory of Gaming* (New York: Elsevier, 1975); and Martin Shubik, *The Uses and Methods of Gaming* (New York: Elsevier, 1975), pp. 2–54.

The Chester Nimitz reflection on war games is worth quoting in full: "The war with Japan had been re-enacted in the game room here by so many people and in so many different ways that nothing that happened during the war was a surprise, absolutely nothing except the Kamikaze tactics towards the end of the war; we had not visualized those." Francis J. McHugh, *Fundamentals of Wargaming* (Newport, R.I.: U.S. Naval War College Press, 1966, pp. 2–54). The Newport games were heavily rule-based at the tactical level, for example, in determining attrition of ships. They were more free-form at the strategic level. See Michael Vlahos, *The Blue Sword: The Naval War College and the American Mission, 1919–1941* (Newport, R.I.: U.S. Naval War College Press, 1980).

A description and feel for free-form war games is given in McHugh, *Fundamentals of Wargaming*; Peter P. Perla, *The Art of Wargaming: A Guide for Professionals and Hobbyists* (Annapolis, Md.: Naval Institute Press, 1990); and Thomas B. Allen, *War Games: The Secret World of the Creators, Players, and Policy Makers Rehearsing World War III Today* (New York: McGraw-Hill, 1987). The difference between free-form games and rule-based games is discussed in Paul Bracken and Martin Shubik, "War Gaming in the Information Age," *Naval War College Review* 44:2 (Spring 2001), pp. 47–60. A description of early cold war games and their shift in emphasis from "winning" to "managing" is in Herbert Goldhamer and Hans Speier, "Some Observations on Political Gaming," *World Politics*, 12:1 (October 1959), pp. 71–83.

The shadow game, the game as seen by the actual players as distinct from their bosses, is described in Paul Bracken, "Unintended Consequences of Strategic Gaming," *Simulation & Games* 8:3 (September 1977), pp. 283–318. Several historical war games are described in this article as well.

2: A MOST USEFUL WEAPON

Paul Ricoeur in *Memory, History, and Forgetting* (Chicago: University of Chicago Press, 2004) describes the tendency to overly forget and remember only certain parts of history. The anthropologist Mary Douglas develops the same theme with an institutional emphasis in *How Institutions Think* (Syracuse, N.Y.: Syracuse University Press, 1986).

The role of nuclear weapons in the cold war is described in Thomas B. Reed and Danny Stillman, *The Nuclear Express: A Political History of the Bomb and Its Proliferation* (Minneapolis: Zenith Press, 2009); Stephen M. Younger, *The Bomb: A New History* (New York: Ecco Press, 2010); Lawrence Freedman, *The Evolution of Nuclear Strategy* (New York: Palgrave

Macmillan, 2003); Paul Bracken, *The Command and Control of Nuclear Forces* (New Haven: Yale University Press, 1983); David G. Coleman and Joseph M. Siracusa, *Real-World Nuclear Deterrence: The Making of International Strategy* (Westport, Conn.: Praeger Security International, 2006); and Henry Kissinger, *Nuclear Weapons and Foreign Policy* (New York: W. W. Norton, 1969).

For the destruction from the use of NATO tactical nuclear weapons in Europe, see Bracken, *Command and Control*, chapter 4, and also Paul Bracken, "Collateral Damage and Theater Warfare," *Survival* 22:5 (1980), pp. 203–7.

For the theme that the cold war was hardly a static rivalry, see Robert Cowley, ed., *The Cold War: A Military History* (New York: Random House, 2005).

The "other cold war," the regional conflicts away from Europe and the direct competition between the United States and the Soviet Union, has received considerable scholarly attention in recent years. It balances Eurocentric treatments of the cold war with a detailed understanding of regional dynamics. The general finding of most of this scholarship is that regional rivalries were driven by local issues and were not mere extensions of the Soviet-American contest. See Odd Arne Westad, *The Global Cold War: Third World Interventions and the Making of Our Times* (New York: Cambridge University Press, 2007); and Heonik Kwan, *The Other Cold War* (New York: Columbia University Press, 2010).

On the size of U.S. forces in the cold war, see Kevin Lewis, "Historical U.S. Force Structure Trends: A Primer," Rand Corporation, P-7582, July 1989. For the argument that the United States was not spending anywhere close to what it could have spent in the cold war, see Paul Bracken, "Mobilization in the Nuclear Age," *International Security* 3:3 (Winter 1978–79), pp. 74–93.

On the Berlin crisis, see Ari Shalom, *The United States and the Berlin Blockade 1948–1949: A Study in Crisis Decision Making* (Berkeley: University of California Press, 1983). My account also draws on the *New York Times* from 1948 for the details of U.S. Air Force exercises; A.M. Giangreco and Robert E. Griffin, *Airbridge to Berlin: The Berlin Crisis of 1948, Its Origins and Aftermath* (Novato, Calif.: Presidio Press, 1988); and W. Phillips Davison, *The Berlin Blockade: A Study in Cold War Politics* (New York: Arno Press, 1980). Modern political science also finds a considerable role for nuclear weapons in the crisis; see Curtis S. Signorino and Ahmer Tarar, "A Unified Theory and Test of Extended Immediate Deterrence," *American Journal of Political Science* 50 (July 2006), 586–605.

3: LESSONS OF THE FIRST NUCLEAR AGE

Books that describe the details of nuclear weapons in the early cold war include Andreas Wegner, *Living with Peril: Eisenhower, Kennedy, and Nuclear Weapons* (Lanham, Md.: Rowman & Littlefield, 1997); Craig Campbell, *Destroying the Village: Eisenhower and Thermonuclear War* (New York: Columbia University Press, 1998); Richard Immerman and Robert B. Bowie, *Waging Peace: How Eisenhower Shaped an Enduring Cold War Strategy* (New York: Oxford University Press, 1998); and Tom Wicker, *Dwight D. Eisenhower* (New York: Times Books, 2002). An indispensable historical account of U.S. nuclear strategy is found in Harold Brown, *Thinking About National Security: Defense and Foreign Policy in a Dangerous World* (Boulder, Colo.: Westview Press, 1983).

Cold war crises are very useful to see the effects of a nuclear context. For the Suez crisis, see David A. Nichols, *Eisenhower 1956: The President's Year of Crisis—Suez and the Brink of War* (New York: Simon & Schuster, 2011); for the 1961 Berlin crisis, see Frederick Kempe, *Berlin 1961: Kennedy, Khrushchev, and the Most Dangerous Place on Earth* (New York: G. P. Putnam's Sons, 2011); and for the Cuban missile crisis, see Michael Doobs, *One Minute to Midnight: Kennedy, Khrushchev, and Castro on the Brink of Nuclear War* (New York: Alfred A. Knopf, 2008).

The Hungarian uprising of 1956, focusing on strategic communications, is analyzed in Victor Sebestyen, *Twelve Days: The Story of the Hungarian Revolution* (New York: Random House, 2007).

The timing of the air strikes on Vietnam comes from my own interviews of SAC commanders and also Daniel Ellsberg, *Secrets: A Memoir of Vietnam and the Pentagon Papers* (New York: Penguin Books, 2003), pp. 11–12. Nixon's 1969 alerts are described in Scott C. Sagan and Jeremi Suri, "The Madman Nuclear Alert," *International Security* 27:150–83 (Spring 2003). I also interviewed SAC officials connected with this event. The JCS order is found in Memorandum from JCS Chairman Wheeler, National Security Archives, on the Web at www.gwu.edu/~nsarchiv/NSAEBB/NSAEBB81/nnp05.pdf. Henry Kissinger's account of the end of the Vietnam War does not mention nuclear weapons but does describe President Nixon's complex combination of threats and efforts to create illusory images of escalation. See Henry Kissinger, *Ending the Vietnam War: A History of America's Involvement in and Extrication from the Vietnam War* (New York: Simon & Schuster, 2003), pp. 49–107. Also, on this same topic, see Robert Dallek, *Nixon and Kissinger: Partners in Power* (New York, HarperCollins, 2007), pp. 104–12.

President Carter's use of the "Doomsday Aircraft" is described in "Flying Command Post Takes Carter to Georgia," *New York Times*, February 12, 1977. The story contained two photographs of the aircraft, a converted B-747. I discussed this topic with President Carter in April 1985, in Plains, Georgia.

The importance of institutions and their alignment with politics is described throughout Henry Kissinger, *Diplomacy* (New York: Simon & Schuster, 1994). Kissinger's discussion is especially gripping in chapters 7 and 8, "A Political Doomsday Machine: European Diplomacy Before the First World War" and "Into the Vortex: The Military Doomsday Machine," pp. 168–217.

For Soviet biological warfare, see Jonathan B. Tucker, "Biological Weapons in the Former Soviet Union: An Interview with Dr. Kenneth Alibeck," *Nonproliferation Review* (Spring-Summer 1999), p. 4.

On the use of analysis for decision making on big decisions, I spoke many times with McGeorge Bundy and Robert McNamara. For misestimating risk, recent research on behavioral economics is especially insightful; see Daniel Kahneman, *Thinking, Fast and Slow* (New York: Farrar, Straus and Giroux, 2011); and for an application of this line of thought to international relations, see Paul Bracken, Ian Bremmer, and David Gordon, eds., *Managing Strategic Surprise: Lessons from Risk Management and Risk Assessment* (New York: Cambridge University Press, 2008).

The misalignment of technology and strategy is widely discussed in business literature. See Margaret A. White and Garry D. Bruton, *The Management of Technology and Innovation: A Strategic Approach* (Mason, Ohio: South-Western, Cengage Learning, 2011).

High-level play in war games by senior officials with respect to American escalation in Vietnam and the Sigma war games of 1964 are described in Harold P. Ford, "Thoughts Engendered by Robert McNamara's *In Retrospect*," on the CIA Web site at https://www.cia.gov/library/center-for-the-study-of-intelligence/csi-publications/csi-studies/studies/96unclass/ford.htm. The Sigma games are also described in Lawrence Freedman, *Kennedy's Wars: Berlin, Cuba, Laos, and Vietnam* (New York: Oxford University Press, 2000), pp. 410–11, and Allen, *War Games*.

The heightened fears of war in 1983 are described in John Prados, "The War Scare of 1983," in Cowley, *Cold War*, pp. 438–53; see also Martin Anderson and Annelise Anderson, *Reagan's Secret War: The Untold Story of His Fight to Save the World from Nuclear Disaster* (New York: Crown, 2009). Also, the CIA analyzes these war fears in Benjamin B. Fischer, *A Cold War Conundrum: The 1983 Soviet War Scare*, on the CIA Web site at https://www.cia.gov/library/center-for-the-study-of-intelligence/csi-publications/books-and-monographs/a-cold-war-conundrum/source.htm; a slightly different account by the same author is in Benjamin B. Fischer, "The Soviet-American War Scare of the 1980s," *Journal of Intelligence and Counter Intelligence* 19:3 (2006), 480–518.

The Proud Prophet war game has not been disclosed before. Phillip Karber promised Secretary Weinberger that he would not discuss any aspects of the simulation for twenty-five years, that is, until 2008. The account here draws on my recent discussions with Karber and my notebook of observations recorded at the time in 1983. I am very grateful to Phillip Karber for his permission and cooperation to describe this game.

4: THE NEW LOGIC OF ARMAGEDDON

The Sartre quote is found in William Barrett, *Time of Need: Forms of Imagination in the Twentieth Century* (New York: Harper Torchbooks, 1972), p. 3.

The emergence of a multipolar nuclear system has received surprisingly little attention, as most discussion has focused exclusively on ways to stop the bomb's spread using the NPT and other tools. For discussion of the characteristics of a multipolar nuclear world, see Paul Bracken, *Fire in the East: The Rise of Asian Military Power and the Second Nuclear Age* (New York: HarperCollins, 1999); Muthiah Alagappa, ed., *The Long Shadow: Nuclear Weapons and Security in 21st Century Asia* (Stanford: Stanford University Press, 2008); Brad Roberts, *Asia's Major Powers and the Emerging Challenges to Nuclear Stability Among Them* (Alexandria, Va.: Institute for Defense Analyses, 2009); and Christopher P. Twomey, *Asia's Complex Strategic Environment: Nuclear Multipolarity and Other Dangers* (Seattle: National Bureau of Asian Research, 2011).

The Suez crisis of 1956 is described in Nichols, *Eisenhower 1956*, and Cole C. Kingseed, *Eisenhower and the Suez Crisis of 1956* (Baton Rouge: LSU Press, 1995). The Soviet nuclear threat to Britain and France is described in Nichols, *Eisenhower 1956*, p. 244.

The White House memo about Israel's nuclear weapons, written July 7, 1969, is found in the Nixon archives and at http://nixon.archives.gov /virtuallibrary/documents/mr/071969_israel.pdf.

On the Israeli bomb test in South Africa, see Jeffrey T. Richelson, *Spying on the Bomb: American Nuclear Intelligence from Nazi Germany to Iran and North Korea* (New York, W. W. Norton, 2006). A CIA officer stationed in South Africa in the 1970s claims definitively that Israel did test an atom bomb, with South African help; see Tyler Drumheller, *On the Brink: An Insider's Account of How the White House Compromised American*

Intelligence (New York: Carroll & Graf, 2006), p. 141. South Africa's nuclear strategy is described in Frank V. Pabian, "South Africa's Nuclear Weapon Program: Lessons for U.S. Nonproliferation Policy," *Nonproliferation Review*, Fall 1995, pp. 1–19; and in Helen E. Purkitt and Stephen Burgess, "South Africa's Chemical and Biological Warfare Program: A Historical and International Perspective," *Journal of South African Studies* 28 (June 2002), 229–53.

That the Israelis mistakenly believed that U.S. intelligence satellites did not monitor the Prince Edward Islands, see Reed and Stillman, *Nuclear Express*, pp. 179–81. South African targeting is discussed here as well, p. 182. The early Israeli bomb program and its two-bomb capability in the 1967 war are described on pp. 120–21.

Game theory was developed by John von Neumann and Oskar Morgenstern. For the qualitative differences in games as the number of players increases, see John von Neumann and Oskar Morgenstern, *Theory of Games and Economic Behavior* (Princeton: Princeton University Press, 1944), pp. 339–403. Martin Shubik of Yale, who studied under both scholars, describes truels in *Game Theory in the Social Sciences* (Cambridge, Mass.: MIT Press, 1985), pp. 20–26.

The interview with Saddam Hussein comes from U.S. Department of Justice, FBI Baghdad Operations Center, June 11, 2004, and is available at www.gwu.edu/~nsarchiv/NSAEBB/NSAEBB279/24.pdf. The distinction between different types of errors is familiar to readers who have taken courses in statistics. They are called Type I and Type II errors. A Type I error is to mistakenly reject a true statement (example: "Israel has no nuclear weapons"). A Type II error occurs where one fails to reject a false statement ("Iraq has WMD" in 2003). Any statistics text describes these two errors.

The case for the 9/11 attacks as an al Qaeda strategy to get the United States to send troops to the Middle East in the expectation that this would lead to a political backlash is described in Lawrence Freedman, *A Choice of Enemies: America Confronts the Middle East* (New York: PublicAffairs, 2008), chapter 16, "Choosing America," pp. 341–70.

On Soviet ham-handed deception programs, on a trip to Moscow in 1992 I raised this point with retired Soviet military officials. I was told that Khrushchev was entirely responsible for putting missiles into Cuba in 1962. He wanted to rush the missiles in, so there was no time for a deception program. I was told that Soviet military engineers simply grabbed the field manuals used in Europe and flew them to Cuba to use there. This reinforces my view that bureaucratic behavior is universal, and probably impermeable even to differences in national culture.

The post–Vasco da Gama era theme is developed in Bracken, *Fire in the East*.

5: THE MIDDLE EAST

The Israeli nuclear program is described in Avner Cohen, *Israel and the Bomb* (New York: Columbia University Press, 1998); Michael I. Karpin, *The Bomb in the Basement: How Israel Went Nuclear and What That Means for the World* (New York: Simon & Schuster, 2006); and Avner Cohen, *The Worst-Kept Secret: Israel's Bargain with the Bomb* (New York: Columbia University Press, 2010). This last book describes the conscious Israeli policy of nuclear ambiguity, of not admitting that it has the bomb. Cohen describes several consequences of this policy. It is relevant to the arguments of this chapter because I offer another result of the ambiguity policy: Israeli leaders and staffers have not thought through how they would use nuclear weapons. They are distressingly unprepared for a nuclear crisis or even a debate about the future of their nuclear posture. (I do not assert that Avner Cohen shares my views on this.) On the future of Israel's strategic posture, see Ronald S. Lauder, "How Subs Could Save Israel," New York *Daily News*, January 5, 2012.

For a description of Israeli foreign and defense policy encompassing the entire history of Israel, see Yehezkel Dror, *Israeli Statecraft: National Security Challenges and Responses* (London: Routledge, 2011); and Freedman, *A Choice of Enemies*. For Arab-Israeli wars, see Chaim Herzog, *The*

Arab-Israeli Wars: War and Peace in the Middle East from the War of Independence Through Lebanon (New York: Random House, 1982).

A description of Israel's nuclear plans against the Soviet Union is found in Seymour Hersh, *The Samson Option: Israel's Nuclear Option and American Foreign Policy* (New York: Random House, 1991), p. 260.

The concept of compound escalation was created by Herman Kahn; see *On Escalation, Metaphors and Scenarios* (New York: Praeger, 1965), pp. 6, 86–87.

For a controversial revisionist account of a Soviet plan to attack Israel's Dimona reactor in the 1967 war, see Isabella Ginor and Gideon Remez, *Foxbats Over Dimona: The Soviets' Nuclear Gamble in the Six Day War* (New Haven: Yale University Press, 2007). I do not know if this account is correct, but I can say that some Israeli military officers serving in 1967 did believe the threat to be real.

Moshe Arens has a PhD in aeronautical engineering, something I've long thought important in shaping his views. His quote is from Moshe Arens, "Facing Iran: Lessons Learned Since Iraq's 1991 Missile Attack on Israel," *Jerusalem Issue Briefs* 9:21 (March 8, 2010).

Iran's quest for the bomb is described in Emanuele Ottolenghi, *Under a Mushroom Cloud: Europe, Iran, and the Bomb* (London: Profile Books, 2009).

6: SOUTH ASIA

For nuclear weapons development in India, see George Perkovich, *India's Nuclear Bomb: The Impact on Global Proliferation* (Berkeley: University of California Press, 2001); for how conventional wars between India and Pakistan have been limited by a nuclear context, see Sumit Ganguly and Devin T. Hagerty, *Fearful Symmetry: India-Pakistan Crises in the Shadow of Nuclear Weapons* (Seattle: University of Washington Press, 2005); and T. V. Paul, ed., *The India-Pakistan Conflict: An Enduring Rivalry* (New York: Cambridge University Press, 2005); and Scott Sagan, ed., *Inside*

Nuclear South Asia (Stanford: Stanford Security Studies, 2009). For the political and strategic dimensions of India's nuclear weapons, see Raja Mohan, *Crossing the Rubicon* (New York: Palgrave Macmillan, 2004).

Pakistan's nuclear program is described in Adrian Levy and Catherine Scott-Clark, *Deception: Pakistan, the United States, and the Secret Trade in Nuclear Weapons* (New York: Walker, 2007). This book also has a good account of A. Q. Khan's nuclear sales efforts around the globe. For insights about Pakistan's nuclear strategies, see Naeem Salik, *The Genesis of South Asian Nuclear Deterrence: Pakistan's Perspective* (New York: Oxford University Press, 2010).

The geopolitics of South Asia and the Indian Ocean are described in Robert D. Kaplan, *Monsoon: The Indian Ocean and the Future of American Power* (New York: Random House, 2010).

For the Indian and Pakistani nuclear tests of 1998, the aftermath, and a candid admission of how India's deception programs convinced the United States that India would not test a bomb, see Strobe Talbott, *Engaging India: Diplomacy, Democracy, and the Bomb* (Washington, D.C.: Brookings Institution Press, 2004). This book also has an excellent account of the interior dynamics of the U.S. government's inability to come to grips with the growing nuclear threats of the 1990s. Apparently, India used information given it in 1995 about U.S. satellite capabilities to thwart these systems in 1998; that is, it learned from the earlier experience. See James Risen and Tim Weiner, "U.S. May Have Helped India Hide Its Nuclear Activity," *New York Times*, May 25, 1998.

Reference to the WikiLeaks cables on Pakistan's nuclear security is from "France Unsure about Pakistan's Nuclear Deterrent: WikiLeaks," *The Times of India*, May 29, 2011, at http://articles.timesofindia.indiatimes .com/2011-05-29/europe/29596590_1_nuclear-warheads-nuclear-energy -technology-nuclear-deterrent.

On the U.S. nuclear power deal with India and its larger consequences, see Harsh V. Pant, *The US-India Nuclear Pact: Policy, Process, and Great Power Politics* (New York: Oxford University Press, 2011). For the Indian arms industry history, see Stephen P. Cohen and Sunil Dasgupta, *Arming Without Aiming: India's Military Modernization* (Washington, D.C.: Brookings Institution Press, 2010).

Pakistan's command-and-control system is described in Paul K. Kerr and Mary Beth Nikitan, *Pakistan's Nuclear Weapons: Proliferation and Security Issues* (Washington, D.C.: Congressional Research Service, 2009). For further analysis of Pakistan's NCA, see Zafar Iqbal Cheema, "Pakistan," chapter 9 of Hans Born, Bates Gill, and Heiner Hanggi, eds., *Governing the Bomb: Civilian Control and Democratic Accountability of Nuclear Weapons* (New York: Oxford University Press, 2010).

For discussion of the formal aspects of Indian command and control of nuclear forces, see Pran Pahwa, *Command and Control of Indian Nuclear Forces* (New Delhi: Knowledge World Publishers, 2002).

7: EAST ASIA

The North Korean missile tests took place on July 5, 2006, in North Korea, and July 4 in the United States. For North Korea's nuclear capabilities, see Bruce W. Bennett, *Uncertainties in the North Korean Nuclear Threat* (Santa Monica, Calif.: Rand Corporation, 2010).

The strategic information transfer discussed here was ordered by President Nixon and carried out by Henry Kissinger. The full details are found in Memorandum of Conversation #196, National Archives, Nixon Presidential Materials, White House Special Files, President's Office Files, Box 87, Memoranda for the President. Top Secret; Sensitive; Exclusively Eyes Only. The meeting was held in the Great Hall of the People. For the full transcript, see The White House, Memorandum of Conversation, Classified Top Secret, Sensitive, Exclusively Eyes Only, February 23, 1972, at www.gwu.edu/~nsarchiv/NSAEBB/NSAEBB106/NZ-4.pdf.

The United States cooperated with Indian intelligence in the early 1960s to place electronic packages in the Himalayas to collect information on Chinese nuclear tests in Xinjiang. See Kenneth J. Conboy and M. S. Kohli, *Spies in the Himalayas: Secret Missions and Perilous Climbs* (Manhattan, Kan.:

University of Kansas Press, 2003). That system was passive; it only received data, it did not transmit. The Hudson Institute project discussed in this chapter, and which I worked on, was active; it was intended to transmit signals.

For China's military modernization, see Denis J. Blasko, *The Chinese Army Today: Tradition and Transformation for the 21st Century* (New York: Routledge, 2006); Richard D. Fisher Jr., *China's Military Modernization: Building for Regional and Global Reach* (New York: Praeger, 2008); Toshi Yoshihara and James R. Holmes, *Red Star Over the Pacific: China's Rise and the Challenge to U.S. Maritime Strategy* (Annapolis, Md.: Naval Institute Press, 2010); Bernard D. Cole, *The Great Wall at Sea: China's Navy in the Twenty-First Century* (Annapolis, Md.: Naval Institute Press, 2010); and Andrew Erickson, Lyle Goldstein, and William Murray, eds., *China's Future Nuclear Submarine Force* (Annapolis, Md.: Naval Institute Press, 2007).

For different views of where China is heading, and implications for the United States, see Henry Kissinger, *On China* (New York: Penguin Press, 2011); William H. Overholt, *Asia, America, and the Transformation of Geopolitics* (New York: Cambridge University Press, 2008); and Aaron L. Friedberg, *A Contest for Supremacy: China, America, and the Struggle for Mastery in Asia* (New York: W. W. Norton, 2011).

For China's anti-access strategy, see Marshall Hoyler, "China's 'Anti-access' Ballistic Missiles and U.S. Active Defense," *Naval War College Review* 63:4 (Autumn 2010), 84–105.

8: HAVE WE FORGOTTEN TOO MUCH?

The Barksdale incident is described in the Report of the Secretary of Defense Task Force on DoD Nuclear Weapons Management, Phase II: Review of the DoD Nuclear Mission, December 2008. See also the DoD Press Briefing on the Secretary's Task Force on Nuclear Weapons Management, Office of the Assistant Secretary of Defense (Public Affairs), January 8, 2009, for discussion of changes in the way the Department of Defense thinks about nuclear weapons since the end of the cold war.

On the development of strategy and think tanks, see Paul Bracken,

"Scholars and Security," *Perspectives on Politics* 8:4 (December 2010), 1095–99.

For details of the cyberwar programs of the United States and Israel against Iran, see David E. Sanger, *Confront and Conceal: Obama's Secret Wars and Surprising Use of American Power* (New York: Crown, 2012).

9: GLOBAL DYNAMICS

For discussion of multipolarity, see Parag Khanna, *The Second World: Empires and Influence in the New Global Order* (New York: Random House, 2008); John J. Mearsheimer, *The Tragedy of Great Power Politics* (New York: W. W. Norton, 2003); and *U.S. National Intelligence Council Global Trends 2025: A Transformed World* (2008).

10: A FIFTY-YEAR PROBLEM

A mangled version of Herman Kahn's argument for seeing nuclear weapons in a longer-term framework is in Herman Kahn, *Thinking About the Unthinkable in the 1980s* (New York: Simon & Schuster, 1984), p. 46. However, Kahn died in 1983. He didn't write or even see this book. Staffers took it on themselves to represent what they thought he meant, and they missed the subtlety Kahn expressed in conversations and briefings.

The Brennan classification is in Donald G. Brennan, ed., *Arms Control, Disarmament, and National Security* (New York: George Braziller, 1961), pp. 19–42. This was the first book ever written about arms control.

For Chinese attitudes about arms control, see Evan S. Medeiros, *The Evolution of China's Nonproliferation Policies and Practices, 1980–2004* (Stanford: Stanford University Press, 2007). Also, for the strategic rationale for mutual restraint between the United States and China, see David C. Gompert and Phillip C. Saunders, *The Paradox of Power: Sino-American Strategic Restraint in an Age of Vulnerability* (Washington, D.C.: National Defense University Press, 2012).

AFTERWORD TO THE PAPERBACK EDITION

For the White House guidance for President Obama's June 2013 speech, see
The White House, June 19, 2013, "Fact Sheet: Nuclear Weapons Employment Strategy of the United States," on the Web at www.whitehouse.gov/the
-press-office/2013/06/19/fact-sheet-nuclear-weapons-employment-strategy
-united-states.

ACKNOWLEDGMENTS

The idea for this book began four years ago, when it seemed to me that an overall account of the second nuclear age was needed to follow up on my book *Fire in the East: The Rise of Asian Military Power and the Second Nuclear Age*, which was published in 1999. Like everyone else, I had not foreseen the 9/11 attacks or the follow-on U.S. intervention in Iraq and Afghanistan. Many people told me that this U.S. action would reverse the nuclear proliferation trends in the 1990s, and that a second nuclear age would be averted. Following Libya's disarmament, and the removal of Saddam Hussein, it looked as if there might indeed be no second nuclear age.

Unfortunately, this has not come to pass. North Korea tested the bomb in 2006. India has become virtually an accepted, legitimate member of the nuclear club. China and Russia are modernizing their nuclear forces. Pakistan is rapidly expanding its atomic arsenal, and Israel is fundamentally rethinking its nuclear posture. Other countries, like Iran, are knocking on the door. Even more than these individual countries, a nuclear context has now taken hold on the rivalries in three critical regions: the Middle East, South

Asia, and East Asia. Terrorist groups have not gotten the bomb, at least not yet, but it becomes easier each year to write the scenario in which they do. Moreover, terrorists in the second nuclear age can cause considerable disasters even if they do not possess a bomb themselves, through catalytic actions and timing of attacks designed to tip a nuclear crisis over the edge.

Despite an enormous U.S. effort in the first decade of the twenty-first century to reverse it, the second nuclear age has kept on developing. An overall description of its complex dynamics is needed now more than ever.

Many people have helped me with advice and ideas on this project. Special thanks to Andy Marshall, Michael Sherman, Martin Shubik, Thomas Schelling, Brad Roberts, Garry Brewer, Phillip A. Karber, Hal Sonnenfeldt, and the late Harvey Sicherman. I would also like to thank my students at Yale, from whom I've learned more than they will know.

Others who have greatly shaped my thinking include Bill Overholt, the late Tom Evans, Jackie Davis, Jerry McWilliams, Uzi Arad, Steve Cimbala, Bob Hurley, Stuart Johnson, Bates Gill, Avner Cohen, Ben Huberman, Bruce Bennett, Paul Davis, John Birkler, and Alf Andreassen. My deepest gratitude also goes to Drs. David Pazer, Larry Fisher, and Cary Passik.

I am grateful to the Smith Richardson Foundation for support of this project. The Foreign Policy Research Institute, in Philadelphia, has been most helpful in arranging early briefings on the subject to get reactions and ideas.

Special thanks to my agent, Jim Hornfischer, for his encouragement and support. At Times Books, Paul Golob has been extraordinarily helpful in making this book come to pass.

Finally, my biggest debt goes to Nan and my family, Kathleen, James, and Meg, who patiently put up with my nuclear exclamations in too many family conversations.

INDEX

disarmament, 6, 33, 218, 248, 261, 271, 273, 276. *See also* arms control
Discovery (space shuttle), 190
domestic politics, 13–14, 46, 222–24
"doomsday airplane," 69, 85
drones, 203, 208
Dr. Strangelove (film), 31, 34, 115
Dulles, John Foster, 42–43, 265
dummy missiles, 24
dynamics. *See also* global dynamics; multiplayer game dynamics
  cold war, 49–50, 58–59
  defined, 49–50
  institutions and, 71–72
  limiting intensity of, 251–52
  second nuclear age and, 50, 59, 94–95
  technology and, 80–81
  tactical dynamics, 280–81

early warning systems, 72, 143, 165, 168–70
East Asia, 2, 9, 95, 189–211, 216, 222, 276, 280
  China and, 195–211, 275
  global dynamics and, 225, 227–28
  North Korea and, 189–95
Eastern Europe, 35, 48–49, 52, 65, 82, 87
economic framework
  cold war and, 44–47
  North Korea and, 192
  second nuclear age and, 123–26, 277
  South Asia and, 163, 172
Egypt, 18, 22–23, 26, 53, 103, 132, 135, 148, 154
  Arab-Israeli wars and, 104, 138
  Israeli peace treaty and, 140
  Suez crisis and, 101
Eisenhower, Dwight D., 46–47, 61, 64–65, 101, 114
ElBaradei, Mohamed, 269
Ellsberg, Daniel, 217
EMCON (emissions control of radios and radars), 68
EMP warheads, 238
energy security, 134

escalation. *See also* compound escalation; escalation dominance; horizontal escalation
  Berlin crisis and, 54
  blocking higher, 232–34
  China and, 208–9
  global dynamics and, 227, 232–34
  great power arms control system and, 268
  limiting intensity of, 251–52
  lower-level, 232–34, 244
  Middle East and, 21–23, 132–33, 137, 140–41
  North Korea and, 194–95
  nuclear vs. conventional contexts and, 22
  reckless, 13–14
  South Asia and, 164–65
  terrorism and, 118, 125
  two-player games and, 106
  Vietnam and, 85
escalation dominance, 130–32
Europe, 4
  cold war and, 39, 42–43, 45–46, 49, 61, 79
  early twentieth century, 71–72
  Iran and, 161, 275
  Middle East and, 156
  missile defense system, 156
  Proud Prophet game and, 87
European Command, 67
"experiential learning," 19
exploitation of nuclear crisis, 254
extended deterrence, 257–58
extreme provocations, 35–36, 149, 259

face-saving exit, 57
false positives vs. false negatives, 113
fear, 30–31
Federal Bureau of Investigation (FBI), 112–13
fifty-year problem, 3, 246, 267
financial warfare, 206
first nuclear age. *See* cold war
"fishbowl effect," 84
Ford Motor Company, 47

Hungary, 65, 102
Hunt for Red October, The (Clancy), 70
Hussein, Saddam, 112–13, 140–41, 157, 167, 180, 221, 248
hydrogen bomb (H-bomb), 37, 38, 166, 175, 233, 253

IBM, 73, 205
ICBMs (Intercontinental Ballistic Missiles), 37, 77, 111, 167, 168, 195, 210, 248, 280–82
conventions on, 253
India, 1, 3, 5–6, 11, 220, 223, 279
arms control and, 263, 266, 268
arms race and, 162–67, 170–72
"bullet-to-the-head" scenario and, 181–87
catalytic war and, 118
China and, 111, 210, 226, 234, 240, 278
Cold Start and, 164–66
conventional forces and, 188
cyberwar and, 180–81
economy of, 163, 172–73
global dynamics and, 123, 226–39, 243
government of, 180
Israel and, 161, 226
as major power, 2, 94n, 228
Middle East and, 156
MIRVs and, 234
modernization and, 243, 272, 275
nationalism and, 116–17
NPT and, 249–50, 278
as nuclear power, 32, 34, 93–94, 100–101, 105, 120–21, 124–25, 163, 166, 277
Pakistan and, 118, 124, 173–81, 278
terrorism and, 175
UN and, 238–39
U.S. and, 164, 176, 210, 241–42, 247, 278
"individuals matter" lesson, 70–71
Indonesia, 35
information technology (IT), 168–71, 180–81, 184, 186, 205–6
information transfer, 197–201, 219, 226, 235

information war. *See* cyberwar
Infosys, 171
institutions
agility of, 207
dynamics of, 71–77
intelligence, 139, 165, 182–86, 226. *See also* information transfer
China and, 202–3, 208
India and, 165, 168–70
Israel and, 159–60, 161
Pakistan and, 170
U.S. and, 180, 190, 202, 208
intensity, limiting, 251–52
interlocking alerts, 72
International Atomic Energy Agency (IAEA), 18, 133, 269
Iran, 5–6, 220, 272, 276, 278, 284
arms control and, 264–65, 267, 282
branch point and, 134–35
China and, 208
cyberwar and, 180, 221
deterrence and, 144–49, 259
game theory and, 18–30, 148
global dynamics and, 111–13, 123
hostage crisis of 1979, 66
Israel and, 26–27, 94, 128–35, 140, 152, 154–55, 156–61, 270, 275
missiles and, 105, 156–58, 161, 226
NPT and, 246, 250, 269
nuclear program of, 28, 34, 93, 121, 127–28, 140, 275
revolution of 1979, 147
Russia and, 228, 231
strategic posture of, 156–59
strategies to manage nuclear, 142–51, 253–54
surrogate war and, 119
Iraq, 112–13, 129, 133, 135, 140–41, 157
Gulf War of 1991, 140–41
war of 2003, 132–33, 166, 180, 221, 236, 248
irrational strategies, 175
ISI (Pakistani intelligence agency), 170, 183
Islam, political, 118, 135

missiles (*cont'd*)
Iran and, 148, 156–57, 159–60
Israel and, 153, 159–60
NATO and, 111–12
North Korea and, 190
Pakistan and, 167–68
underground silos, 24–25
Mitchel Field, 56
mobile missiles, 24–25, 37, 49, 111, 153,
158, 160, 201–4, 208, 210, 272
modernization, 6, 95, 171–72, 216, 238,
243–44, 272, 283–84
"moment of choice" dramas, 44
Morgenstern, Oskar, 108
Mossadegh, Mohammad, 147
Motorola, 205
"MSGs" (major powers, secondary
powers, groups), defined, 94–95.
See also groups, subnational; major
powers; secondary powers; *and
individual countries, groups,
and regions*
Mubarak, Hosni, 154
multinational companies, 171
multiplayer game dynamics, 25, 106–14,
186, 227–44
multipolar nuclear order, 3, 8, 276–79,
282
arms control and, 260–70
evolution of, 229–30
major power dynamics and, 229–44
Mumbai attacks (2008), 169
mutual assured destruction (MAD),
106, 230–31, 268

Nasser, Gamal Abdel, 117
national command authority (NCA),
177–79
nationalism, 114–17, 125
national liberation wars, 50
National Security Council, 84
National War College, 83, 85–86
Naval War College, 17
near-doomsday machines, 37
Netherlands, 52, 62, 87
neutron bomb, 37, 49, 104–5

"new look" nuclear force, 256
New York Times, 56, 69
"next moves" strategy, 41
Nimitz, Chester W., 17
9/11 attacks, 14, 118, 161, 178, 223
Nixon, Richard M., 66–69, 89, 102–3,
108, 114, 132, 197–98, 200–201,
218, 266
no first use, 26, 233, 262–68, 284–85
"nonaccidental" accident, 174
nonaligned nations, 100
nonproliferation treaty (NPT), 4, 7, 10,
31, 62, 94–95, 260, 269, 278
crisis games and, 18–19, 25–29
great power arms control system and,
268–69
Iran and, 150
Israel and, 27–29, 103
Japan and, 241
new theory of victory and, 249–51
North Korea and, 105, 246, 249–50,
267, 269–70
second nuclear age and, 94, 120, 123,
154, 218–20, 225–26, 228–29, 241
tightening of, 246–47
non-zero sum games, 73
NORAD (North American Air Defense
Command), 67, 236
North Atlantic Treaty Organization
(NATO), 39, 48, 57, 62–64, 82–83,
87, 111–12, 172, 237, 257–58, 263
North Korea, 1, 4–6, 10, 189–95, 220,
223, 231, 233–35, 251, 272, 275, 277,
280, 284
accidental war and, 237
arms control and, 264–65, 267, 271
China and, 110–11, 208, 233–34
containment and, 247–48
deterrence and, 192–93, 216
East Asia and, 189–95, 275
global dynamics and, 227
information transfer and, 226
Japan and, 94, 239, 280
nationalism and, 115–16
NPT and, 105, 246, 249–50, 267,
269–70

ABOUT THE AUTHOR

PAUL BRACKEN is the author of *Fire in the East* and *The Command and Control of Nuclear Forces*. He is a professor of management and political science at Yale University, and was previously a member of the senior staff of the Hudson Institute under Herman Kahn and a consultant to the Rand Corporation. He serves on several Department of Defense advisory boards and works with global multinational corporations on strategy and technology issues. He lives in Connecticut.